# Culture
# and Society in
# Seventeenth-Century
# France

STUDIES IN CULTURAL HISTORY

SERIES EDITOR:

Professor J. R. Hale

# Culture
# and Society in
# Seventeenth-Century
# France

DAVID MALAND

Charles Scribner's Sons

NEW YORK

# Contents

# Acknowledgments

The author and publishers wish to thank the following for permission to reproduce illustrations appearing in this book: the Courtauld Institute of Art for plates 3, 5 and 24; the Earl of Derby for plate 21; the Gobelins Museum, Paris, for plate 33; Mr A. F. Kersting for plate 27; the Mansell Collection for plates 6, 8, 17, 18, 20 and 23; the Musées Nationaux for plates 14 and 15; the National Gallery, London, for plate 30; the Radio Times Hulton Picture Library for plates 1, 2, 7, 9, 10, 16, 19, 22 and 34; and Mr Peter Smith for plate 12.

# List of Plates

# Introduction

The qualities of an individual artist defy explanation but the quality of a civilisation lends itself to historical analysis and provokes a legitimate quest to identify the spirit of the age. There are undercurrents of opposed forces which cannot be reconciled, survivals from preceding ages, anticipations of future ones and a mass of internal contradictions; yet, in spite of these complexities the dominant ideas of any age stand out to attract the principal attentions of historians. 'Whenever you look at any particular civilisation, I think you will find that its most characteristic writings are dominated by a particular pattern of life; and those who are engaged in these writings, or paint these paintings, or produce this particular music in some sense are dominated by it. And in order to identify a civilisation, in order to explain what kind of civilisation it is, in order to understand the world in which men of this sort thought and felt and acted, it is, I think, of importance to try so far as possible to isolate the dominant pattern which that culture obeys' (Isaiah Berlin in a broadcast lecture 'In Search of a Definition'). This is what this study sets out to do for the culture of France in the seventeenth century.

Among the varied factors which underlay, reinforced and in some cases determined the direction taken by artists and writers, one of critical importance was the restoration of royal authority by Henri IV, and this is therefore our first concern in chapter 1. The long period of civil war had wasted the resources of France and diverted attention from the arts, and Malherbe expressed the gratitude felt by all writers and artists. When Marie de' Medici arrived in France to marry Henri he welcomed her in an ode designed to attract the attention of the bridegroom as well as the bride, extolling the royal achievement in establishing peace.

> *Ce sera vous qui de nos villes*
> *Ferez la beauté refleurir.*
> *Vous qui de nos haines civiles*
> *Ferez la racine mourir.*\*

Within two years of Henri's recognition by both Catholics and Huguenots a dozen anthologies of contemporary verse had appeared and, as one of the editors commented, 'The Muses, scattered by the horror of our recent and widespread disorders, and shrouded as it were in shades of darkest night, begin at last to see the light once more with the coming of this new dawn and of this most happy peace.' The swift and dramatic reconstruction of Paris was a yet more tangible expression of this mood, and the new developments in building styles and poetry, epitomised in the work of Salomon de Brosse and Malherbe, reflected the new vigour in the arts and the growing taste for restraint, self-discipline and order.

The roots of anarchy and civil war could not be eradicated in one short reign, as the events of Louis xiii's minority were to show, but the reigns of Louis xiii and Louis xiv established securely the power of the crown and led to the creation of a centralised administration which won the envy of every other state (a process described at the start of chapter 3 and developed in chapter 8). The stage was thus set for a blossoming of the arts, though the new environment was not without its own dangers. The total suppression of disorder in the final period covered by this book, the period of Colbert's administration from 1660 to 1685, led to the impoverishment of inspiration in the arts by the imposition of too great a degree of control and uniformity. Moreover, the administrative dependence of the provinces upon Paris weakened the quality of provincial culture, as we see in

---

\* It will be you who make the beauty of our towns blossom again, you who will kill the root of all our private enmities.

chapter 10. In the early sixteenth century, during the reigns of
François I and Henri II, both powerful monarchs and both patrons
of the arts, when the court had made a constant progress through the
kingdom, Lyon had rivalled Paris as a cultural centre, and Bordeaux
had pursued an independent course as the leader of intellectual life
in the south-west. Writers and artists had been passionately attached
to their local regions, and Montaigne, for example, had spent most
of his life with great contentment in his native Gascony; but, as a
result of the Bourbon monarchs who made Paris the permanent
centre both of their court and of their administration, provincial
life was denuded of talent and the capital became the glitering source
of patronage. French culture in the seventeenth century, therefore,
was virtually the product of one city.

It was also the product of a very restricted social group. Most
Frenchmen were ignorant of the cultural activity of their age since
they were eking out a hand-to-mouth existence in which the struggle
for survival preoccupied their minds. The precarious balance between starvation and sufficiency was a factor which far outweighed
all others in the lives of most of the 16 million inhabitants of France.
'A wet season, a late frost, a July storm could throw an entire
province into anguish and starvation' (R. Mandrou, *Introduction à la
France moderne*), and the detailed work of Pierre Goubert and René
Baehrel had indicated both the frequency and the severity of sub-
sistence crises throughout the century. In a history such as this,
therefore, the peasantry plays no part. Its labour made possible the
wealth of the other classes, but it made no contribution to the cultural life of France. Illiterate, isolated and perennially threatened by
starvation, the peasants were the derided beasts of burden in French
society—'fit only to appear in some farce', said La Bruyère. The
*État de la France*, a study of contemporary society by Nicolas Beson-
gne, described the wealthier categories of the *Tiers État* and added,
'one could add a fourth category of this estate, the peasant, but there
is nothing important to say about him.' What was important was
the wealth of the courtiers, of the society of the Paris salons and of
the horde of *officiers* who battened off royal service. Collectively we
find them described repeatedly as the society of *la cour et la ville*. This

was the group whose wealth and patronage made possible the great achievements of seventeenth-century art, literature and music.

The existence of a wealthy, leisured élite does not necessarily result in a flowering of the arts. Dr Charles Burney, writing in the eighteenth century about the connection between the economic rise of the Netherlands in the fifteenth century and the great development which occurred there in music, affirmed that, 'as the polite arts are children of affluence and dependent upon superfluity for support, it is natural to suppose that they would thrive well at this period'. Wealth of course is a necessary factor, but it is too simple a view that a coefficient of economic development might render any significant clue to the cultural quality of an age. What mattered was the motivation of the patrons.

The monarchs had always been associated with the arts. Traditionally their social duty was to provide for musicians, poets and painters at their courts, but their concern went deeper than this. They had recognised that posterity remembered them as often for the works they commissioned as for their great victories, and it was Colbert who expressed this in its crudest form: 'It is by the size of their monuments that kings are measured', and, 'His Majesty, loving the fine arts as much as he does, will cultivate them with even greater care that they may serve to immortalise his great and glorious actions.' But policy without taste can achieve little and it was of tremendous importance that the Bourbon kings should have possessed such genuine enthusiasms—Henri IV for town-planning, Louis XIII for music and Louis XIV for the theatre and landscape gardening—that they were able to recognise and to prefer the best talents of the day to the second-rate. The patronage of the court was surpassed in many ways by the patronage of such royal ministers as Richelieu, Mazarin and Fouquet. They too kept a shrewd eye on posterity and the acclaim of their contemporaries but unlike, say, Sully or Colbert, they enjoyed a sophisticated taste which inspired and informed their patronage. Richelieu in particular played a vital role in establishing the classical mood in France and his contribution is discussed at some length in chapters 3 and 4.

Outside the court, the salon of Mme de Rambouillet, and those of her successors and imitators, not only provided an independent and influential source of patronage but also, and of far greater importance, a novel degree of sophistication and a taste for elegance, refinement and order which had a remarkable effect on French sensibility in general, and on literature and the theatre in particular (this is the theme of chapter 2). As a result the nobility of the court and the ambitious well-to-do bourgeoisie were provided with exemplars of patronage and of taste which they swiftly imitated. The reasons for this imitation are complex, but so far as the nobility was concerned its conversion from illiterate philistinism was achieved by the fact that the court, led by Henri IV, Louis XIII, Richelieu, Mazarin and Fouquet, and Parisian society, led by the salons of Mme de Rambouillet, Mme de Sablé and Mlle de Scudéry, made literature and the arts fashionable and good taste popular. The new concept of *l'honnête homme* established a taste for the arts as a characteristic of noble behaviour which the nobility, sometimes reluctantly, came to accept, and which the middle classes zealously sought to imitate. Bourgeois ambition became in the middle years of the century one of the most potent factors in the history of French culture. Its nature and its achievement are analysed fully in chapter 5; briefly, the bourgeoisie despised its own image and sought by every means to behave like the nobility. Once culture, patronage and good taste had become fashionable at court, the middle classes followed suit with great enthusiasm.

The quality of the artists and writers who received this patronage is less susceptible of analysis. If the creation of circumstances in which larger numbers of artists of all kinds could find profitable employment must have encouraged the growth of talent, the historian nevertheless hesitates to find explanations of the genius displayed by a Mansart, a Racine or a Poussin. What is possible is to identify the common characteristics of the greatest exponents of the arts and to relate these to the society which commissioned them. In the first place the majority were formally trained in their craft—their training, their social position and the rewards they enjoyed are described in chapters 3 and 4—and, consequently, no matter how original their observation or their inspiration, they were brought up to look at things in a certain way, to subscribe to accepted models; and this is true too of the poets and other writers who, without formal training, were nonetheless profoundly influenced by the masters of their day. This training in the techniques of their craft was therefore an important factor, but it was capable of modification in order to meet both personal tastes, as was the case with Poussin who found himself ill at ease with the Italian schools, as well as the changing tastes of patrons. These in turn were affected by social and economic factors, as we have seen, but also by many others. Political absolutism, Cartesianism, the Catholic revival and the Jansenism of Port-Royal were equally significant factors which influenced both patrons and artists alike, and which are therefore given full weight in this book.

There were many artists and writers who still offered the public a multitude of styles and genres, as we shall see from the popularity of mannerist paintings, romantic novels, *pièces à machines*, burlesques and rumbustious tragi-comedies, but the market for these began to contract as classicism gained ground, and there were few who could afford to ignore this fact. Yet it was not simply the profit motive which accelerated the trend towards classicism. Unlike the Pléiade of the previous century who had deliberately sought to be esoteric, the artists and writers of the seventeenth century retained a close community of interest with their neighbours, and themselves shared in the changing assumptions and preferences of their age. Most of them did not have to prostitute their art to make it acceptable; and men of genius, whose ability it was to transcend the particular situation and to give it a universal significance, reflected, along with lesser men, the essential features of their common environment.

We shall see this clearly in the development of the individual styles of such artists as Vouet, Philippe de Champaigne and Poussin. It is apparent too in the literary concepts of Malherbe, of the Académie Française and of Boileau, in Lully's modification of baroque opera to French taste and in the dramas of Corneille, Molière and Racine. The reaction against mannerism in architecture led by Salomon de Brosse reached its triumphant conclusion in the work of Le Vau and Mansart, and the classical mood is even more obvious in the garden settings to their country houses and palaces. When the American Arthur Lovejoy put forward the hypothesis of the essential unity of the ideas of an age he wrote that 'the history of landscape gardening becomes a part of any truly philosophical history of modern thought'. In seventeenth-century France his theme is exemplified by the work of Le Nôtre and his predecessors which, in chapter 7, is demonstrated as the most tangible expression of French classicism.

All references to a common culture are potentially misleading, for as Nikolaus Pevsner has warned, 'it is an understandable desire of the historian to establish that one style ruled at one time everywhere. A kind of mental tidiness demands it and also the historian's imperative faith in a *Zeitgeist*, that is one character pertaining to one epoch' (*Listener*, 5 March 1964). Yet it is even more misleading to exaggerate or emphasise the divisions between those who disagreed with each other, unaware in their own day that they shared basic assumptions which could be totally discarded by later generations. In France the disorder of the Fronde has been similarly exaggerated, especially by those who have sought for its cultural equivalent in the novels of Mlle de Scudéry and the vogue of burlesque. The general progress throughout the period was towards a settled absolutism in the state, and, in the arts, though individual poets or painters pursued separate courses, the general tendency was undeniably towards a form of classicism.

The classical mood, so often identified as the expression of the well-ordered society of Louis XIV at Versailles, was in fact established by an earlier, more turbulent generation. Throughout the conflict of antagonistic trends in both political and cultural life, a small social élite, for all its crude manners and its unbearable violence in settling disputes of all kinds, began in the midst of intrigue and disorder to crave for the attainment of order, and this desire for restraint, regulation and refinement soon became general among the society of *la cour et la ville*. With the single exception of Racine, the men whose names epitomise French classicism—men such as Mansart, Philippe de Champaigne, Poussin, Corneille, Molière and Pascal—had all established themselves before the age of Louis XIV. The nature of

this classical mood is therefore analysed separately in chapter 7 before
we move on to the cultural life of Versailles.

In his *Notes toward the Definition of Culture*, T. S. Eliot reminds us
that 'culture is the one thing that we cannot deliberately aim at. It is
the product of a variety of more or less harmonious activities, each
pursued for its own sake: the artist must concentrate upon his canvas,
the poet upon his typewriter, the civil servant upon the just settlement of particular problems as they present themselves upon his
desk, each according to the situation in which he finds himself.' His
comment has a particular significance for the period we are studying.
The classical mood was established as the sum of so many individual
efforts, acting within an environment influenced by certain determining pressures; it lost its vigour when, under Colbert, these individual techniques were rationalised to produce a coherent, uniform
system, and imposed on the next generation of artists and writers.
When a rapid stream is transformed into a well-ordered *pièce d'eau*
we seem to be confronted with a clear example of *l'œuvre classique*,
but all is relative. To achieve this from a passionate desire to establish
order out of chaos is one thing; to do so because all rapid streams are
frowned upon by official patrons is merely pseudo-classicism.

# one

# Henri IV and the Return to Order

'There are no such things as Wars of Religion, only civil wars', wrote Sir Walter Raleigh, a shrewd observer of events, and the conflict which preoccupied France at the end of the sixteenth century confirmed the wisdom of his views. Though Roman Catholics and Huguenots slaughtered each other with missionary zeal, the basic fault was the inability of the royal family to assert its authority and terminate the disputes of its overmighty subjects. This, finally, is what Henri IV succeeded in doing by 1598.

When the last of Henri II's ineffective sons was killed in 1589, it was Henri IV who claimed the succession as a direct descendant of Charles V through the dukes of Angoulême and the royal house of Navarre. With the strongest claim to the throne, and an army of Huguenots at his back, he presented the Catholics with a problem they could neither ignore nor solve. To make matters worse, their only effective rival candidate, Philip II of Spain, was unacceptable to most of them. Henri timed his action very cleverly. He waited until his competent soldiering and brilliant public relations had convinced his enemies that no other man but he could ever unite and pacify the kingdom. He then resolved their dilemma by a politic conversion to Rome in 1593. One by one the Catholic leaders made their peace, and the tact and generosity of the king in his hour of victory did much to heal the rivalries of two generations. The last stronghold, Brittany, surrendered in 1598 when the duc de Mercœur acknowledged Henri—in return for four million livres and the governorship of the province. In this unheroic but eminently practical manner, Henri pacified France. The Huguenots of course were aghast at his conversion, but without an alternative leader they had no option but to accept. After much recrimination and hard bargaining at Nantes in 1598, Henri recovered their loyalty by granting them extensive powers of self-government and toleration, guaranteed by their retention of military bases in 100 French towns. In the same year Philip II of Spain abandoned his claim and made peace with Henri by the Treaty of Vervins.

Henri's problem thereafter was simple to define but difficult to resolve. His predecessors, a poor, sickly lot since 1559, had abandoned or surrendered much of their power to the great nobles, and Henri himself, by his agreements with the Huguenots and with many Catholic leaders, had made the situation worse. Once recognised as king, however, he began to recover the crown's authority. His reputation as a soldier, as a notorious lover, as a Gascon wit, and as the champion of the people's interests—*le roi de la poule au pot*—made him a king to be admired; his swift action in breaking conspiracies and his execution of a former comrade for treason made him respected and feared. If he ruled in the guise of a popular monarch he made no pretence of seeking popular authority for his actions. The États-Généraux, a national assembly akin in part to the English Parliament, was never summoned, and the church assemblies, the municipal authorities and the legal corporations of the *parlements*, were treated in a conciliatory but firm way that brooked no opposition. Nor were the majority of Frenchmen eager to oppose: after two generations of civil war they had come to recognise that what mattered more was not the legality of royal power but its effectiveness.

Though it was impossible to undertake the wholesale reform of French society, to destroy the privileges of the nobility, disarm the Huguenots and make all classes equally subject to taxation, Henri recovered the powers held two generations back by Henri II. Royal commands began to take precedence over the interests of the great provincial nobles, and the king's writs began to override the jurisdiction of provincial courts. It was a slow process, made more difficult by the fact that Henri's agents were not directly accountable to him. For more than a century the officers of the royal administration, the *officier* class, had purchased their positions and enjoyed not only lucrative perquisites but considerable independence. For financial reasons Henri carried the process further in 1604 by allowing an *officier*, in return for an annual payment to the crown, to insure himself against dismissal and to secure the right to sell or bequeath his office as he chose. This represented a serious check to royal power, but so far as Henri IV's reign was concerned the consequences were not too serious; most *officiers* recognised that Henri's rule brought them immeasurable advantages, and that the extension of royal authority could only result in the extension of their own importance as its guardians.

Henri's predecessors had lacked his personality and authority, but this was not the only reason for their failure. The crown had never recovered from the series of bankruptcies which had forced Henri II to make peace with Spain in 1559 after 50 years of war, and unless Henri IV could solve the problem he too would fail. By great good fortune he had in the duc de Sully a tireless, painstaking treasurer, who looked after Henri's finances as carefully as he husbanded his own—a rare quality in seventeenth-century administration. His achievement was deceptively simple. It involved no dramatic reforms since none were possible. Nothing short of a social revolution could abolish the privileges of the nobility, the clergy, the *officiers* and the middle class in general, which for one reason or another exempted them from the full force of taxation. Instead, Sully accepted the harsh fact that the king's income came from the largest but poorest section of society, the peasantry, but he secured a higher standard of honesty in its collection by establishing a more efficient system of book-keeping. A simple solution, it required tremendous courage and persistence to carry it out, but the result was to leave Henri solvent.

The great attraction of Henri's reign for most Frenchmen was the opportunity provided to improve their lot, though in comparison with Englishmen or Dutchmen they seemed peculiarly reluctant to do so. The nobles scorned agriculture and refused to settle on their estates in order to farm them directly, and the middle classes were so preoccupied with the notion of living like nobles that they abandoned commercial and industrial ventures as soon as they had enough capital to invest in government loans, to purchase a title or to become *officiers*. All the same, the noble derived his revenue from his peasants, and middle-class success stories had to start somewhere in a workshop or a booth. For 50 years the civil wars had led to the devastation of the fields, the decline of industry and the dislocation of trade. After 1598 the peasant had only the elements and the tax-collectors to contend with in his unequal struggle against starvation, and the merchant was free to travel the country safely with his goods. Compared with this, the well-advertised steps taken by Sully to improve agriculture, and the proposals of other members of the council to reform old industries and introduce new ones, were of little consequence. It was the advent of peace and the opportunities it afforded which gave new life to the economy.

In 1610 Henri was assassinated as he set out on a dangerous, and probably ill-conceived, expedition to renew the war with Spain. The consequences of his death revealed how much the peace and good order of the previous 12 years had depended upon his personal government. Sully knew that the great provincial nobles had begun to find the years of royal authority irksome, that they hankered after a decentralised type of government which would leave them masters of their local areas, and when Henri's death left a nine-year-old boy on the throne he prophesied, 'France will fall into strange hands.' Henri's widow, Marie de' Medici, was made regent on behalf of her son Louis XIII, but she was totally unsuited to the task. An Italian banker's daughter, however exalted, was unable to withstand the haughty disdain of the French nobility, and though she loved political intrigue she could not govern. Her authority, such as it was, was immediately eroded by the nobles who flocked to her court demanding pensions, titles and positions of authority. It was men like the Italian adventurer Concini and the French prince de Condé who inherited the powers of Henri IV, and France reverted to the unhappy tradition of palace revolution and civil war. Fortunately, the young Louis XIII had the spirit of his father and in 1617 he seized control. At first his efforts, though fairly successful, lacked direction, and it was not until the appointment of Richelieu to the royal council in 1624 that the policies of Henri IV were again resumed with skill and energy.

'France and I both need time to draw breath' was Henri's comment when in 1593 his conversion opened up to him the gates of Paris, and no place had more need of recuperation than Paris itself. The last ten years of the civil war had been essentially a struggle to control the capital, with serious consequences for its buildings. Many were demolished by the defenders to establish a clear field of vision from their strong points; many more were destroyed by the attackers in their efforts to take the city by storm. In 1592, for example, when the citizens had been on the brink of surrendering to a prolonged attack by Henri, a swift expedition by a Spanish army from Brussels had saved the day, but it was a salvation that the city could scarcely endure: 'More than 1,400 houses in the suburbs', read one civic report, 'have been flattened by cannon balls or burnt to the ground.' Henri, once inside the city in 1593, immediately undertook a massive rebuilding programme. 'As soon as he became master of Paris you could see nothing but masons at work', recorded the *Mercure François*, and to such good effect that the Spanish envoys who arrived in 1598 to negotiate the Treaty of Vervins were astounded at the progress which had been made. When they asked Henri how it was done, he was too astute not to miss an occasion to indicate his rightful presence. 'When the master is never at home, everything falls into ruin, but once he is there to embellish his house everything profits by it', and it was with official encouragement that contemporaries compared him to Amphion, the legendary builder of Thebes, at the sound of whose lyre the very stones slid gently into place.

The comparison was well made. The great rebuilding was not undertaken merely to repair the damages inflicted by war; it was conceived and directed by a king who was passionately interested in the development of his capital. Unlike the Valois kings who had paid only sketchy attention to Paris, Henri chose to make it the permanent centre of his administration and the permanent setting for his court. No doubt there was a strong measure of political calculation behind his plan—the ambition of a man who has fought his way through many years to gain a throne and who seeks to establish some permanent memorial to his reign. It was Cosimo de' Medici, the unofficial ruler of Florence in the fifteenth century, who said, 'I know my fellow citizens. In 50 years time they will only remember me by the few poor buildings I leave them.' But both Cosimo and Henri were moved by a genuine love of building for its own sake, a love which Henri was at last free to indulge. The poets complained that the fount of royal patronage had dried up in his reign, but his employment of architects and builders was a very different story—as he himself indicated: 'People say I am stingy, but I do three things far removed from avarice; I make war, I make love and I build.'

It was in keeping with his personality and his political interests that his building programme should have been practical rather than grandiose. One of his first tasks was to make his palaces inhabitable. At that date the Louvre, for example, was nothing more than the south-west corner of the present Square Court, an undistinguished neighbour of the Tuileries which Catherine de' Medici had built for her own use. Henri spent over eight million livres on repairs and extensions. At the Louvre he completed the Petite Galerie on lines sketched out by Catherine, and then began the Grande Galerie to run at right angles from it along the old ramparts of the Seine, to connect with the Tuileries. Just before his death he was playing with the idea of clearing away the ground to the north in order to build a second gallery in parallel, but this was never realised.

Much more important than the improvements to the Louvre was his work in reshaping the city. The first step was the construction of the Pont Neuf. Henri III in 1578 had commissioned Jacques Androuet du Cerceau and his brother Baptiste to link the west end of the Cité to the north and south banks of the Seine, but the project had been held up by the wars. Henri IV had it done between 1599 and 1607 by Guillaume Marchant but, if the idea was not entirely his, the treatment was wholly characteristic of him. He stripped the project not only of such frills as triumphal arches but also of the houses which were to have been built on the bridges: the result is that instead of two separate bridges, each with its own decorations and houses, the Pont Neuf appears as a single architectural unit spanning the Seine with elegance and without clutter. In addition, Henri realised that the bridge alone would never ease traffic congestion in the Cité unless it was fed by a new road. For this reason he decided to open up the area south of the river by cutting through a warren of back streets to link the Pont Neuf to the Faubourg Saint-Germain by the Rue Dauphine. This raised the thorny problem of property rights, but his retort to the Augustinian monks who objected to the loss of a cabbage patch ended the matter in the most practical way: *'Ventre saint gris!* The houses you will be able to build along the new road will be worth a whole lot more to you than your cabbages.'

These schemes were very much Henri's own, and men like Marchant and his own architect at the Louvre, Louis Métézeau, acted more or less under his direct orders. It was Henri, too, who wanted to make the Rue Dauphine attractive as well as serviceable. He wrote of his plan to make those who built there conform to a common standard of construction and decoration, 'for it would make a fine sight from the bridge to see the whole street as one single façade'. Unfortunately for Paris, this intention was never made binding in law, and we have to look elsewhere in the city to see what Henri sought to achieve.

In the Place Dauphine, for example, he left nothing to chance. It resulted indirectly from a project of the queen's. Where the Pont Neuf cut across the eastern tip of the Cité, Marie de' Medici conceived the notion of an equestrian statue of her husband, to stand magnificently in view of his subjects at the prow of the old ship of Paris. Since France had no tradition of public effigies of her sovereigns, it was the Colleoni statue in Venice which Marie must have had in mind, and it was to her relatives in Italy that she wrote for assistance in finding a sculptor capable of carrying out her plan. The statue was not erected until 1614, but the discussion about it drew Henri's attention to the area of waste land which would face it. In 1607 he decided to erect the Place Dauphine, triangular in shape to follow the configuration of the island, with the statue to stand at its apex. Achille de Harlay, a president of the Paris Parlement, was granted the lease under pain of forfeiture if he did not complete the job in three years, and with precise instructions to build houses of uniform design.

There was nothing grandiose about them. They were to be simple, indeed small, houses, three stories high with pairs of arched openings for shops on the ground floor. The chief material was brick, decorated uniformly with stucco *chaînes*, with stone from the limestone quarries of Montmartre for the quoins, and slate for the high roofs with their dormer windows. Order, regularity and practicality were its virtues, and the total effect must have been most satisfying. Unhappily, there is little left of it today. The base was destroyed in 1874 to make room for the Palais de Justice, and the uniform façade of the remaining sides has been broken. It is only from such plates as those of Turgot's plan of Paris (1737) that an idea of its original dignity can be gained.

Even before any plans had been considered for the Place Dauphine, Henri had been planning to develop the site, to the north of the river, of the old palace of Tournelles, where Henri II had been killed in a tournament and where his widow had hoped to create a Place de Valois. As with so much of Henri's urban planning, practicality took precedence over grandeur and display. He issued letters patent in 1605 to build a silk factory on the northern half of the site, and commissioned Claude Chastillon to draw up plans for a Place Royale (now the Place des Vosges) in the south. The plots were leased out at nominal rents, on condition that the tenants accepted a uniform style of building.

The style was essentially that of the Place Dauphine, but modified to suit a rather more prosperous clientèle. There were no shops and the ground floor became an arcade of simple, regular arches with four bays to each house. Unlike the Place Dauphine, where the first and ground floors were of equal height, the first floor was given special prominence, heightened by the introduction of French windows opening to the floor—though it is maintained by Babelon that these were added some 20 years later. With greater spaciousness came greater dignity, but decorative motifs remained essentially simple. The arcade was done in stone, the other floors in brick with long-and-short stonework around the windows, and with stucco *chaînes* to continue the line of the pillars in the arcade below. Though the arcade provided a unifying motif, each house marked its independence by its own separate roof with dormer windows. In the centre of the southern side stood the Pavillon du Roi. This was not only more substantial and loftier than the other houses, but also more elaborately decorated, particularly on the ground floor where the arcading was made more monumental by raising its height and by using double columns to support each arch. Behind the arcading, and under the Pavillon itself, the residents of the Place could walk through to a special access road which led to the busy thoroughfare of the Rue Saint-Antoine.

When a consortium of merchants failed to establish the factory which Henri had planned, he decided to repeat the pattern of houses to make a symmetrical square, with a Pavillon de la Reine facing the Pavillon du Roi. Two roads cut into the Place Royale at the north-east and north-west corners, but there was no question of through traffic. Henri conceived of the Place in its final form as something more than a prosperous residential area; it was to serve as an ordered setting for Parisian recreation. Here the citizens could escape the noise and smell of the Rue Saint-Antoine and take the air as they strolled under the arcades. On special days it became a place of assembly for fêtes and public celebrations, as in 1612, when a famous Carrousel was held to celebrate the marriage of Louis XIII to Anne d'Autriche. 20,000 spectators crammed into the Place Royale for three successive days to watch a series of military parades, tableaux and processions, in which elephants and court poets alike were welcomed with rapturous applause.

In its quieter moments the Place Royale became the centre of a very fashionable quarter, the Marais, and the first to buy lots there were nearly all men of the royal household and the administration. These included Jean de Fourcy who worked under Sully's direction as *intendant des bâtiments*, Claude Chastillon, *ingénieur topographe du roi*, who had first surveyed the site, four of Sully's secretaries, and Président Jeannin, a *parlementaire* and one of Henri's chief ministers, whose enthusiasm for building was such that Tallement wrote of him, 'this man has built and rebuilt so many homes that I have lost count'.

For most Parisians, certainly for those who prided themselves on being fashionable, the Place Royale was referred to simply as 'the Place'. This distinguished it from the more humble milieu of the Place Dauphine, and also from a third Place which Henri began just before his death. This was to be less of a residential square than an impressive, indeed spectacular, entry to the city on the north-east side. Claude Chastillon's engraving reveals Henri's intention of a vast semicircular Place de France, with the city wall as its diameter and with eight major roads fanning out into the city from a magnificent gateway at its centre, the Porte de France.

It was typical of the character of Henri's reign that of all his town-planning projects it was only the most spectacular and least practical which was not achieved. No other ruler in the seventeenth century had so practical a nature or was so concerned to relate his policies to the solution of immediate needs. The aesthetic appeal, for example, of his town houses, the brickwork decorated with stone quoins and frames, sprang directly from his building regulations to reduce fire hazards in the city. He forbade any further construction in wood and plaster and, since stone was expensive, it was used instead of brick only for those parts of the building where the load was at its greatest, at the wall angles, the doorways and the window frames. He was also concerned to remedy the condition of the streets, a task in which he relied upon the enthusiastic support of François Miron, *Prévôt des Marchands* in the city. Together they undertook the provision of better water supplies, and installed a large hydraulic pump, 'La Samaritaine', to serve the area around the Louvre: they also widened streets where possible and paved them. Without so obvious an appeal to enlightened self-interest as Henri's retort to the Augustine fathers over their cabbage patch, it was not possible to touch the most congested zones of the old city and the university where the problem was at its worst. Equally insoluble was the problem of the mud, the Parisian *crotte*, a notorious amalgam of general rubbish, animal dung and nightsoil whose adhesive qualities defied both brush and water. Malherbe, one of the court poets, wrote in 1608 to a friend in the provinces: 'There is a great to-do here in Paris about the mud, but I am afraid it will be just as filthy as before', but he added, in reference to Henri's general improvement of the city, 'if you come back to Paris in two years time you will no longer recognise the place'.

The style of building which Henri preferred had a significance far beyond its relation to fire regulations. The wars of religion had been a bad time for architecture since few had cared to undertake more than defence works and repairs. What there is of French architecture betwen 1560 and 1600, however, shows the desertion of the principles of rationalism and classicism acquired from Italy in the reign of Francis 1 for the newer style, also from Italy, of mannerism. Mannerism as it is now generally understood is best considered first of all as a reaction against the tremendous achievements of the High Renaissance. It is not simply that the mannerisms of artists like Raphael or of architects like Bramante were adopted; the whole mood was altered as the mannerists, conscious of their inability to surpass their mentors, refused to accept a future of pointless emulation. Instead, they deliberately flouted the rules deduced from classical art in order to attract attention to themselves, relying of course on a small but highly intellectual public which knew these rules and could thus recognise, and perhaps appreciate, the point of abandoning them.

At its best this could produce a degree of sophisticated elegance, as when the smooth band above the windows of the rusticated ground floor of Giulio Romano's own home at Mantua was broken discreetly by the keystones of the windows; but more frequently the self-conscious effort to establish novelty resulted in an unbalanced, even discordant style, in sharp contrast to the balance and harmony of the High Renaissance. In a classical structure the parts are strictly regulated and related to the whole so that, as the Renaissance architect Alberti put it, 'the harmony and concord of all the parts are achieved in such a manner that nothing could be added or taken away or altered except for the worse'. The mannerist architect tried to impress his public by the novelty of his inventions, which frequently disrupted not only the accepted canons but also the balance of the structure itself, since he failed to relate the novel details to the overall design. An extreme and capricious example can be seen at the

Palazzo Zuccari in Rome, where a window is modelled as the gaping mouth of a giant, whose forehead, nose and glaring eyeballs break grotesquely into the pediment. It glares from the wall, distracting, perturbing and a little ridiculous.

Mannerism was not just a movement in reaction against the High Renaissance giants. The giants themselves, Raphael and Michelangelo, had reacted against the style of their youth and middle age. With them it was not a vogue for eclecticism but a genuine surfeit of humanism. For them the classical ideal began to appear too well-ordered, and they felt a great need to flout the established principles of discipline, restraint, balance and learning. We can see the handling of Renaissance motifs in a deliberately alien way in Michelangelo's Laurentian Library, where the columns of the anteroom, instead of projecting from the wall to carry the architraves, are recessed. Consequently, it is the wall panels which appear to be left with the work of load-bearing. Even more perverse, by classical standards, are the corbels at the foot of each column. Not only do they seem far too unsubstantial for their function of giving support, but in any case Michelangelo uses them solely for decoration. The whole room in fact reflects a mood of frustration and unresolved conflict.

An explanation of this frustration may lie in the increasing doubts that artists felt about their own status. Unlike the medieval artisan who knew where he stood, enjoying the protection of his gild, maintaining the traditions of his craft, the Renaissance artist was in many ways both exalted and liberated. This, as Arnold Hauser suggests, 'provided him with innumerable openings that were not available to the medieval artist, but it set him in a vacuum of freedom in which he was often on the point of losing himself'. For this theory he finds evidence in the despair experienced by Michelangelo in old age, in Rosso's suicide, in the mental disturbance of Tasso and El Greco and in the melancholia of Parmigianino.

Mannerism, an uneasy, restless style which reflected in some measure the disturbances wrought in Italy as a result of Spanish domination and the Counter-Reformation, was well suited to the disrupted climate of France after the death of Henri II. This is not to propose a rigid thesis of cause and effect, nor to deny that had a genius appeared in full and competent mastery of classical rules then French architecture might have been led along a different path, but to explain in part the general tendency to emphasise the decoration of surface at the expense of structure. It also explains the greater element of fantasy in surface decoration, the preference for the ingenious and the complex in place of the simple and direct. In the work of Hughes Sambin at Dijon we see the effect of this. His Maison Milsand has a distinctive charm, but imagination has clearly run amok. The surface is encrusted with a medley of animal heads, *chaînes* of thick foliage, and an overabundance of vegetation.

In the work of the later sixteenth century can be discerned a sense of tension and conflict, parallel to the political and religious tensions of the period. Much of this is apparent in the work of Jacques Andronet du Cerceau the elder. Born in 1520, it was clear by 1559, the year of Henri II's death, that his style was moving consciously away from the rules of strict classicism. His first *Livre d'Architecture* appeared in that year, followed in 1576 and 1579 by the two volumes of *Les Plus Excellents Bastiments de France*. The engravings, which won him greater fame than his own buildings, concentrate in the main on the decoration of surfaces, and reveal a considerable degree of fantasy. The plans of the châteaux at Charleval and Verneuil-sur-Oise, for example, indicate his wanton use of classical forms. Entablatures are interrupted by column heads and keystones, or disappear behind a mass of encrustation. At Charleval, the chimney stacks appear like electric toasters on pedestals, the lofty arches of an arcade are made to alternate with stubby, square porticos, and the rustication spreads across everything, even across the pilaster strips. It is not the rational development of classical forms which we see in the baroque (see chapter 6), it is mannerist, a hotchpotch of fiddling detail, incoherent and unrelated.

In contrast to this, Henri IV showed a marked preference for simplicity, order and practicality, and approved the straightforward execution of rational design. Decoration was kept to a minimum. Examples of this style can be seen not only in Paris but in the stable gates erected at Fontainebleau, in Sully's château of Rosny, and in many others throughout the Île de France. Mannerism did not disappear immediately Henri IV became king, but examples of it are found either in districts well removed from the capital, or else they date from the years of aristocratic reaction and civil disorder following his assassination. The château which Charles de Cosse, duc de Brissac, built near Angers in 1606 is a case in point. Not only is the structure wholly unbalanced, which may have been a necessary consequence of renovating what was essentially a military keep, but the surface decoration gives the eye no rest. The motif of long-and-short stonework around the windows is typical of Henri IV's reign, as we see in the Place Royale, but the windows are so close together that the decoration virtually masks the wall—and what remains is covered with heavily rusticated pilaster strips and arches.

To equate political order with classicism, and chaos with mannerism, is too simple a formula for comprehensive application—and Henri IV's own taste for building was too genuine and too intense to be explained solely in terms of his political achievement—but the generalisation contains the essence of the truth. The rational conception of Henri's buildings, their coherent, logical style, reflect his political concepts. His power in France did not rest upon tradition or force alone; it was acceptable because it was felt by most Frenchmen to be practical and reasonable, two qualities most apparent in his building style. We find them again in the renovations and extensions to the royal palaces at Fontainebleau amd Saint-Germain where his influence was dominant, though the works were undertaken by his architects, men such as Louis Métézeau and Rémy Collin. At Fontainebleau, where he spent over 2,400,000 livres and where the Florentine ambassador described him scrambling tirelessly about the scaffolding, giving urgent directions to his masons, his new buildings around the kitchen court and stables were sober and restrained in their ordered domesticity. It reflects the general pattern of his reign that at both these palaces he employed Claude Mollet to undertake the first large-scale works of landscape gardening, establishing a tradition of reducing nature to order which Le Nôtre was to make famous at Versailles. At Fontainebleau, in addition to the ordered parterres and well-cut shrubberies, Mollet created a canal over 1,300 yards long; at Saint-Germain, where the Seine flowed

200 feet below the palace, he devised the delightful and ordered progression of arcades, terraces and stairways, preserved in the engraving of 1654.

One architect whose work epitomised in a remarkable way the essential characteristics of Henri's reign was Salomon de Brosse, and because in addition he was the best architect of his day he established a new trend of order and classicism of great significance for the future. He was the first architect for several generations to abandon the mannerist preoccupation with surface decoration and to think instead in terms of the mass of a building. In view of his upbringing this was rather unexpected, since he was born at Verneuil in 1571 and grew up on the scaffolding of the strange palace designed by his grandfather, Jacques Androuet du Cerceau. He came to Paris when the edict of Nantes made it safe for Huguenots to work there, and eventually secured a commission of great importance from Marie de' Medici. Since her arrival in Paris in 1601 she had been horrified by her undistinguished apartments at the Louvre, and had resolved, like Catherine de' Medici before her, to build her own. It was not until 1612, however, that she finally found the ideal site. Well away from the centre, in the Faubourg Saint-Germain, stood the house and gardens of the duc de Luxembourg: she paid 90,000 livres for the site and immediately set to to build the splendid palace she had had in mind. From the very beginning her ideas of splendour had been influenced by her youth in Italy; in 1611 she wrote to her aunt, the grand duchess of Tuscany, for the plans of the Pitti Palace, and at the same time despatched Louis Métézeau to Florence to make his own notes.

In the event the commission went to de Brosse, and his treatment of the *corps de logis* shows that he was advancing to his own novel concept of what a palace or château should look like. While at work on the Luxembourg de Brosse was also building a château at Blérancourt, where he designed a *corps de logis* with four pavilions at each corner, but without the traditional wings and courtyard. In other words, he created a solid, free-standing, symmetrical block with a sense of mass unattained before in France. Once this was achieved, the need for a fuzz of decoration was removed. At the Luxembourg, however, where Marie demanded a large inner court, de Brosse could not escape the four-sided plan of *corps de logis*, two flanking wings at right angles to it and a linking screen to enclose the space, but he clearly sought to achieve an effect similar to that of Bléran-court.

First of all he designed the *corps de logis* as a simple rectangular block with four square, symmetrical pavilions at each corner. The pavilion roofs, high-pitched, are cut off at the apex. They cannot, therefore, dominate the main block nor demonstrate their separation from it, and so the sense of compact unity is strengthened. In addition, the dormer windows are made into an attic storey by putting them behind a cornice and balustrade. Consequently, the entablature runs along the entire roof edge—save for the discreet interruption of shallow pediments above the central window of each pavilion—and holds the whole building together. This unifying feature is repeated in the lines of the balustrade and the cornice which mark out the first and second storeys respectively. As for the wings, de Brosse made them long and low, and the sense of a free-standing main block is largely unimpaired. Marie insisted upon the stonework being rusti-cated, as at the Pitti Palace, but as this was the only ornamentation, and as de Brosse achieved it with a very light touch, there is little sense of fuss or disturbance. The total effect is of a well-ordered mass, of carefully balanced proportions, and of details related to the whole composition.

This is the architectural parallel to the order and restraint revealed in Henri IV's policies and in his town planning. It was fortuitous in the sense that de Brosse was never trained in the style, nor did he visit Italy; but not only did he himself derive satisfaction from the stricter use of classical forms, it is clear that his work also appealed to many others who discovered in it a welcome contrast to the manner-ism of the du Cerceau family.

Two other buildings are worth mentioning. When he was com-missioned to repair the church of Saint Gervais in 1616 he had the interesting problem of constructing a classical façade for a Gothic church. The Italian technique was to produce a two-tier design, but as the Gothic nave was extremely tall, de Brosse was able to build

1. Government—Henri IV, after a portrait
by Frans Pourbus (see pages 17–20)

THE RETURN TO ORDER

2. Poetry—François de
Malherbe (see pages
35–44)

L'ADMIRABLE DESSEIN DE LA PORTE ET PLACE DE FRANCE AVEC SES RUES COMMENCÉE A CONSTRUIRE ÉS MARESTZ DU TEMPLE A PARIS DVRANT LE REGNE DE HENRY LE GRAND 4 DV NOM ROY DE FRANCE ET DE NAVARRE L'AN DE GRACE MIL SIX CENS ET DIX PAR CLAVDE CHASTILLON CHAALONNOIS

3. Claude Chastillon's design for a Place de France (see page 26)

a three-tier façade, with the three orders, Doric, Ionic and Corinthian, correctly superimposed at each stage. With a straight pediment over the main door, and a curved one to crown the whole work, the result was logical, ordered and satisfying. The most classical of all his buildings, especially for the manner in which he anticipates the style of François Mansart, is perhaps the Palais du Parlement at Rennes. If this is set beside du Cerceau's engraving of the château at Charleval, we can see the full extent of the transformation achieved by de Brosse. From a world in which classical motifs are used without logic or order, in which fantasy of invention is valued apparently above all else, and in which the decoration of the surface is the chief concern of the architect, we move to the building at Rennes with its solid proportions, its simple design, its dignity, restraint and mass. It is a transformation as remarkable as that achieved by Henri IV in ending the civil wars and establishing the rule of law.

A great deal of money was spent by Henri IV and Marie de' Medici on the internal decoration of their palaces, but there was no such figure as de Brosse to dominate the art of painting. Painting in Paris was at a very low ebb, and what little there was was mostly in the mannerist style. We have already analysed mannerism in architecture: so far as painting is concerned the same generalisations apply about the reaction from humanist self-sufficiency and the deliberate repudiation of the rules. Even in the final work of Raphael and Michelangelo we see a challenge to the Renaissance ideals of classic beauty, of noble gestures and strong bodies, of well-balanced compositions inducing a mood of harmony and rest; and their successors went further in flouting what had become conventional. Parmigianino, for example, faced with the problem of painting a madonna more graceful and more elegant than any by the acknowledged master of the genre, Raphael, exaggerated the delicacy of the fingers, elongated the limbs and strove to emphasise the flowing line so far that he gave his madonna a swan neck. In addition he disturbed the composition of the group, so that with one side crowded with angels the other is left out of balance. 'He wanted to show that the classical solution of perfect harmony is not the only solution conceivable; that natural simplicity is one way of achieving beauty, but that there are less direct ways of getting interesting effects for sophisticated lovers of art' (Gombrich).

The style spread quickly to France. Primaticcio, Francis I's finest artist, had fallen increasingly under Parmigianino's influence, and for three generations French painting was obsessed by the desire to achieve elegance, sinuosity and complex relationships of gesture and body; one most easily recognised is the device of a figure in the foreground, cut off at the waist by the edge of the frame, twisting round to face into the heart of the picture. The taste, too, was for scenes of ceremony and allegory, in which the importance of the symbol is a secret shared by the painter and the small world of his sophisticated patrons. This element of *préciosité* was highly valued by the Valois court, and survived in the salons of the early seventeenth century where there was a vogue for the work of Claude Vignon, and the Lorraine artist, Claude Deruet.

Henri IV's chief painters, Ambroise Dubois, Toussaint Dubreuil and Martin Fréminet, were in this tradition, but little has survived of their work. Dubreuil decorated the Petite Galerie at the Louvre which was burnt in 1661, and his allegories at Saint-Germain were dispersed in the eighteenth century, but most of his work was with Fréminet at Fontainebleau, producing such scenes as the Surrender of Amiens to Henri IV, with Henri as Mars and his mistress, Gabrielle d'Estrées, as Diana. What is interesting about Dubreuil is that in his painting there is a discernible trend from the mannerist tradition, some sense of restraint and balance, which, if never so clearly marked as in de Brosse, is nevertheless a first step in preparing the way for Poussin and the revival of classicism.

A great many of Henri's commissions were designed to serve the interests of propaganda. Consequently there was much emphasis on his victories over disorder, his championship of France against Spain, and his vital act of conversion to the faith expected of all French kings. Dubreuil's 'Surrender of Amiens' was clearly in this category, and so was the equestrian statue which Marie de' Medici secured from Giovanni da Bologna to stand on the Pont Neuf. Pierre Biard, the best of some very moderate French sculptors, commemorated the battle of Ivry in bas-relief at Fontainebleau, and produced a massive allegory of Henri IV as Jupiter allied with the Giants, scattering with thunderbolts the forces of the Catholic League. Guillaume Dupré produced some very fine medals and coins to record the great moments of Henri's reign, and the printing presses produced an astonishing flood of engravings to popularise Henri's deeds—especially in 1594 to assert the validity of his conversion.

Marie de' Medici's most important act of patronage was her commission to Rubens in 1622 to paint the gallery of the Luxembourg. In this she showed herself a typical Medici. For her new palace nothing less would do than the premier artist in Europe, and for a theme nothing less than the story of her life. Though many of the scenes are as splendid as any done elsewhere by Rubens, and though his reputation excited tremendous interest in his works, his visit to France was curiously without consequence. His baroque spirit was so alien, both to the tradition of mannerism and to the slowly reviving classicism, that it made no impact at all on artists and public alike. In this respect, the minor Flemish painter, Frans Pourbus the Younger, was of greater importance. He had made a name at the court in Brussels, and Marie employed him to continue the decoration of the Petite Galerie after Dubreuil's death. He satisfied her demands extremely well since he combined great skill in depicting the trappings of royalty—the jewels and the formality—with a gift for portraiture. In his less formal commissions for nobles and Parisian bourgeois he revealed a much greater degree of naturalism, which was not only very popular but foreshadowed the style of sober realism and balanced portraiture which Philippe de Champaigne was to establish in mid-century.

The imposition of order upon a turbulent society by Henri IV was closely paralleled by the achievement in literature of François de Malherbe. Born in Caen in 1553, the son of a *parlementaire*, he was trained in law, served as a soldier and, from 1576, settled in Provence as secretary to the provincial governor. Among the cultured circle of humanist magistrates in Aix, he won a reputation for his verses, but it was too restricted a public to satisfy him and he tried unsuccessfully in 1586 to secure the patronage of Henri III by presenting to him 'Les Larmes de Saint Pierre'. In 1600 he tried again, with an ode to

Marie de' Medici on her disembarkation at Marseilles. This too failed, but finally a fellow Norman and poet, Cardinal du Perron, mentioned his name at court, and in 1605 Malherbe came to Paris in a final gamble to win royal approval. His arrival coincided with Henri's departure on a routine expedition to maintain order, and his '*Prière pour le Roi, Henri le Grand, allant en Limousin*' was skilfully directed to the occasion.

> *La terreur de son nom rendra nos villes fortes.*
> *On n'en gardera plus ni les murs ni les portes,*
> *Les veilles cesseront aux sommets de nos tours;*
> *Le fer mieux employé cultivera la terre,*
> *Et le peuple qui tremble aux frayeurs de la guerre,*
> *Si ce n'est pas pour danser, n'aura plus de tambours.**

Henri liked the subject, with a clear eye to its value as propaganda, but he also liked the direct simplicity of the style. He ordered the duc de Bellegarde, his master of the horse, to look after Malherbe, who was generously provided with board and lodging, a servant, a horse and a pension of 1,000 livres. Ultimately, Malherbe hoped for more direct patronage from Henri himself; to Peiresc, one of the magistrates at Aix, he wrote, 'the king has promised me a pension on the first abbey or bishopric which falls vacant', but it was not until after Henri's death that Marie de' Medici gave him a pension of 2,500 livres and, later still, that Richelieu found him a profitable office as a *trésorier de France*. Henri gave very little to poets, though he valued their services. Malherbe, du Perron, Desportes and several others, '*les poètes du Louvre*', were required to produce a perpetual series of odes, stanzas, epithalamiums and funeral hymns to celebrate the events of the royal household, eloquent variations on the eternal themes of peace, war and death. Sometimes, too, of love. In the last year of the reign, for example, Henri became infatuated with the 15-year-old bride of the prince de Condé. The young couple fled to Brussels, and

---

* The terror of his name will strengthen our towns. No longer will they guard the walls and gates, and the vigils will cease from the summits of our towers. Iron will be better employed in cultivating the earth, and the people who tremble at the terrors of war will have no need of drums except for dancing.

Henri ordered his poets into action to lure the young girl back. When she returned to the court for a few weeks in the summer, Malherbe was called to celebrate the occasion, ludicrous though it was, with his 'Pour Alcandre [Henri IV] au retour d'Oranthe à Fontainebleau', a poem of interest for its description of Claude Mollet's gardens and canal.

If this seemed humiliating Malherbe affected not to notice. Unlike the poets of the Valois court, the Pléiade in particular, who esteemed themselves as purveyors of immortality, and who refused to submit their inspiration to the demands of a mere patron, Malherbe was apparently content to do his duty as Laureate without violating any artistic scruples. He tended to disparage himself. To his disciple Racan he wrote; 'if our verses survive us all the glory we can expect from them will be that we were both excellent arrangers of syllables ... that we have both been quite mad to pass the best years of our life in an exercise so useless to the public and ourselves.' Such extreme nonchalance is suspect. Malherbe is truer to himself, and to the arrogance of poets of all ages, when he writes; 'Common or garden works last several years, but what Malherbe writes will last for ever.' It is quite clear that he valued both his position and his work; he had used every trick and waited more than a generation to secure the one, and the other he composed and polished with the utmost professional care.

His poetry was of great importance because it embodied the ideals he stood for as a critic; ideals of clarity, reason and order, which explains not only why Henri IV liked his verse, but why he so epitomised the reign of Henri IV. Up in his room in the Hôtel de Bellegarde he held what were virtually seminars on French language and literature. 'Do you remember the old pedagogue at court', wrote Guez de Balzac, 'and how we used to call him the tyrant of words and syllables?' His 'tyranny' was exercised to repel the forces of disorder and confusion, with whom he identified the Pléiade, and to establish order, rule and discipline. The Plèide, the group of sixteenth-century poets which included Ronsard, du Bellay and Jodelle, was excessively aristocratic and excessively erudite: aristocratic in that they identified themselves with the nobility, finding more attraction in warfare and other noble occupations than in anything else; erudite in that they wrote deliberately for an educated minority which knew the mythology as well as the vocabulary of Greece and Rome. *Odi profanum vulgus* was their device, and by 1600 they were out of touch. *La vie noble* stood less for dignity and splendour and exciting forays into Italy than for the evils of civil war; and pedantry was becoming a vice in French society. 'Liberating himself from the aristocratic and pedantic views of the Pléiade, this Norman gentleman, with the practical common sense of a bourgeois, set out to reconcile reason and art' (Lanson).

The Pléiade had done much to enrich the language. In a revolutionary manifesto, *La Deffence et Illustration de la langue française* (1549), Du Bellay, with Ronsard, argued the need to plunder other languages, to adopt, adapt and invent words, until the French language became a worthy instrument for a new French literature. The Pléiade were so successful that before the end of the century Montaigne was calling for a halt to the unbridled borrowing of words. 'In our language', he wrote, 'I find plenty of material, but it lacks style.' After a period of enrichment, digestion was at a premium: 'France and I both need time to draw breath.'

It was Malherbe who reversed the trend. Inheriting a rich fund of vocabulary in a state of prolific disorder, he pruned and refined it. He did so by making usage the test by which to judge a word; a word was useless unless it could be understood by the man in the street. This was not a plea for working-class realism nor for a democratic approach to language. Malherbe believed that if the language of the court was cleared of dialect, patois, slang and neologisms, it could then be comprehended by the common man, even though the latter would not expect to speak himself in the same manner. An interesting example of his pruning in action comes from the *Vie de Malherbe* by his pupil Racan. 'M. de Bellegarde who was a Gascon, sent to ask of him if it were better to say *dépensé* or *dépendu*; and he replied immediately that *dépensé* was better French, but *pendu, dépendu, rependu* and all the other compounds of that disgusting word were more suitable for Gascons to use!' Clearly there was some loss of variety and vitality in a pruning operation on this scale, and many attacked Malherbe and his friends on the grounds that because they had such limited imaginations they had clearly no use for a large vocabulary. 'These fellows', wrote Mlle de Gournay who hated Malherbe, 'want everyone to go on foot because they have no horse.' This was unfair, since Malherbe was making the language intelligible to a much larger circle than the Pléiade had ever written for.

Malherbe also opposed the Pléiade in their views on poetry as an art. He rejected the spontaneous improvisation they approved, and stuck out for close-knit composition. In the face of the adherents of nonchalance and easy naturalism, he imposed respect for technique and craftsmanship. He established, for example, the rules for the use of the Alexandrine—the verse of 12 feet in which most of the trage-dies of the century were to be written—forbidding *enjambement* and hiatus, and determining the caesura. Above all he had a close ear for rhyme, distinguishing feminine rhymes, masculine rhymes and rich rhymes (these last occurred when the rhyming syllables began with the same consonant, e.g. *terreur*, *horreur*). An interesting speculation has been proposed to explain this emphasis. Many of Malherbe's lyrics were probably composed to be sung to a set air, and in the *air de cour* it was usual to end-stop the lines, to establish a cadence in the middle of the line and to emphasise the rhyme at the end. There-fore, 'the emphasis on rhyme corresponds to the importance given by Malherbe to rich, difficult rhyme, the end-stopping of lines corre-sponds to Malherbe's rule prohibiting *enjambement*; and the cadence in the middle of the line corresponds to his rule demanding a caesura at the hemistich' (Weingarten).

In addition to regulating construction and rhyme, Malherbe urged all poets to avoid tautology and superfluous epithets. He disliked the mythological allusions, fantasies and conceits to be found in the verses of the Pléiade, and advised great caution in the use of images. The meaning was always to be direct and immediately accessible, and he insisted that the writing of love poetry gives no man the right to compose nonsense. Above all he loathed padding. His copy of Desportes's verse was scribbled with his indignant comments— '*bourre*', '*cheville*', padding. In all this he was justly claimed by Boileau to be the initiator of classicism in French literature. It was he who,

*D'un mot mis en sa place enseigna le pouvoir,*
*Et réduisit la muse aux règles du devoir.*
*Par ce sage écrivain la langue réparée*
*N'offrit plus rien de rude à l'oreille épurée.**

One accusation made against Malherbe, and against classicism in general, is that spontaneity and inspiration are forfeited by the concentration on technique. Malherbe, in comparison with most poets, lacked spontaneous lyricism, but this is chiefly because he tried to discourage it. He sought a measure of self-discipline in the emotions as well as in the vocabulary and prosody. In his view the Pléiade had given too much public expression to their private emotions, and he deliberately chose to conceal his own. He wrote, for example, a *'Consolation à M. du Périer'* on the death of his daughter. The theme is that of the Stoic philosophy which accepts the human condition for what it is; sentiment is spurned and the treatment is as objective as possible. It ends, referring to Death:

> *De murmure contre elle et perdre patience*
> *Il est mal à propos;*
> *Vouloir ce que Dieu veut est la seule science*
> *Qui nous met en repos.†*

For some the restraint in composition is moving; for many it is too cold, with more eloquence than sensibility. Malherbe, of course, is deliberately appealing to intellect rather than to emotion, is deliberately attempting to cultivate a detached, rational and analytical view. It is worth remembering that he too could write verse in which formal restraint is abandoned and emotion is deliberately invoked. It happened on the death of his own son who was forced into a duel and killed. The violence of the emotion and of the language in the final stanzas compares interestingly with the *Consolation*.

---

* Taught the powerful effect of the right word in the right place, and compelled the Muse to obey the rules of her craft. Because of this wise author, the French language was purged and no longer offended the refined ear with anything uncouth.

† To murmur against death and to lose patience is inopportune: to desire what God desires is the only knowledge which gives us any rest.

*O mon Dieu, mon Sauveur, puisque par la raison*
*Le trouble de mon âme étant sans guérison,*
*Le vœu de la vengeance est un vœu légitime.*

*Fais que de ton appui je sois fortifié:*
*Ta justice t'en prie, et les auteurs du crime*
*Sont fils de ces bourreaux qui t'ont crucifié.**

The trend towards logical order and self-discipline in literature originated with Malherbe, yet, in his own lifetime, it was not readily apparent. Two influential writers who went their own way regardless of him were Honoré d'Urfé and Alexandre Hardy: one the author of a turbulent, diffuse romance, a disjointed but highly popular amalgam of pastoral idylls and chivalric derring-do; the other the playwright for a turbulent stage, whose melodramas and tragi-comedies lacked form and discipline but played to packed houses. Their works and their significance are described below, but at this stage we should bear in mind that Hardy in particular would have been hailed as the first great literary figure of the century had the classical mood not triumphed.

Among his own kind, the poets, Malherbe had only two avowed disciples, Mainard and Racan. The remainder tended to abuse him. They condemned him as a mere craftsman, devoid of inspiration and weighed down by the mechanics of his prosody, but they did not form a coherent group. Their reactions were too individual, too much the expression of their separate personalities, for them to be identified as an alternative force in French literature. Saint-Amant, for example, represented no group at all. A libertine and a man of the world, he lived a life of great variety, of action and adventure, yet his verses are intensely personal, inspired by a sense of mystery and fantasy. No one else at that time could write such beautifully evocative lines.

---

* O my God, my Saviour, since my troubled spirit has no solace, by natural law my cry for vengeance is legitimate. May I be strengthened by your aid: I beg from you your justice, for the authors of this crime are the children of those murderers who crucified you.

*J'écoute, à demi transporté,*
*Le bruit des ailes du silence*
*Qui vole dans l'obscurité.*\*

His major poem, '*La Solitude*', expresses a concept wholly alien to the dominant mood of his time. It begins:

*Oh! que j'aime la solitude!*
*Que ces lieux sacrés à la nuit,*
*Eloignés du monde et du bruit,*
*Plaisent à mon inquiétude.*†

Indeed, it was the nineteenth-century public which found his life story satisfactorily in the tradition of La Bohème and which appreciated the romantic response to nature in his poetry.

Many of Malherbe's critics had far more in common with him than they imagined. Mathurin Régnier, for example, a successful court poet who was more assiduous than his rival in turning out the formal verses for court occasions, claimed to espouse the cause of the Pléiade. But it was too late to turn the clock back. Between 1600 and 1630 none of the published anthologies of verse included Ronsard, save one, and the edition of his work published in 1630 was the last until 1781. Régnier himself was the last man to imitate the languid eloquence—and the mawkishness—of Ronsard's disciples, and his own works, the 17 Satires, are derived less from the Pléiade than from his own gifts of observation, a satiric temperament and a strong, even crude, sense of realism. His literary battle with Malherbe was not over content, vocabulary or prosody; it was a personal issue. Régnier found him far too prosaic for a poet —'*C'est proser de la rime et rimer de la prose*'—and, as Desportes's nephew, rushed to avenge his uncle's reputation.

Théophile de Viau, another individualist like Saint-Amant, was more generous to Malherbe.

---

\* I listen, half-transported, to the sound of the wings of silence, floating in the darkness.

† Oh! how I love solitude! How these places sacred to the night, far from the world and from noise, satisfy my unquiet mind.

*Imite qui voudra les merveilles d'autrui*
*Malherbe a très bien fait mais il a fait pour lui.**

He shared Malherbe's contempt for the manner in which the Pléiade bowed to classical authority—'*la sotte antiquité*', he called it; and he affirmed, 'We must write as moderns. . . . We must, like Homer, describe things well but not with his very words and epithets: we must write in the way he wrote, but not what he wrote.' He also had the wit to perceive the direction that Malherbe was taking, that light odes would give way to satires and elegies, fantasy to intellectual analysis. For his own part he did not like it.

*Mon âme imaginant n'a point la patience*
*De bien polir des vers, et ranger la science;*
*La règle me déplaît; j'écris confusément;*
*Jamais un bon esprit ne fait rien qu'aisément.†*

De Viau was the only poet whose natural gifts might have enabled him to challenge Malherbe in the theory of the art as well as its practice. Aware that Malherbe was leading towards intellectual abstraction, he preferred to write vigorously of his personal sentiments and emotions, his love of nature and his joy in sensation. 'I love a fine day, clear fountains, a view of the mountain, the layout of a great plain, beautiful forests; the ocean with its waves, its calms and its storms; I love even more everything which involves the senses; music, flowers, fine clothes, the hunt, beautiful horses, good smells, good living.' But though his verse was popular, he himself became suspect. Born of strict Gascon Huguenots in 1590 he became a central figure of the Libertins who championed sensual pleasures and regarded conventional religion with scepticism. Their leader was the Italian Varini, but he was burned in 1619 as a free-thinker, and though de Viau hastily announced his conversion to Rome this did not save him from being condemned to the same fate in 1623. He

---

* Let him who so desires imitate the marvels of others. Malherbe has done very well, but he has done it for himself.

† My inventive spirit has not the patience to polish its verses properly, and rules displease me; I write confusedly and there never was a man of spirit who wrote but easily.

appealed, and after two years in prison was granted a second trial. Here he was acquitted but banished from Paris. He died in 1626, under the protection of the powerful family of Montmorency.

The Libertins were defeated not only by the Church but also by the powerful forces working in French society to establish a stable, centralised administration, especially after Louis XIII had recovered power in 1617. With de Viau's trial and death the movement collapsed. Guez de Balzac and others who had stood on its sidelines hastily drew aside the hems of their skirts and turned to the new star in the ascendant, Richelieu. The consequence for literature was important. The orthodox, conformist group around Malherbe, and his disciples of the next generation, was consolidated. The trend towards discipline, order and reason was confirmed.

# two

# Order and Civility in Society and the Theatre

The restoration of peace made it possible for the economy to be revived, but it was only by the action of individual merchants that the opportunity could be exploited; in the same way, the political achievements of Henri IV's reign made possible, but could not of themselves promote, a more civilised society. For two generations, social life had been more or less confined to castle keeps and provincial towns, and standards of civility, never very sophisticated at the best of times, had deteriorated. The most significant consequence of Henri's enthusiasm for Paris was that the court, instead of wandering from château to château, settled permanently in the capital, and it was in Paris that 'society', *le monde*, at last came into its own.

Henri himself did not assist the reform of manners: in its tone and behaviour his court resembled a barracks. It was all very well for Malherbe to make the court the arbiter of taste in matters of vocabulary, but the vulgarity of court life exposed it to criticism. The wives of several courtiers found it so disgusting that they withdrew to their own *hôtels* in Paris to establish there their own society of nobles, who were prepared for the occasion to accept the standards of their hostess, and of men of letters, who were delighted beyond measure to find a sympathetic audience. Of these few women, the most famous was Catherine de Vivonne, wife of the marquis de Rambouillet. She was physically rather weak, and so could easily excuse herself from court, but her personality was radiantly strong.

She had great charm and beauty, and a genuine gaiety and wit which helped her to combine a keen intelligence with the qualities of good friendship. A contemporary novel describes her: 'Her features are the most noble and the most beautiful that I have ever seen, and there is such tranquillity in her face that it clearly springs from her own true nature. You can see at a glance that there is no inner conflict within her and that all her emotions are controlled by reason.'

Mme de Rambouillet left the court in 1607 when her daughter Julie was born. Within a few years the court had begun to come to her, and every Thursday from 1617 until 1665 she was regularly at home to her guests, in the rue Saint-Thomas du Louvre. Her salon became one of the most civilising and educative influences of the period. In the first place it allowed women to meet men on terms of equality; indeed the women were increasingly acknowledged to be the arbiters of good taste. Terms of mutual respect replaced the insipid gallantry which was the best the court had to offer, and the court's worst features were avoided altogether. The contemporary satire that her *hôtel* was 'a haunt for coquettes' was inaccurate and undeserved. Mme de Rambouillet was unfashionably chaste, devoted to her husband, her family and her faith. In the second place she brought together the most aristocratic of nobles and the most talented of men of letters; this made literature fashionable and good taste popular. The bourgeois writer was acceptable only on the noble's terms, but this had positive advantages. It brought an ill-educated nobility to an appreciation of literature without loss of face and, by keeping the writers firmly in their place, prevented the salon from acquiring too self-consciously a literary air.

Most of the great names of the first half of the century were regular guests at the Hôtel de Rambouillet: Richelieu himself, his enemy the duc de la Rochefoucauld, the great Condé, and another successful soldier, the comte de Guiche, who became a marshal of France. Among the women who held their own as equals were Charlotte de Montmorency—princesse de Condé, and unhappy object of Henri IV's final passion—her daughter the duchesse de Longueville, a notorious Frondeuse, and Mme de Combalet, Richelieu's favourite niece who kept house for him after her husband's death.

There were many too who subsequently established their own salons in direct imitation of their hostess—Mme de Sablé, Mlle de Scudéry, Mme de la Fayette and Mme de Sévigné, whose novels, letters and salons are described below. The writers too—Malherbe, Conrart, Chapelain, Corneille, Voiture and Vaugelas—were the important ones to whose achievement much of this book is devoted.

Conversation was the *raison d'être* of the Hôtel de Rambouillet, and the house had been redesigned to assist it. Following a pattern already established in a few *hôtels*, the staircase was removed from the centre and put to one side of the *corps de logis*, leaving a suite of communicating rooms in which small groups could hold intimate conversation and yet be free to move easily to others. In the central room, the famous Chambre Bleu, was Mme de Rambouillet's day bed. Not physically strong, she had in addition a skin complaint which made it painful for her to be exposed directly to sunlight or to the warmth of a fire. In consequence her day bed was set back in a screened alcove and she received her guests in the *ruelle*, the space between the bed and the wall. *Ruelle*, in fact, was the current word for salon; and we find it defined a little later in the *Dictionnaire* of the Académie Française as an 'assembly which meets at the house of a lady for the sake of lively conversations'.

Lively conversations is not a good translation of '*conversations d'esprit*', though the first condition of such conversations was that they should not be dull. This was due to the presence of the women since, as Diderot explained a century later, 'women compel us to discuss with charm and clarity the driest and thorniest subjects. If we wish them to listen, and are afraid to tire or bore them, we develop a particular method of explaining ourselves easily, which method passes from conversation into style.' Pedantry was the worst offence. It was resented equally by the nobles and by the women, since neither had had much education, and few were versed in Latin and Greek. 'There is no other place in the world where there is more good sense and less pedantry', wrote Chapelain, yet he was probably the worst offender. In general the *galants* set the tone, and the *savants* like Chapelain were forced to wear their learning lightly. Wit was considered a vital attribute of *esprit*; not so much the production of *bans mots*, since a learned society had plenty of time in which to polish up its fine phrases, but the facility to hit a point spontaneously. Mme de Rambouillet was once hearing out an over-credulous abbé, who kept repeating how many steps had been taken by some saint after decapitation. Finally she broke in, 'But, Monseigneur, it is only the first step which counts.' Malherbe, too, had a reputation for wit. Tallement tells of a Provençal *parlementaire* who put a hideous coat of arms in the centre of the chimney piece. Seeking admiration he turned to Malherbe: 'How does it seem to you?' 'I should put it a little lower', he said.

It is true that conversation was enjoyed at times as much for its form as its content, and contemporary criticism of the shallowness of salon life had some justification. The abbé Goussault, in the midst of several reflections on the faults of mankind, added, 'with the ladies, provided that a man is very respectful, and that he relates the latest gossip . . . then he is accepted as a very fine, *honnête homme.*' But conversations did not lack content at the Hôtel de Rambouillet. When we consider the men of affairs who were present, the discussions must have been at least well-informed, though political matters were wisely excluded. Much of the conversation was devoted to the social ideal which the salon itself was doing much to establish, the concept of the *honnête homme*, and since this ideal was largely a reflection of themselves the guests of Mme de Rambouillet may be pardoned for taking such pleasure in talking about it and in trying to give it definition. The concept was derived in part from one of the most famous books to come from Renaissance Italy, Castiglione's *Courtier*, and several books had appeared in France in imitation, among them the *Guide des Courtisans* by Nervèze (1606), *Gentilhomme de Cour* by Pasquier (1611), and *Traité de Cour* by de Refuge (1616).

Courtly academies, the one sector of formal education in France to have any social significance in the seventeenth century, were greatly influenced by Castiglione's ideal of *l'uomo universale*. The curricula of schools in general had little bearing on social behaviour and less on the enjoyment of the arts. Even the best schools, those of the Jesuits and the Jansenists, were almost exclusively academic

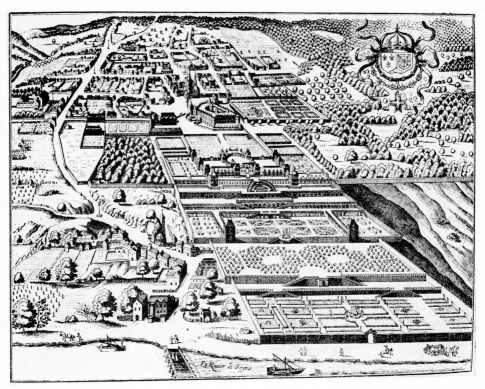

4. The gardens at Saint-Germain-en-Laye, designed by Claude Mollet for Henri IV (see pages 30–1).

5. Château de Charleval. This engraving by the architect, Jacques Androuet du Cerceau, illustrates the mannerist style in France (*cf* plates 12 and 13, and see pages 27–9)

6. The Hôtel de Rambouillet by Paul Mérivart (see pages 45–6)

7. Pierre Corneille, after a portrait by Charles Le Brun (see pages 108–13)

in their emphasis, but the priests of the Oratory, who founded the courtly academies, set out to provide a social education. So valuable was this for the sons of the nobility, and so necessary, that Louis XIII and Richelieu encouraged the Oratory to set up several academies across France. The priests who taught were men of wide education and culture, and though Latin naturally held the honoured place, history, geography, politics and modern languages were given considerable time and emphasis in the curriculum. It was not thus surprising, for example, that when the scientific and philosophical ideas of Descartes began, in the mid-century, to challenge the inherited systems of thought, the Oratorians were the first to adapt their teaching to the new ideas. Any young noble, therefore, who pursued his studies with any thoroughness was as well primed as the scholars of other schools, though this was not the only object of the academies. Fencing, riding and dancing were given a great deal of attention, courage and athletic skill were highly valued but, above all, the academies fostered and controlled the very qualities most admired in the salons—courtesy, civility and enough knowledge of the world and of letters to maintain a serious conversation in good company, and sufficient taste to make the right comments on such matters as food, sermons or plays.

Most of this was summarised in 1632 by Nicolas Faret in his *L'honnête homme, ou l'art de plaire à la cour*. Though he is clearly translating much of Castiglione's work, he is also establishing *l'honnête homme* as the product of the salon, not least when he demands the ability to hold one's own in conversation. 'I prefer my *honnête homme* to be passably knowledgeable in several disciplines than to be profound in one only; . . . since he who can only speak well on one subject is obliged to keep silent too often.' This concept of social and conversational skill was developed further by Vaugelas in *Remarques sur la langue française*, where he agrees that all the obvious qualities of education and physical prowess must be accompanied 'by a certain manner which . . . can only be acquired in the company of the great nobles and the ladies'. There is much to criticise in the ideal. It was essentially aristocratic, confined to a virtually closed community, and it reflected and confirmed the sharp divisions within French society with singular complacency. Moreover, as Faret indicated in his title, the *honnête homme* sought to please. In consequence, it became possible to judge a man less by his conformity to the traditional codes of morality than by his adaptability to the swiftly changing standards of social custom in fashionable society.

The repudiation of pedantry and the genteel affectation of ama- teurishness could too easily lead to a suave manner concealing ig- norance or indifference. Abbé Goussault attacked this superficiality as we have seen, and a later moralist, La Bruyère, put it more bluntly still: 'The *honnête homme* stands somewhere between Mr Cleverdick and Mr Goodman, but not at an equal distance from both, for the difference between him and Mr Cleverdick gets less with every day, and is on the point of disappearing altogether.' Against this obvious weakness, we must set the uncivilised standards of society in 1600, and recognise the tremendous importance of the salons and the aca- demies in securing the acceptance by a roughshod, even boorish, nobility of a more polished and urbane ideal of social behaviour. This educative role of the Hôtel de Rambouillet, and of its concept of *l'honnête homme*, was more vital to the development of French civilisa- tion in the seventeenth century than the provision of money to pay for it.

The Hôtel de Rambouillet was also attracted to discussions on the nature and psychology of love, a subject prompted directly by Honoré d'Urfé's novel *L'Astrée* which was welcomed with rapture in the salons and which, for all its inchoate literary form, exercised a powerful influence in civilising the French nobility. D'Urfé's own story was as romantic as any in his novel. At the age of 17 he had to leave home, supposedly for falling in love with his sister-in-law, Diane de Châteaumorand. He joined the Knights of St John, and fought for the Catholic League against Henri IV. Captured in 1595, ransomed by Diane, then recaptured, he was finally released in the service of the Duke of Savoy. Diane meanwhile secured the annul- ment of her marriage, d'Urfé left the Knights of St John, and came home to make his peace with Henri IV and to marry Diane. Between 1607 and 1613 he published the first two parts of *L'Astrée*; he then separated from Diane for six years in which he returned to Savoy,

and published part three in 1619. Soon after this he was reconciled
with his wife, went soldiering again abroad, died of pneumonia in
1625 and was followed within a month or so by his wife. The manuscript for part four was edited posthumously by his secretary Baro,
who wrote the fifth and final part himself from notes left by his master.

L'Astrée is narrated in a diffuse style which today is virtually un-
readable, but which did not prevent it being a bestseller in its day.
Set in the fifth century, on the banks of the Lignon (in d'Urfé's own
district of Forez in the Lyonnais), it is the story of the shepherd
Céladon and his love for the shepherdess Astrée. When Astrée falsely
suspects him of infidelity she banishes Céladon from her sight. He
tries to lose his life in the waters of the Lignon but is saved by three
nymphs who then try to seduce him. Resisting their charms he re-
tires to the forest and builds a rustic temple dedicated to the worship
of Astrée. He meets a Druid, disguises himself as the Druid's daughter
Léonide, and in this guise is reintroduced to Astrée. He wins her
confidence in a long series of conversations on the subtle psychology
of love and finally persuades her to call for Céladon to reappear. At
this he reveals himself, but Astrée is so angry at his deceit that she
banishes him yet again. After many vicissitudes, and despite 45 incidental narratives and by-plots, interspersed with madrigals and sonnets, the lovers are finally reconciled when they meet by a magic
fountain.

This tale of suffering, of an enduring and infinitely faithful love,
was a theme so refined and divorced from real life that it attracted
the admiration of readers in the salons, from whose windows 'real
life' seemed so lacking in good taste. After the long civil war, and its
sporadic revival between 1610 and 1617, they found great delight
in this idealised picture of pastoral tranquillity, in which country
noblemen appeared not as warriors but as shepherds—not, of course,
to tend sheep, but to discuss the nature of love with elegant shepherdesses of their own class. This picture so enthralled the habitués
of the Hôtel de Rambouillet that periodic excursions were made,
in the appropriate costumes, to the Château de Rambouillet where
they held their picnics à l'Astrée to the music of violins concealed in
the shrubbery. Much more important than this was the effect of

*L'Astrée* in helping to establish a new ideal of courtly gallantry. Mme de Rambouillet had done much to win respect for women as the social equals of men, and had raised the tone of society by insisting on the universal acceptance of moral conventions in her salon. *L'Astrée* reinforced her efforts by disassociating love from vulgar sensuality and blind passion, and by showing it to be an honourable sentiment of which virtue, modesty and constancy were the prime characteristics. After the much-publicised love stories of the Vert-Galant himself, Henri IV, in which women were merely the object of man's overriding lust, the effect of a story whose hero obeyed the heroine's every command was most salutary. Virtuous womanhood was glorified, her courtly lover idealised.

Discussions on the nature of *l'honnête homme* and of courtly love, for all their interest, cannot by themselves explain the prolonged popularity of Mme de Rambouillet's salon. It was her achievement to make of it a place not only of wit, intelligence and refinement but of genuine gaiety. The nobility attended her *hôtel* for so long because primarily they enjoyed her company and the fun she engendered; and because they did not wish to be excluded, the most boorish would endeavour to restrain themselves. Practical jokes were very popular, if not to our taste today, and we must remember not only the discussions on *L'Astrée* but the incursion of two performing bears, released by Voiture behind the screens of his hostess's *ruelle*. She, in turn, scored heavily off him, in a joke as carefully prepared as the *bons mots* of salon conversation. Taking one of Voiture's new poems, she had it printed, paginated and bound in an earlier collection of his verse, and left it lying around for him to discover. The comte de Guiche suffered greatly after over-eating one night, not from indigestion but because, while he slept, the other guests took in his doublets. The next morning, convinced that he had mysteriously swollen up, he attended mass in a dressing-gown and consulted his friends for a remedy. Finally, one who claimed experience of the disease wrote him a prescription: '*Recipe de bon ciseaux et décous ton pourpoint*' (take a pair of scissors and cut open your doublet).

But, as gossip could rise to the level of conversation, so games and jokes did not have to degenerate to mere horseplay. There was a great vogue for parlour games of a literary sort; *jeux de la lettre*, in which all replies to questions had to begin with a chosen letter, riddles in verse and *bouts rimés*, in which verses are composed to a given set of rhymes. On one occasion, in 1641, a symposium of 91 poems by habitués of the salon was composed, decorated, bound, and presented to Mme de Rambouillet's daughter Julie. It was entitled '*La Guirlande de Julie*'; each poem represented the praise accorded to Julie by a separate flower. Versification was indeed very popular in the Hôtel de Rambouillet, though not with all its critics: 'The value of a poet was measured by his capacity for turning a somersault in verse, for constructing ingenious word puzzles with which to express exaggerated sentiments' (Lytton Strachey). While all this is true, it misses the point that many of the verses were composed by nobles, who a generation earlier would have shot a poet as soon as look at him.

One poet whose intelligence and good taste saved him from mere cleverness and banality was Vincent Voiture. His father was a well-to-do wine merchant at Amiens with a contract to supply the court, and he was able to send his son to the Collège de Boncour and on to the university at Orléans to read law. One of the most valuable results of his education was the friendship he made with the comte d'Avaux, who helped him greatly by introducing him to influential and important men. In 1626 he became *conseiller du roi* and in the following year Gaston d'Orléans, the king's brother, gave him a post in his household. Since Gaston was frequently in conspiracy against Richelieu, and in exile from 1631 to 1636, Voiture was under suspicion at court and spent the years of Gaston's exile in Lorraine, Madrid and the Spanish Netherlands. On his return he retained his salary from Gaston but was also employed by Richelieu on a series of diplomatic missions to Italy, Spain and Morocco. As a result of this he was nominated to the Académie Française, but his fortune was finally made when d'Avaux became *surintendant des finances* and appointed Voiture his *premier commis*. Thereafter he was worth 18,000 livres a year.

Voiture's reputation as a brilliant conversationalist was first made at the Hôtel de Rambouillet which he dominated from his first appearance in 1625 until his death in 1648. He combined the most remarkable qualities of social grace with wit and intelligence, a fact of especial significance since it reconciled the nobility to his bourgeois birth and enabled him to interest them in matters of literary criticism and good taste. A discussion on the spelling of *muscadin*, for example, which could well have been left to the pedants, was transformed into a lively salon issue with Voiture's witty attack on those who spelled it *muscardin*, by making it rhyme with other words to which he added a wholly superfluous *r*. It begins,

> *Au siècle des vieux palardins,*
> *Soit courtisans, soit citardins,*
> *Femmes de cour ou citardines,*
> *Prononçaient toujours muscardines,* etc.

Another celebrated literary issue was his defence of the word *car*, threatened first by Malherbe and then by the Académie Française which wanted to replace it by the clumsy *pour ce que*. In a charming letter to Julie he wrote; 'If anyone had told me some years back that I might have to live longer than *car*, I would have thought that I had been promised a longer life than any of the patriarchs. However, it has come about that after having been employed in the most important treatises, and been ever honourably present in the councils of our kings, it falls suddenly into disgrace and is threatened with a violent end.'

Though his verses were elegant and refined, and his '*Sonnet d'Uranie*' most charmingly composed and very popular in its day, the sentiments were artificial. As Lanson wrote of him, in a phrase worthy of the salons, he was 'passionately attentive, but more interested in the gentle compliments he paid than in the women to whom he paid them'. His wit and skill were more evident in the *bouts rimés* competitions, and especially in his revival of the complex *rondeau* form. This demanded the repetition of certain phrases and the use of only two rhymes. Voiture's version is quite untranslatable, but the complexity of the rules, and the ingenuity and wit with which he achieves them, are evident at a glance.

*Ma foi, c'est fait de moi, car Isabeau*
*M'a conjuré de lui faire un rondeau.*
*Cela me met en une peine extrême.*
*Quoi! treize vers, huit en eau, cinq en eme!*
*Je lui ferais aussi tôt un bateau!*

*En voilà cinq pourtant en un monceau.*
*Faisons-en huit en invoquant Brodeau,** 
*Et puis mettons, par quelque stratagème:*
   *Ma foi, c'est fait.*

*Si je pouvais encore de mon cerveau*
*Tirer cinq vers, l'ouvrage serait beau;*
*Mais cependant je suis dedans l'onzième,*
*Et ci je crois que je fais le douzième;*
*En voilà treize ajustés au niveau.*
   *Ma foi, c'est fait.*

Though they have little lasting value as literature, the *rondeaux*, *bouts rimés*, riddles and sonnets of Voiture were vital in awakening a measure of literary taste among the French nobility. Men who would have fled the company of Malherbe spent hours in conversation with Voiture, and because he aroused their interest, sugared the pill with wit and indicated the causes of good taste, they were more ready to appreciate the excellence of the other writers of their age.

This in essence was the role of the Hôtel de Rambouillet. Providing very little save accommodation for a few, it was scarcely a source of patronage, but it educated the patrons. It served as a nursery for an influential reading public; it refined manners and, as an arbiter of taste, it surpassed the court. Because of its existence the French nobility was less likely to boast of its own illiteracy; its manners were refined and its sensibility extended. The price paid for this was a measure of artificiality. Writers generally became preoccupied with salon society. For all that they gained an insight from the psychological analysis of *l'honnête homme* and the classical hero, they gave no thought to man in his struggle with nature, disease and

---

* A contemporary dictionary of rhymes.

poverty. Town life—indeed salon life, alone—became the norm for writers; the countryside was ignored save for what was seen from the terraces at Saint-Germain or at a *fête champêtre* at Rambouillet. Within this artificial milieu, the end product could well be the eighteenth-century marquis whose indifference to life as it was lived by the human race was expressed in his aphorism, '*Vivre?—nos valets le feront pour nous*'.

This aristocratic detachment, and its preoccupation with a very restricted world, is closely related to another feature of salon life, its *préciosité*. This was the attempt to be different for its own sake, a form of artificial refinement and of ostentation which was deliberately cultivated at the Hôtel de Rambouillet. As originally used, the word had no pejorative overtones, and we must forget at this stage that later in the century Molière was to link, it seems for ever, *précieuses* with *ridicules*. In the salon it was nothing more or less than the attempt to distinguish oneself from others by a show of refinement. There was nothing new in this. A wave of *préciosité* had already passed over Europe at the end of the sixteenth century. In England, for example, John Lyly had encouraged the adoption of a formal, elaborate style of writing, characterised by rhetorical antitheses, copious alliteration and the frequent citation of classical and medieval lore. The same degree of artificiality is found too in Robert Green's *Carde of Fancie*, a blend of allegory and romance, and similar movements had appeared in Spain, Italy and France. Daniel Mornet has shown how *préciosité* of an extreme sort had led to the exaggerated refinements of authors like Nervèze and Escuteaux; and what could be more far-fetched, more 'conceited', than the title of a best-selling book by François Desrues, 'Flowers of fine speaking, gathered from the salons of the most refined spirits of the age, for expressing amorous passions whether for men or for women.'

The *précieux* of the Hôtel de Rambouillet were much more restrained. In a highly conversational and aristocratic milieu their object was to distinguish themselves where possible by originality of thought or expression. It was given to only a few, such as Voiture, to achieve originality of thought, and the others, wisely, concentrated on the art of rendering their ideas more striking by the piquancy of their vocabulary or by the ingenious construction of their phrases. It was a natural development, in effect, of the skill required for *conversations d'esprit*. It set out to achieve effect by use of the unexpected, by contrast, by archaism, by exaggeration; superlatives, for example, were overworked, as were words like *furieusement* and *ravissant*. Precision was used to good effect, as in distinguishing *aimer une dame* from *goûter un melon*; and some of the neologisms invented for effect soon passed into the language at large: *s'en-canailler*, to degrade oneself, and *féliciter*, to congratulate.

There was a marked aversion for words which were too technical or too frankly working-class, and great ingenuity—and wit—was required to find substitutes such as *le supplément du soleil* for candle, and *l'instrument de la propreté* for brush. This of course was to base literary usage on class distinction, but it was to be the theme of Vaugelas's *Remarques sur la langue française* (1647), where he equated good usage with court usage: 'We must not forget the rule that *honnêtes hommes* must never use low words or phrases in conversation, unless they are trying to be funny.' Periphrasis was necessary, too, to avoid words which were too harshly realistic, physical or suggestive. *Vomir*, to vomit, *cracher*, to spit, and *poitrine*, breast, were therefore abhorred; Balzac even jibbed at a line from a famous sonnet, 'Job', by Benserade, '*vous verrez sa misère nue*', because of the suggestive overtones of the word *naked*. This was indeed being precious; so was Mme de Longueville who applauded an Italian castrato by exclaiming, '*Mon dieu, que cet* incommodé *chante bien*'.

We must remember that the immediate fun of inventing new words and phrases, or of giving old ones a new emphasis, is not to be confused with the slavish repetition of them; indeed, those who invented them were the ones least likely to take them too seriously. There was literary gain in the exercise, too, since the salon writers developed considerable skill in the use of metaphor, though there was less when they prolonged their metaphors with too great subtlety. The pursuit of refinement could lead easily to mere affectation and coterie jargon, but Mme de Rambouillet was too robust in her sense of humour to allow either of these to go unchecked. Moreover, the easy, aristocratic self-confidence of most of her guests discouraged affectation. The great nobles did not have to model themselves on others; they set the tone of society by instinct and tradition, and their presence prevented the salon becoming an over-precious literary clique. 'High society purifies', wrote Chapelain, who knew the dangers of his own pedantry and how he restrained himself to avoid rebuff by men like Condé or the comte de Guiche.

The *précieux* of the Hôtel de Rambouillet were not effeminate. If the influence of their hostess, and of *L'Astrée*, succeeded to some extent in civilising their manners, it did not tame their natures, since there were the men who fought violent duels, intrigued against the government and led their separate armies in the Fronde. Yet, though they do not appear so obviously as Malherbe or de Brosse, they stand as necessary forerunners of the classical tradition in France. In the first place they rejected the extreme forms of euphuism; they introduced a degree of restraint and good taste in place of the absurd over-elaboration and over-emphasis of writers like Nervèze. In this, '*ils ont fait œuvre classique*' (Mornet). Moreover, the language of the classical age owed a great deal of its purity and precision to them. They continued the work of Malherbe in refining vocabulary, and in developing the notion of what is deemed suitable for use in fine literature. At the same time they enriched the language by neologism and periphrasis, by the epigram, by teaching the force a word acquires when put in its proper place. They added a further dimension to Malherbe's criterion. He sought to make language universally intelligible; they wanted it to give pleasure as well. The identification of the *précieux* with the classical tradition which triumphed in France has not always been accepted, but there is much to recommend it. However self-conscious their effort, they were nonetheless seeking after literary form. Learning to develop a sense of style often results in fussy over-elaboration—the unnecessary flourishes of the tyro—yet it marks an important step forward from the stage of indifference to form.

The epigrams and *conversations d'esprit* led directly to the clarity and simplicity of Pascal, Mme de Sévigné and La Bruyère. The parlour games and *questions d'amour* gave way to the penetrating analysis of the passions by La Rochefoucauld, Mme de la Fayette and Racine. This taste for psychology lies at the bottom of classical literature, and it is the predicament of the human soul which is treated in the great tragedies of the classical age. Above all, we must remember that the great classical authors wrote for the sophisticated public of the salons; without it there would have been no great body of literature. The blend of delicacy and dignity, the sensitivity to language, the taste for psychological analysis, and the concentration on man and his moral predicament—hallmarks of the classical age—could not have been achieved without *la société précieuse* which gathered in the Hôtel de Rambouillet.

Though *préciosité* was essential to the development of classicism, it was not in itself uniformly classical. There was often too much affectation, too much emphasis on refinement, and this provided a reaction. If propriety is the essence of *préciosité*, burlesque deliberately flouts it, and the elaborate gallantry and high-flown emotions of courtly shepherdesses and pastoral cavaliers were met with a fruity belch and a belly laugh. In 1622 Charles Sorel published the *Histoire Comique de Francion*, and in 1627 the *Berger Extravagant*, in which he deliberately burlesqued *L'Astrée* and revelled in using the very language to which the *précieux* took exception.

The greatest exponent of burlesque was Paul Scarron. The son of a *parlementaire*, he was pushed into the Church and became a canon at Le Mans under the bishop's patronage, without taking full orders. In 1637, aged 27, he was crippled by rheumatism, returned to Paris as a helpless hunch-back and married Mlle d'Aubigné, who later became Mme de Maintenon. In Scarron's work there is buffoonery, coarseness and realism of the most explicit kind combined with a tremendous zest and an acute observation of the human animal. The first part of *Le Roman Comique*, the adventures of a troupe of players around Le Mans, was so popular that for the second part he secured a quite exceptional advance of 1,000 livres. He then proposed a burlesque of the *Aeneid*, a *Virgile Travesti*, and was given 11,000 livres to produce 11 cantos. This was very successful. He preserved the form of the classic epic, but parodied the content, making his gods and heroes talk in slang.

One essential point to remember about Sorel and Scarron is that they wrote for the very people whose tastes they were satirising; otherwise the whole point of their work would have been lost. Like the mannerist painters, their success depended on a sophisticated public which was aware of the rules they were flouting. In other words, the burlesque writers do not represent a rival tendency, appealing to a rival public. Theirs is a reaction to the excesses of *préciosité*, written by and for those who understood its nature. *Le Roman Comique* is as essentially a product of the salon environment as '*La Guirlande de Julie*'.

The improved standards of civility and order, achieved by the influence of the Hôtel de Rambouillet, acting within a context of greater internal peace and political stability, were also achieved during the same period in the Parisian theatre. This theatre had its origins in the dramatic presentation of simple Biblical scenes before the altar of Notre-Dame; as the plays became more complex, and as other themes from the lives of the saints were added, the performers moved into the cathedral precinct. Across the west front they erected a long platform stage with all the necessary scene settings, or *mansions*, placed side by side. Hell was usually at the audience's extreme right, Heaven at its left. As the action of the play switched from one scene to another, the actors would move in front of the appropriate *mansion*. The plays were intensely realistic but lacked any conscious form in their composition; indeed, so many extra passages were added in relating the adventures of a saint that the entire work could only be performed as a serial play. The realism sometimes got out of hand with the actors playing up to their audiences to give them extra thrills or belly laughs. One exasperated contemporary complained that 'in order to lengthen the Acts of the Apostles they have added several apocryphal things, and at the beginning and end of it have introduced loose farces and pantomimes, and have extended their play productions to the length of six or seven months, which led and leads to the neglect of divine service, indifference in almsgiving and charity, adultery and incessant fornication, scandals, mockery and scorn.' The theatre, it seems, has always had much to answer for.

The organisation responsible for the presentation of these plays was a religious and charitable brotherhood of well-to-do merchants, established by letters patent in 1402 as the Confrérie de la Passion et Résurrection de nostre Sauveur et Rédempteur Jésus-Christ. In 1548 it purchased the Hôtel de Bourgogne, a converted tennis court, for its secular productions; in the same year, coincidentally, those who shared the views of the captious critic already quoted carried the day with the authorities and secured a ban on all Mystery and religious plays. Soon after this the Confrérie changed its function. No longer presenting plays itself, it exploited its monopoly by leasing out the Hôtel de Bourgogne to troupes of players, and maintained its charitable works, processions and masses from the proceeds. In terms of hard cash this meant raising 2,000 to 2,500 livres annually by renting out the theatre, and there were very few troupes who could hope to do sufficiently well to pay the Confrérie its high rentals as well as make a profit for themselves—especially when there was competition from the mountebanks and players of the Pont Neuf, the Foire Saint-Germain and the Foire Saint-Laurent. Attempts were made to evade the monopoly by leasing other premises. One company took over a tennis court in 1609, renaming it the Hôtel d'Argent, but the authorities upheld the Confrérie and fined the actors. The same thing happened in 1622, and on this occasion a general prohibition was published against the use of tennis courts for theatrical productions.

Several Italian companies, the Gelosi, the Andreini and the Alfieri, ran successful seasons of *commedia dell'arte* at the Hôtel de Bourgogne, but the first company to establish itself there with any semblance of permanence was Les Comédiens Français Ordinaires du Roi led by Valleran Lecomte, an actor of great repute who was largely responsible for their long run from 1610 to 1622. In 1622 they could no longer meet the rental charges, and for 12 months there were no theatrical productions in Paris. A rival company, the Troupe de M. le Prince d'Orange, made occasional forays into France from the Netherlands and ventured as far south as Paris, where it was joined by Guillaume Montdory. In 1625, on the death of their patron, the actors decided to settle in Paris under Montdory's leadership, and leased the Hôtel de Bourgogne. They too failed to survive there. Fortunately, however, public taste for the theatre was growing, receipts began to improve, and in 1629 the Comédiens du roi settled in as permanent tenants of the Confrérie. In the same year Montdory and his colleagues set up a rival theatre in a tennis court in the Marais, and Paris, at last, possessed two theatres, each with its regular company.

This was still very little to boast about. London, for example, had five, and the Parisian theatre was remarkably crude both in its subject-matter and its physical form. The Hôtel de Bourgogne betrayed its original function as a tennis court—as did the Marais until it was burned in 1644 and rebuilt. It was a long narrow box. The stage was at one of the short ends, and the audience was accommodated in a double row of *loges* around the other walls and in the parterre in the middle. As most of the audience were facing each other, it was therefore difficult for the actors to secure their attention. In addition, they could not spread out the long line of multiple settings as they had been accustomed to do in the open air; instead they crammed them together in a complex setting which must have caused confusion among both actors and audience. An illustration from the basic seventeenth-century authority on stage-management, *Le Mémoire de Mahelot*, shows one such stage plan for a play called *L'Agarite*, which required a castle, a seat, a ruined church, a tomb, a throne, a palace and a bedroom.

One possible solution was the erection of a double-decker stage, or at least a semi-permanent structure ready for use when necessary. Lawrenson believes it was done by the Confrérie when they first experimented with indoor productions at L'Hôpital de la Trinité in the fifteenth century, and it is quite clear from the following explicit order to the builders that it was done at the Marais after the fire of 1644: 'Up above the stage you must make another one, 12 feet high and of the same length as the other, supported on eight pillars.' Another device, recorded in the *Mémoire du Mahelot*, was to cover up part of the scenery until it was needed. In *Lisandre et Caliste*, for example, there had to be a butcher's shop and opposite it a barred window; 'this window must be hidden during Act One and must not be seen until Act Two. It must then be covered up again.'

The best solution to the problem of the *décor simultané* was to abolish it, but this was not possible until the new theories of dramatic art after 1630 demanded that all the action should occur in one place. It was first done at the Marais for the plays of Jean Mairet but, within a decade or so, the company adopted a new fashion for *pièces à machines*, a species of pantomime and musical spectacular which involved prodigious changes of scene (see chapter 4). For this, of course, special machines were imported from Italy, but to conceal their action a proscenium curtain had to be introduced for the first time. It was not used at the Hôtel de Bourgogne where the new tradition of the single scene struck root. From 1640 onwards, the stage became an unchanging *palais à volonté* or *chambre à quatre portes*, the staple setting of classical drama in the seventeenth century.

In the early seventeenth century, plays were put on twice a week, and in the afternoon because the civic authorities were suspicious of evening assemblies. The staple fare seems to have been a *prologue comique*, a tragedy or tragi-comedy and finally a farce. Expert authorities disagree very strongly about this, but it seems likely that both the prologue and the farce were boisterous and obscene in their humour. This was only to be expected since the tone of public comedy was set by the entertainers of the fairs and markets, when a man like the famous Tabarin drew the crowds in order that his brother might sell them patent medicines or draw their teeth. Performances such as these must have been crude in word and gesture. Then there were the Italian companies. The tradition of the *commedia dell'arte* was that of a stylised pantomime, with stock characters like the ridiculous old man Pantalone, the soldier, Matamoros, the picaresque trickster, Scaramouche, and the lovers, Harlequin and Columbine, who were identified by masks or flour and paint make-up. The dialogue was improvised, but it counted for little before an audience ignorant of Italian, and the action depended upon mimicry, gesture and broad clowning.

The companies at the Hôtel de Bourgogne and the Marais were no less crude. It is true that Henriette du Rohan, writing in 1618 about the Troupe de M. le Prince d'Orange, seems to deny this—

'They were very decent, and there was no foul language'—but we must either question her interpretation of a '*vilaine parole*' or accept the weight of the evidence against her. Most of the plays were stories of seduction and adultery, which were told with a wealth of obscenity. Take, for example, the lines addressed to the ladies of the play in the *Ballet des Quolibets* (1627):

> *Je porte un baton de mesure*
> *Dont quinze pouces de longueur*
> *Par les efforts de la nature*
> *Amortiraient votre langueur.*

We must also remember that Gros-Guillaume, a coarse and popular *comédien*, played the Place Dauphine as well as the Hôtel de Bourgogne, and the printed versions of Bruscambille's obscene *prologues comiques* sold like hot cakes on the Pont Neuf. Even the central item on the programme, the tragedy, though neither comic nor obscene, was packed with violent scenes of vengeance, rape and murder.

The traditional explanation of the crudity of the drama was that it was played to a crude audience, an audience which was assumed to have been largely plebeian and wholly masculine. This view was supported by Tallement's much-quoted dictum, 'Decent women never went to the theatre', and when one play, *Les Corrivaux*, began with a greeting to the audience, 'Messieurs, God grant you joy, and to you also mesdames, and to you beautiful wives and daughters', it was taken by later critics as an ironic reference to the prostitutes who haunted the theatre. The argument was further reinforced by quoting the abbé d'Aubignac who wrote in 1657, 'Fifty years ago no decent woman dared to go to the theatre', but Lough challenges the thesis by quoting the abbé's next phrase, 'unless she went veiled and incognito'. But there is no need to exchange quotations to demonstrate that nobles, and noble ladies, attended the theatre. As Lough points out, when Marie de' Medici, a very devout woman, retired to Blois in 1617 after Louis XIII had seized power and driven her from the court, she enlivened her exile by sending once for Gros-Guillaume and twice for Tabarin, 'and those of his company to act the plays they have frequently done for us in the past for our

8. Louis XIII crowned by Victory, by Philippe de Champaigne. The background scene commemorates the siege of La Rochelle (see page 78)

9. Nanteuil's engraving of Mazarin inside the Palais Cardinal

10. Philippe de Champaigne's triple portrait of Richelieu, possibly intended as a preliminary study for a statue (see page 94)

pleasure and our service'. It is possible that Tabarin modified his act, but this is unlikely when we consider that the lines from the *Ballet des Quolibets* were written specially for the entertainment of the court. Moreover, the court attended the Hôtel de Bourgogne so frequently that the notion of two standards of entertainment is not tenable. 'There can be no reasonable doubt that the King and his courtiers, male and female, saw the same plays—French and Italian— as were presented to the normal audience in the Paris Theatre' (Lough).

Those who went to the parterre were generally rowdy and drunken, but socially they were the superiors of Shakespeare's groundlings. Most of them were nobles and army officers, mixed with a few middle-class merchants and intellectuals. They paid five sous, the equivalent of sixpence in seventeenth-century England, and by mid-century the price had been increased to 30 sous for a new play and 15 for a repeat production. The *loges*, at double the price of the parterre, were occupied almost exclusively by the nobility and royalty, but a bourgeois who wanted to take his wife with him could secure one.

The refinement of the theatre after 1620, a process we shall examine in the following pages, cannot be attributed therefore to any social change in the composition of the audience. Rather, the audiences began to adopt the new standards which were gaining ground in society through the influence of the salons. The fashion for propriety and *préciosité* put an end to coarse gesture and foul language on the stage. Violence, too, became objectionable, and a growing feeling for form and order was expressed in distaste for the disorganised, rambling scripts of the early 1600s. To reform comedy it was enough to bowdlerise the obscenities, but it was in the development of tragedy that the process of refinement and the taste for order led to the most remarkable developments in the very concept of tragedy itself.

A significant step had already been taken in the sixteenth century when some of the poets and scholars had begun to write tragedies, even though their inspiration owed more to a reading of classical literature than to any experience of the tennis courts and other improvised theatres. Accordingly, the first stage was one of mere translation—*Électre* (1537), *Hécube* (1544)—but during the winter of 1552–3 Étienne Jodelle entertained the court of Henri II with his *Cléopâtre Captive*, the first original tragedy in the French language. It was intellectual drama in the worst sense, not for being a pastiche of Plutarch, but because it had no chance of survival on the stage. It was written for a play-reading, not for acting. It was nonetheless important for its influence. The play was in five acts; violent episodes, including Cleopatra's death, were kept off stage and reported by a chorus; and the plot was concentrated upon the situation after Anthony's death. This pattern of treatment was repeated in Jodelle's later plays, and was developed theoretically by another playwright, Jean de la Taille. Aristotle had laid down that no good play could be written without unity of action, but de la Taille went much further in advocating the case for concentration by demanding acceptance of three unities—of action, time and place.

In 1572, when these theories were proposed, the public found them unacceptable—for a very simple reason. Tragedy was handicapped by the failure of Jodelle and others to grasp its essential nature. Their concept was too immature, too static and too dull. Instead of demonstrating the building up of unbearable tensions and inner conflicts as the tragic hero began to find himself caught up in events, they were content to produce a series of solemn lamentations before and after the inevitable death of their hero. Tragedy, in short, instead of being an analysis of human nature under attack, was nothing more than the mournful relation of a sad story. It is not surprising that audiences preferred the long-winded, poorly constructed, complex, prolix and prolific tragi-comedies which poured in from Spain and Italy, because these, for all their faults, had the power to move and excite them.

The first French tragedies to be written by men of letters with any understanding of the theatre were by Robert Garnier, whose plays were produced by a troupe which toured the north and west, with occasional stands in Paris. He developed Jodelle's practice of eliminating physical violence from the stage because he saw that the representation of spiritual and mental conflict could be much more powerful in its effect. In *Sédécie, ou Les Juives* (1583) he confined the action to the supplications and lamentations of the Jews, but gave them an extra dimension and greater impact by reported scenes of the horrors perpetrated offstage by Nebuchadnezzar and his agents. Garnier's style was important; it was imitated by Antoine de Montchrétien, whose *L'Écossaise* was successful at the Hôtel de Bourgogne in 1601, and it could have set the trend towards refinement and order in the theatre. Instead, a counter-blow was suddenly struck by Alexandre Hardy.

Hardy was the *poète à gages*, the company's own author, at the Hôtel de Bourgogne until his death in 1632. He is credited with having written—or put together—600 plays, but less than 40 have survived because the Comédiens du Roi forbade their publication lest other companies produce them. Hardy was first of all a man of the theatre; he worked with actors, derived his living from them, and came to know instinctively what could be successfully put across to an audience. He abandoned the chorus as a deadening device, and set out to produce exuberant plays, full of action, suspense and conflict. His tragedies were frank melodramas, his pastorals the stage equivalent of *L'Astrée*, and his tragi-comedies full of complications, surprise encounters and magical transformations. Hardy was also a poet, though not a gifted one, and in touch with the intellectuals of his age. Aware of the rules which were being discussed he generally observed them in the letter though rarely in the spirit. He refused to accept that Malherbe's doctrine could apply to the poetry of the theatre; drama, he claimed, demanded *éclat*, a brilliance of style and richness of imagery and language which was more in the tradition of the Pléiade. He loved sentences which, he wrote, 'thunder in the actor's mouth, and resound right into the spectator's soul'.

Hardy's plays were extremely popular and held the field for 20 years, but they failed to establish his ideas as the dominant ones in the French theatre. By 1630 the taste of the audience was changing and only a poet with the gifts of a Shakespeare could have reversed the trend towards classicism, but Hardy's poetry was not good enough to reconcile later audiences to the turbulence of his plots and of his language. The day was being won by less talented men whose dramatic techniques were more in accord with salon taste. This taste demanded adherence to the two great principles of *bienséance* and *vraisemblance*. The first was an extension of the notions of propriety already current in the Hôtel de Rambouillet. It disapproved of violence in public, of foul language and of buffoonery; consequently, the programme of the Hôtel de Bourgogne had to undergo a radical transformation between 1620 and 1640. In addition, the principle of *bienséance* involved a preference for lofty themes, noble characters, and for these to be treated with appropriate dignity in verse—especially in the stately progression of alexandrine couplets.

The principle of *vraisemblance* was well put by the abbé d'Aubignac in his *Pratique du Théâtre* (1657): 'It is a general maxim that the theatre does not set out to present the truth.' Cruel, foul and horrid events take place in life, but these cannot be staged for they would offend our sense of propriety. Truth, moreover, is often stranger than fiction; people do in fact drop dead, but 'everyone would laugh it to scorn if it happened in a play that, in order to round it all off, the hero's rival died suddenly of apoplexy'. *Vraisemblance*, therefore, demands that our credulity should not be strained; plots involving the confusion of twins, changes of identity and over-happy coincidences had to be abandoned, and this was not all. It was difficult enough, argued the habitués of the salons, to suspend one's disbelief sufficiently to allow a play to have any effect in the first place, but in the Hôtel de Bourgogne it was virtually impossible. The primitive stage furnishing was bad enough, but when the scene was changed every 15 minutes from forest glades to Illyrian seacoasts, then the artificiality of the convention became too apparent. Finally, it was argued, there was nothing more infuriating in this respect than to have an actor pretend to age 30 years in as many minutes. To meet these objections the doctrine of the three unities had much to offer.

To those who accept and, indeed, think in terms of the Shakespearian tradition, the notions of the salons may seem over-precious, but they had a logic of their own and were genuinely felt. If France could not produce a Shakespeare to bring the discordant elements of her theatre to their great fulfilment, then it was only reasonable to reform these elements and bring them to order. In 1631, therefore, when Jean Mairet used the preface to his play *Silvanie* to make a plea for the adoption of the three unities, he awoke a response denied to de la Taille 50 years earlier. Unlike de la Taille, Mairet brought forward a new principle. Making no appeal to the authority of Aristotle, or of anyone else, he rested his case on the basic premiss that poetry and drama exist to give pleasure. This cannot be achieved, he argued, if the plays lack credibility or if the production offends good taste. The acceptance of rules—and in particular, of the three unities of time, place and action—is therefore designed to increase the pleasure of a discriminating audience.

It was also of value to the playwright since the chief effect of the unities was to achieve a greater emotional intensity. Unity of action and place compelled him to achieve greater clarity in composition; unity of time made him single out the most intense moment of his story and construct everything tightly around it. There remained the problem of reporting to the audience the actions which had taken place in the past, or were taking place offstage, but this was a challenge to authors to make their narratives more vigorous and exciting than the events themselves would have been if seen. This was not an impossible task by any means, and the effect achieved was often far greater in its emotional impact by narration than by putting the action on the stage. Moreover, a more sophisticated concept of tragedy emerged. It is not the incidents themselves which matter, but the effect of them upon the characters. The interest lies no longer in what the characters do, but in what goes on in their minds.

*three*

# Richelieu and Mazarin

## I

Periods of growth are often more fascinating than periods of attainment. The political and cultural antecedents of Versailles have an interest denied to Versailles itself because in studying the development of movements, trends and fashions we become aware that in the initial stages things could have gone so very differently. The commonsense tastes of Henri IV in building and town planning, and the refining influence of Mme de Rambouillet in social life, were not the product of their environment but factors which helped to alter it. No matter how important the social pressures, the availability of money, the questions of war and peace, of government and anarchy, there remain not only the inexplicable facts of genius but also the chance circumstances which serve to influence the course of events. Given a longer period of anarchy after the death of Henri IV or a less able minister than Richelieu after 1624, given a greater poet than Hardy or a less talented critic than Malherbe, then the patterns of political and literary development could have been significantly different. We must therefore regard the appointment of Richelieu to the royal council in 1624 as one of the most critical events of the century, for in him Louis XIII discovered the one man capable of renewing the trend begun by Henri IV towards the creation of a strong centralised government. Louis was not a nonentity: he was too much the son of Henri IV to lack physical courage or common sense, but he lacked his father's robust spirit. Because of a lonely and neglected childhood, he became too moody and too indolent to sustain the burden of day-to-day administration, and too withdrawn to meet the challenge of political life with its perpetual clash of strong personalities. Richelieu was the ideal agent to undertake all this for him. If he was physically inferior to Louis— a thin, slight figure, perpetually suffering from migraine and other nervous disorders—he yet had the strength of will and the emotional stability to ride out crises, and the industry and enthusiasm to apply policies in detail and with thoroughness.

To many contemporaries it seemed that Louis XIII had abdicated in favour of Richelieu, but the cardinal himself knew how dependent he remained on royal favour. 'The four square yards of the King's cabinet are more difficult for me to conquer than all the battlefields of Europe', nor was this mere lip service to the principle of royal authority. The vulnerable nature of Richelieu's position was dramatically revealed in the so-called Day of Dupes in 1630. Already he had had to contend with the enmity of those who opposed his policies or who coveted his position, but none of these was as dangerous to him as Marie de' Medici, Anne d'Autriche and Gaston d'Orléans. As Louis's mother, wife and brother, respectively, they were peculiarly privileged to enjoy conspiracy without responsibility—it was their accomplices who were punished. Marie loved power although she had exercised it singularly ineffectively after Henri's death, and she hated Richelieu because she had once supported him in the belief he would serve her interests. In 1630 she set out to destroy Richelieu's position, demanding of Louis that he appoint her nominee to the army in Italy in preference to Richelieu's. The court awaited the outcome with excitement, recognising that behind this simple issue was a tremendous struggle for power. If Marie triumphed, the forces which had led to anarchy between 1610 and 1617 would again be in the ascendant.

Louis XIII had been ill, and during his convalescence he was exposed unremittingly to Marie's relentless emotional blackmail. Finally he gave way and, after appointing her protégé, Marillac, left Paris for the peace of his hunting lodge at Versailles. Here Louis recovered his nerve and, on the Day of Dupes, when the court celebrated Marie's triumph, ordered Marillac's arrest. Marie's power over him was broken for ever and she went into exile at Brussels, Gaston fled to Lorraine, Marillac was executed and Richelieu was confirmed in his office as chief minister. It was unwittingly symbolic that the decision which assured the extension of royal authority should have been taken at Versailles.

Richelieu had observed from the events after Henri IV's death that the greatest threat to royal authority came from that section of the nobility which was unable to reconcile itself to a life of peace on its estates, and which regarded itself as above the law, free to settle its disputes with neighbours or with the crown by force. For this reason he tried, not very successfully, to enforce laws against duelling, and to secure the destruction of private fortresses. This, of course, brought him up against the organised military power of the Huguenots. 'So long as they have a foothold in France', he wrote, 'the King will not be master in his own house, and will be unable to undertake any great enterprise abroad.' Huguenot rebellions in 1625 and 1627 did in fact sabotage Richelieu's policies at home and abroad, and there was nothing left for it but to gamble on a trial of strength. La Rochelle, the major Huguenot port, was attacked in 1627 and despite attempts to relieve it by the English it fell in 1628. Another royal army swept down the Rhône valley into Languedoc, the very heart of Huguenot country, seizing one stronghold after another. By 1629 the contest was over. The Grace of Alais left the Huguenots free to enjoy religious and civic liberties, but the military powers which had made them a privileged and dangerous state within the State were abolished. Thereafter, the Huguenots as a group never again disturbed the peace of France.

Representative institutions, identified today with government by the people, represented only the vested interests of certain privileged classes. Richelieu took care that they did not prevent the extension of royal authority. Condé and others had compelled Marie de' Medici to summon the États-Généraux in 1614, but what they had gained by it is not clear since it merely echoed the divergent views of different pressure groups. Richelieu never allowed it to meet, but its role was to some extent sought after by the Paris Parlement. This was essentially a judicial and administrative body, made up of lawyers and *officiers*, with no political responsibility beyond the registration of royal edicts. Its members had been angered by Richelieu's practice of setting up his own tribunals to meet special circumstances, and they were ambitious, not merely to protect their interests but to extend them into affairs of state. For this they were ill-qualified. As royal servants they could not withhold obedience when the King, whose authority they upheld, confronted them in a special audience known as a *lit de justice*. Moreover, they chose their ground unwisely by electing to support Gaston d'Orléans after his flight to Lorraine. Louis XIII immediately silenced them in a *lit de justice*, and Richelieu attacked them piecemeal by increasing the number of offices for sale in the Parlement, thus disparaging their importance and their financial value. In 1641 the members meekly registered an edict which denied them the right to discuss affairs of state.

In the provinces the key post in the administration was that of governor. It was generally held by the head of the most powerful local family who frequently modified royal policies to suit his own interests and those of his clientèle. Very gradually Richelieu replaced them with men whose loyalty was assured, since they were making their career in the royal service, and whose ability was sufficient to overawe the provincial nobility. Outlying provinces, such as Brittany, Bourgogne or Dauphiné, were a special problem since these had been the last to be joined to France and still retained special liberties derived from their charters of incorporation. Among these was the right to hold assemblies of their own Estates—hence their name of *pays d'état*—and with this right the power to vote taxes. Since this meant that the *pays d'état*, comprising a third of the kingdom, contributed only one-tenth of its revenue, Richelieu began tentatively to diminish their status. This was to attack them at their most sensitive point but, by a skilful mixture of persuasion and political blackmail, he succeeded in getting the Estates of several provinces to pay more taxes. In Languedoc, however, he was faced with rebellion. The issue was complicated by local rivalries, by the fact that the Huguenots of the province took no action as Huguenots, and by Gaston's sudden irruption from Lorraine. In the event the rebels were defeated and Gaston was reconciled to Louis XIII—

though Richelieu deemed it prudent to shelve the taxation issue for the time being.

In other fields of government Richelieu encouraged without success the foundation of overseas trading companies, built up an excellent navy and intervened with increasing self-confidence in European affairs. From his assumption of office we can date the transition of power in Europe from Spain to France, even though this was due to Spain's inner weakness rather than to France's growing strength. France, indeed, was peculiarly vulnerable to attack since Spain had bases along her entire land frontier—from Dunkirk to Luxembourg, in the Rhineland and north Italy, and along the Pyrenees. The most that Richelieu could do initially was to intervene in local disputes along the frontier in order to establish bridgeheads where possible across the Spanish supply routes. The Thirty Years War in Germany offered many opportunities to do this, and he exploited the rivalries of German princes and the territorial ambitions of the kings of Denmark and of Sweden with great skill; but despite some dramatic moments of triumph, his allies each in turn met defeat and in 1635 France was forced to abandon her policy of indirect action and to declare war on Spain.

This very nearly led to disaster. Spanish armies invaded from the Netherlands in 1636 and advanced as far south as Corbie, with their outriders in the Paris suburbs. The timely arrival of a French ally on the Spanish flank halted the advance, and when winter came the invaders left France. Thereafter the French began to win the war. The capture of Breisach (1639) and Turin (1640) severed Spanish supply routes with the Netherlands; in 1641 French armies crossed into Spain to exploit revolutions in Portugal and Aragon; in 1643 Condé's son, the duc d'Enghien, defeated a Spanish army at Rocroi, destroyed the legend of Spanish invincibility and established a new legend of French might; in 1648, when a separate peace was made in Germany, most Spanish bases had been cleared from the Rhineland.

By this time both Richelieu and Louis XIII were dead (1642 and 1643). Promptly the provincial États, the parlements, and the nobility set out to recover their powers and prerogatives—an attempt which

Louis XIII had anticipated. Recalling only too well what had happened after his father's death in 1610, he had set up a regency council to govern after his own, but Anne d'Autriche wanted full power for herself. Her enmity to Richelieu was well known, and with this in her favour she persuaded the great nobles and the Paris Parlement to set aside Louis's will and to appoint her as Regent on behalf of the five-year-old Louis XIV. In a wholly unexpected and fortuitous manner Richelieu's policies were nonetheless maintained, since Anne chose to marry in secret the very man whom Richelieu had trained to succeed him as chief minister.

Such a *dénouement* in a play would have been criticised as lacking in *vraisemblance*, and in real life it was no less unpopular with those who felt cheated of power. In appearance and character Cardinal Mazarin was altogether different from Richelieu, more self-indulgent, more avaricious, a smooth Italian administrator, 'who was exceedingly sorry that his dignity as cardinal prevented him from humiliating himself before you as much as he would have liked' (de Retz); but in ruthlessness and skill he lacked nothing as Richelieu's successor. Conspiracies broke out immediately and the *importants*—the name with its overtones of scorn was coined in the Hôtel de Rambouillet to denote the ambitious princes and nobles involved—were exiled or imprisoned.

The problem of royal bankruptcy could not be solved so easily. Richelieu had gone headlong into debt to pay for the war against Spain, and Mazarin was compelled to continue this war even though the revenues were pledged for three years in advance. Serious though the situation was, his solution made it worse by adding the bourgeoisie to the number of his enemies. More than any other group the *officiers* were offended by the expedients he adopted, since these affected their status, the value of their offices, their salaries and their investments. In 1647, therefore, the Paris Parlement refused to ratify a further list of expedients, and declared itself ready to challenge the authority of a *lit de justice* during a royal minority. From this proceeded a confused succession of events until both crown and the Parlement summoned to their aid the troops fighting against Spain. So began the Fronde, a period of rebellion and civil war which got its name from de Retz's contemptuous reference to some of his own followers, 'who sling mud [*qui frondent*] like schoolboys in the gutters of Paris'.

It is possible to interpret the Fronde as a constitutional movement which fell into the wrong hands; it is better to regard it as an anarchic reaction to the growing power of the crown, brought about by the double dangers of a royal minority and royal bankruptcy. The Parlement and its legitimate grievances was soon ignored—indeed, after six months it made its peace with the crown without anyone taking the slightest notice. This left the Frondeurs united only by their common ambition to destroy Mazarin and to seize for themselves whatever could be gained by wrecking the government. The young prince de Condé, newly come to the title, and whose arrogance had been fed by the victories he had won as duc d'Enghien, sought to control the queen as his father had controlled Marie de' Medici in 1614; with him were his brother Conti, his sister Mme de Longueville and the men like Turenne and La Rochefoucauld who fought to win her favours. Gaston d'Orléans was involved, of course, but his daughter, La Grande Mademoiselle, raised her own army in order to bargain for Louis xɪv's hand in marriage; de Retz, an ambitious cleric, merely coveted Mazarin's position. In the provinces, moreover, old scores were settled in a series of local struggles for power which took little count of events in Paris.

From 1648 until 1653 the combinations of vested interests formed and re-formed with a rapidity that baffled even Gaston: 'I remember every intrigue of the League', he confessed, 'every faction of the Huguenots, but I have never found anything so baffling as the present situation.' Mazarin realised that if he were out of the way the Frondeurs would soon fall out among themselves, and twice he left France for this purpose. It was dangerous, since it left Anne at the mercy of those who planned to remove her to a convent and to gain possession of her son, but Anne played her role with courage, and Mazarin's counter-intrigues soon achieved their effect. As in 1598, most Frenchmen had had enough of civil war, and were looking to the restoration of royal authority to guarantee them peace and order. Even the nobles began to tire of a conflict which had become so confused as to be unprofitable. All that they wanted was to make peace without too obviously recognising Mazarin's triumph; this was afforded by the astute declaration of Louis xiv's majority, four years in advance, so that those who had fought the regents were free to make submission to the King. The only exception was Condé, who left France in disgust to spend the next eight years in Spanish service. Mazarin, secure behind the throne until his death in 1661, restored the authority of the crown, and the machinery by which to enforce it—and did so with astonishing speed, in part because Richelieu had shown him what needed to be done, but even more because the fruitless and costly years of the Fronde had made opposition to the King unfashionable.

The extension of French power abroad was meanwhile carried further. By 1648, when peace was made in Germany, French armies had established the bridgeheads desired by Richelieu across the Spanish lines of communication and encirclement. The war with Spain continued, of course, but by sheer chance the years of the Fronde were also years of rebellion in Spain. When Mazarin was at last free in the mid-1650s to prosecute the war with any vigour, the hollowness of Spanish power had become apparent. Her finances ruined beyond any remedy save peace, her allies lost during the German war or later seduced by French diplomacy, and her king-doms of Catalonia and Portugal still in revolt, she could not hope to survive. When Mazarin added to his strength the army and navy of republican England, Spain sued for peace. It was the greatest moment in French history over the past 100 years, and Mazarin pressed home his advantage. The only concession he made was to cut off aid to the Catalan rebels and to pardon Condé for his treason. For the rest, France acquired a series of frontier bases and provinces in the Pyrenees and in the Spanish Netherlands, and Maria Theresa was married to Louis xiv. The basis of Louis xiv's power in Europe as in France had been firmly laid.

Although royal power was strengthened by Richelieu and Mazar-in, it was to some extent at the expense of royal prestige. It is clear to us how much Richelieu was dependent upon Louis xiii's support, but contemporaries were not mistaken in regarding him as the dominant figure of the age. There is a similar pattern, too, so far as the arts were concerned. Richelieu was one of the most important and influential patrons of the century, whereas 'royal patronage', writes Crozet with deliberate irony, 'lacked a little lustre between the reigns of Henri IV and Louis XIV'. By virtue of being king, of course, Louis had a number of commissions to dispense if only to maintain the fabric of his properties, and indeed he went further than that. Philibert Le Roy rebuilt the half-ruined château at Versailles, which Louis used as his favourite hunting lodge, and produced a well-balanced, simple design in the style of the Place Royale. It still encloses the forecourt of Louis XIV's palace, and, with its blue slates, red bricks and white stone facings, we can see why Saint-Simon described it as '*le petit château tricolore*'.

At the Louvre Louis decided to extend the south-west corner of what is now the Square Court. Here, in the previous century, Lescot had built two blocks at right angles with two storeys and an attic floor articulated by Corinthian and Composite orders, and decorated with some rather fussy stonework. Le Mercier, who was commissioned to double the length of the west wing, simply repeated Lescot's dimensions and motifs in order to maintain a sense of unity. In the centre of the wing, however, he decided to build a clock tower, the Pavillon de l'Horloge. Since this had to rise above Lescot's attic floor, and since no orders could strictly be employed above a Composite order, he dispensed with pilasters altogether and used groups of caryatids around the clock face to support a squat dome. In its mannerist effect it is closer in spirit to the du Cerceau family than to the final work of de Brosse.

At Saint-Germain and Fontainebleau Louis employed the best painters of the day, Vouet and Philippe de Champaigne, to immortalise the great occasions of the reign in the traditional, allegoric way. The fall of La Rochelle, for example, notable as a double triumph for the victory of orthodoxy over heresy and of monarchy over rebellion, was celebrated by Champaigne in a picture of Louis being greeted by Victory, with a panoramic view of La Rochelle thrown in for good measure. There were also many commissions to restore or to decorate churches and abbeys, for Louis was extremely devout—although an element of propaganda was not excluded even here; in the church of Saint-Eustache de Paris was a sculpture of Saint Louis by Simon Guillain, whose face, moustache and beard recalled the features of Louis XIII, while the Virgin bore a close resemblance to Anne d'Autriche.

All this kept architects and painters at work, but it had no significance beyond that. Louis encouraged no new style, confirmed no trend, nor did he show much interest. To poets he appeared wholly antagonistic. When Richelieu died he cancelled the literary pensions he had granted, saying with brutal frankness, '*nous n'avons plus affaire de cela*' (Tallement). Plays, however, he greatly enjoyed. His doctor Jean Héroard recorded his actions as a child, and from this we see that when he was 13 years old he attended over 100 performances between January 1613 and February 1614. It was an enthusiasm which remained throughout his life, but it did not surpass his passion for music. As he grew older, especially when he was no longer able to go hunting, he turned to music for consolation, and there is a touching account in Dubois's *Mémoire fidèle des choses qui se sont passées à la mort de Louis XIII* of an incident after he had received the last unction. 'He ordered M. de Niel, *premier valet de garde robe*, to fetch his lute and to sing praises unto God: *Lauda anima mea dominum*, and he made Saint-Martin, Cambefort and Ferdinant sing the part songs which he had composed for Godeau's paraphrases of the Psalms of David, and nothing but sacred hymns were sung and the King even joined in the bass part with the Marshal de Schomberg'.

Pierre de Nyert, or de Niel as Dubois calls him, played a relatively important part in the development of French singing techniques. To understand these we must bear in mind that in France the link between verse and music had been very close, and that Ronsard had urged most forcibly that a musical accompaniment was necessary for the enjoyment of poetry, 'for poetry without instruments, or without the charm of one or several voices is not at all pleasing'. We have already seen how Malherbe's rules for the writing of verse had been influenced by this connection, but the influence could also work the other way. It was because of the emphasis given to the accompaniment of verse that polyphony declined in the sixteenth century and harmony was impoverished. Instead, the French became masters of melodic invention, producing beautifully finished phrases to go with lines of verse. One of the finest composers of this was Pierre Guédron, Henri IV's *surintendant de la musique du roi*, whose work and that of other masters is preserved in a collection begun by Gabrielle Bataille, *Airs en tablature de luth* (1608). So successful were these *airs de cour* that many foreigners, Italians in particular, came to Paris to study them. Because French poetry tended to be very clear and definite in form, usually in alexandrines, the composers had to follow the rhythms of the verse instead of working out preconceived musical rhythms. In musical terms this involved a great measure of rhythmic freedom in which bar lines were left out and strong beats were not stressed. The rhythmic flexibility which this produced created an impression of ceaseless movement— wholly different from the heavily measured Italian tradition—and a clear, passionless line full of charm but lacking intensity.

Pierre de Nyert had been brought up in this tradition—and was successful enough as a performer to be appointed *premier valet de garde robe* by Louis XIII, who left him 600 livres in his will—but he had also been to Italy in the household of the duc de Créqui. He could not forget the impact of the operas staged by the Barberini cardinals, and he wanted to adapt some of the Italian techniques to improve the French tradition (for features of Italian music, see chapter 4). This required caution. Guédron, who had been fascinated by the Italian recitative, had tried to introduce an element of lyrical declamation into French singing but it was held that the French language was unsuitable for this kind of treatment. Moreover, there was a profound prejudice against Italian singing. Apart from their hostility to castrato singers, the French disliked the emotional intensity and dramatic emphasis of the Italians. Tallement tells a revealing story of a Mlle Sandrier who went to sing in north Italy: 'She returned to Paris 17 years later and began to sing the Italian songs she had learnt in Turin. She caused a great sensation, but it was short-lived: several people concluded that she could not even sing properly, *for this is quite in the Italian tradition*, and she

11. Multiple stage setting from the *Mémoire de Mahelot* (see page 62)

12. Château Maisons by François Mansart, one of the finest examples of the French classical style (see pages 165–6)

13. Château de Vaux-le-Vicomte, built by Louis Le Vau for Nicolas Fouquet. The castle is reflected in the *parterre d'eau* by André Le Nôtre (see pages 168–9)

pulled the most horrible faces.' Worse still, 'she seemed to be suffering from convulsions'.

De Nyert's reforms were valuable but not radical. He established straightforward rules to ensure distinct pronunciation of the words, and to regulate breathing so that there was no interruption of a phrase. He also introduced a great degree of ornamentation following the Italian practice of diminutions. He passed the test of royal approval, and greatly influenced both Michel Lambert, one of Louis's most important musicians, and Bénigne de Bacilly, whose *Remarques sur l'art de bien chanter*, was accepted as an authoritative textbook throughout France. In his book Bacilly included several examples of the new ornamentations, among them the *double*. The *air de cour* is sung through without ornament in order to establish the melody in everyone's mind; it is then repeated—the *double*—with variations, sometimes improvised but often, as in the following case, written by the composer.

As the *air de cour* was the musical form in which the French excelled, so the instrument best suited to accompany it was the lute. Indeed it was generally regarded as a French instrument, the tablatures and the techniques of playing it were derived from France, and French lutanists had won an international reputation. Richelieu prided himself upon his skill with it, and Anne d'Autriche took lessons from Le Vieux Gaultier, the most famous of all French virtuosi. Denis, Le Jeune Gaultier, was more of a composer, famous for his dance suites of preludes, pavanes, courants and sarabandes. His music was very popular in the salons, and there was a degree of *préciosité* about his compositions which were based upon a theory of modes associated with the Greeks. The notion was that each mode was particularly apt for expressing a certain mood; the Lydian mode, for example, was melancholy, while the Ionian was most suitable for dancing. Modes were assigned key signatures, and in the famous collection of lute compositions, *La Rhétorique des Dieux*, the pieces, including many by Denis, are grouped together according to their modes. The third member of the Gaultiers, Pierre, spent most of his time at the English court, where he developed *le style brisé*, remarkable for its prolific use of grace notes and other embellishments.

Mersenne, whose *Harmonie Universelle* (1636) was one of the greatest works of seventeenth-century musical theory, refers to Pierre's ornamentation, and cites a bewildering number of techniques. He also records that the violin was nonetheless beginning to rival the lute: 'Its sounds have more effect upon the spirit of the hearers than those of the lute or other string instruments, because they are more vigorous and indeed penetrating, by reason of the great tension of their strings and their shriller tones. And those who have heard the Vingt-Quatre Violons du Roi maintain that they have never heard anything more ravishing or more powerful.' The creation of the Vingt-Quatre Violons was Louis XIII's greatest service to music. It was the first permanent orchestra of this period in France; it comprised six first violins, four second, four third, four violas and six basses, and the leader, Guillaume Dumanoir, was so outstanding a performer that the gild of musicians, the Confrérie de Saint Julien, awarded him the coveted title of *roi des violons*. Technically the royal players were limited to first position for most of the time, but they cultivated so great an agility of bowing that Mersenne was prompted to comment on their gay and lively movement. They also developed a particular style of intricate ornamentation, *broderies* and improvised diminutions of great complexity, with the result that French players as well as French singers appeared to be

much more delicate and intellectual, and much less robust and emotional, than the Italians.

They were, however, much inferior to the Italians in ability. No
matter how skilfully they operated within their genre, the genre
itself was too thin, too undemanding; and French musicians were
so wrapped up in their own limited achievement that they seem to
have been wholly deaf to the lovely melodies, the pulsating rhythms
and the rich orchestration of Italian music. Mersenne saw the fault
and criticised it. Italian composers, he wrote, 'portray the passions
and moods of the soul and the spirit—anger for example, frenzy,
rancour, rage, faintness of heart and several other emotions—so
vividly that we might imagine they were inspired by the self-same
passions that they portrayed, while our Frenchmen are happy simply
to caress the ear with a never-ending sweetness in their singing which
drains the life out of it.' The reason he proposed was lack of courage;
Guédron had had the right idea in trying to adapt the Italian form of
recitative, 'but our musicians are too timid to introduce this style of
singing in France'. André Maugars, a talented viol player who had
been in Richelieu's service, made a similar point after spending some
years in Rome. In his *Response faite à un curieux sur le sentiment de la
Musique* he admitted that both countries had weaknesses—'we err
by default, the Italians by excess'—but that the richness and variety
of Italian music surpassed anything that the French could offer.

Whatever Louis XIII's limitations as a patron of the arts, he performed a vital function by continuing Henri IV's practice of making
Paris his permanent home, with the consequences for society and the
theatre which we have already examined. Without this concentration of society in one place even Richelieu's influence could not
have been so profound. It was a necessary corollary of his administrative policies that Paris should not merely be the centre of
government, but that its proud buildings, its fine paintings, its
sophisticated salons, its theatre and its academy of letters, which he
himself established, should set the tone for the rest of France. He
was horrified by the sluttish conditions in which Louis XIII was
prepared to live; the dignified setting of noble buildings, luxuriously
appointed, was in his view a necessary adjunct to political greatness.

This of course reflected his private conviction that the arts are an essential element in life and not a secondary or ancillary function of society. Because of this they merited the same watchful control by the State as everything else. He was never politically supreme and could not therefore be in any sense a director or controller of French culture, but by his influence and patronage he encouraged in all art forms the trend towards the qualities he most valued in the State, towards civility, order, restraint, discipline and a rational spirit. In short, he encouraged the growth of classicism.

There was also a good deal of personal prestige involved. Père Arcère, historian of La Rochelle, wrote of the great fortifications constructed there by Richelieu, and of his coat of arms which embellished them, as 'monuments to the vigilant care of this great statesman and perhaps to an over-keen desire to let posterity know about it'. He was certainly aware of the immortality to be conferred by poets and artists on one who might at any moment be destroyed in politics, and he enjoyed the reflection of his grandeur in the town he built and named after himself, in the splendour of the palace he erected in full view of the Louvre, and in the noble portraits of himself by the greatest painters of the day.

But to attribute everything to political calculation and self-aggrandisement is to ignore the fact that his enthusiasm for all the arts was wholly genuine. 'It is not necessary', he wrote, 'that a man should attend without interruption to public affairs; on the contrary, concentration of this kind is more likely than anything else to render him useless.' He would never discuss politics late at night, and always enjoyed the elegant and intelligent conversation at the Hôtel de Rambouillet. He composed verses, turned his hand to writing plays, played the lute, was passionately fond of the *ballet de cour*, and retained an eight-piece orchestra to play to him daily and to accompany him, even on campaigns. He was also a discriminating patron of artists, and his private collection included a dozen works by Poussin, and many others by Rubens, Van Dyck, Dürer, Titian, Caravaggio, Mantegna and Georges de la Tour. He had begun building when he first became bishop of Luçon; there he restored the cathedral and the palace which had been extensively damaged in the wars of religion. His first private venture was in 1623 when he bought Limours, one of Francis I's châteaux, and had it transformed and redecorated, selling it in 1626 to Gaston d'Orléans.

Naturally enough it was not until his increased security after the Day of Dupes that he began the great buildings on which his fame was to rest, and so varied and so many were the projects that he had to set up a kind of general staff to administer them. This included Michel le Masle, a canon of Notre-Dame, Léonor d'Estampes, bishop of Chartres, himself a keen patron, and Alphonse Lopez, a shadowy figure, probably a Morisco Jew, whom Richelieu employed on secret missions and for seeking out works of art to add to his collection. There was also Henri de Sourdis, archbishop of Bordeaux, who spent his life serving Richelieu as a provincial governor, as admiral of his newly created fleet, and also as an agent of his patronage.

The most important adviser of all was Richelieu's chief architect, Jacques Le Mercier. Born in the early 1580s, the son of a master mason of Paris, he left for Rome in 1607, and returned seven years later. In 1623 the duc de Liancourt set him an interesting problem: having bought the Hôtel de Bouillon built by de Brosse and a plot of land adjacent to it, he wanted the *hôtel* redesigned to occupy the full site. Le Mercier executed this well and undertook a similar commission for Louis XIII when he extended the Lescot wing at the Louvre. Thereafter he was employed almost exclusively by Richelieu.

Some years earlier, Richelieu had bought the former Hôtel de Rambouillet—not the more recent *hôtel* whose salon he attended— and had it improved and extended. As a neighbour of the Louvre, however, it remained too insignificant for Richelieu's taste and, after ruthlessly buying up adjoining land from the Tuileries to the Porte Saint-Denis, he ordered Le Mercier to build him a palace—the Palais Cardinal. It was an imposing building of great size grouped around two main courtyards. In the first court there were, in addition to the main *appartement*, the great theatre, inaugurated in 1641 by Richelieu's own play, *Mirame*, and a gallery for his collection of objets d'art. The second court, set out on a different axis, contained on three sides a smaller theatre, the chapel and the Galerie des Hommes

Illustres which in subtle flattery of his own position celebrated the achievements of those who had served the previous kings of France. The fourth side, bounded by an ironwork screen, opened on to the gardens. Splendid though it was, especially in comparison with the Louvre, Richelieu had hoped to give it an even more splendid setting by creating behind it an enormous square, 100 metres across —a Place Ducale of uniform pavilions in which he would have housed his new founded Académie Française. This project was never realised.

Outside Paris one building project succeeded another. At Rueil, for example, he bought the château in 1633 for 147,000 livres, and spent over a million in rebuilding and extending it. Nothing, however, not even the grandiose concept of the Place Ducale, could match up to what he achieved on his ancestral estates in Poitou. He bought up whatever land came on the market, until he could order Le Mercier to build him, not merely a palace, but a small town to be called Richelieu, with a château and park adjoining it. The town was designed like a neat, logical chequerboard. One main road, La Grande Rue, ran from north to south, linking the two main squares, and both it and the squares were flanked by *hôtels* built in the simple style of Henri IV's domestic architecture. Unlike Henri's squares and roads, however, Richelieu's town served no good purpose. Whereas the Pont Neuf became the most crowded thoroughfare in Paris, Richelieu was virtually deserted. The cardinal's own men dutifully moved in to build *hôtels* there, Henri de Sourdis, of course, Lopez and Le Masle, and the members of the administration who hoped for promotion, such as Bouthillier and Pierre Séguier, the ambitious Keeper of the Seals. But this was all, and those who built never went so far as to live there. With a great deal of charm but no *raison d'être*, Richelieu remained half-empty.

The town survives, virtually unchanged, but the château no longer exists. Le Mercier designed the main building around three sides of a square court, enclosed on the fourth side by a low wall, and with a series of forecourts, each opening into the other, to receive the road from the main gates. Le Mercier's great opportunity to demonstrate his ability on the grand scale was missed, and he produced a dull building of no architectural significance. What struck contemporaries was not the château at all, but the canalised waters of the river Mable, and the peacocks and statues which thronged the lawns. The surface decorations seem to have been in the idiom of the mannerist tradition, fussy and incoherent. From this and from his other work we must recognise that Le Mercier, though proficient in the classical idiom, seems to have been unaffected by his years in Rome and, so far as the development of classical architecture was concerned, was considerably less advanced than de Brosse, his senior by ten years.

In this respect the tidy-minded historian who likes his patterns to cohere would be much happier if Richelieu, whose influence generally did much to promote a classical mood in all the arts, had chosen instead to employ such a man as François Mansart, born in Paris in 1598. His father, a master carpenter, died when he was young and he was therefore trained by a brother-in-law, Germain Gaultier, who had worked with de Brosse at Rennes. Possibly Mansart too worked for a time under de Brosse at Coulommiers. Unlike most artists, he never went to Italy and was in many ways technically less proficient in the classical style than Le Mercier; nevertheless, he began to develop a feeling for mass and a technique for handling it which revealed a far greater understanding of the essential qualities of classical architecture than that of any other contemporary, whether Italian-trained or not. Unhappily, he also developed qualities of arrogance, obstinacy and dishonesty which made him impossible to work with and difficult to employ.

Any account of Mansart's work must owe much to Sir Arthur Blunt who traces the evolution of his style. For the church of the Feuillants (1623) he imitated the two top storeys of de Brosse's Saint-Gervais, but added mannerist ornaments so that 'it is less classical than the model on which it is based' (Blunt); at Berny (1623) he tried to construct a château as a free-standing unit, like de Brosse's Blérancourt, but it is less successful and he could not leave it without mannerist decoration. In 1626, at Balleroy, he succeeded. The massive blocks of the *corps de logis*, the two wings and the two flanking pavilions on the garden side are grouped in a most harmonious and satisfying way, and the surface decoration is in the simple style of

Henri IV's buildings. The dignity of composition and the restraint in decoration indicate that Mansart had arrived at a fuller understanding of classicism.

Balleroy's owner, Jean de Choisy, was chancellor to Gaston d'Orléans, and it was through this connection that Mansart was invited to undertake the transformation of Blois. This was a fine Renaissance château on which Francis I had lavished a great deal of effort, but Richelieu proposed its reconstruction in order to keep Gaston out of the way after his part in the Languedoc rebellion of 1632. Gaston's own enthusiasm for the project was genuine enough; his tastes in art were much more sophisticated than those of Louis XIII, and he was passionately fond of collecting pictures, jewels and objets d'art. His plans for Blois were nothing less than monumental. Everything, including Francis I's wing, was to be destroyed, and a new palace built very much on the lines of the Luxembourg. Mansart designed an immense *corps de logis* flanked by double pavilions, with two long wings at right angles where Gaston's vast collections could be displayed in style. On the fourth side the court was to be enclosed by a wall, in the centre of which a massive rotunda porchway would give access to a forecourt on the east side and to terraced gardens on the west.

Very little of this ambitious plan was achieved. Much of the old château was preserved, including Francis I's wing, and only the central block of the new *corps de logis* was built—the present Orléans wing. The quadrant colonnades give it a particular air of refined elegance, but the rest of the decoration is simple enough. From a pedantic viewpoint there are indeed errors in the handling of classical detail; the entrance motif is in the form of a triumphal arch but Mansart has extended it to include the second storey as well, and, above it, the semicircular pediment with its scrollwork and foliage is more mannerist than classical. But the superimposed orders are scrupulously articulated, with Doric, Ionic and Corinthian capitals successively for the three storeys, and the pilasters, instead of being inset on each façade, are placed right at the corners of the block, so that the line of the edge is strengthened and the effect of mass intensified. Above it all there is the solid, high-pitched roof to which

Mansart gave his name. It is, therefore, a building which combines simplicity and elegance with a sense of mass, and all the parts are satisfyingly related. Mansart's evolving concept of a building as a whole rather than as a series of unrelated façades is illustrated at Blois by his treatment of the other side of the block where the ground level was higher than at the front. Here he replaced the Doric floor by a low, unarticulated basement, which means that the Ionic and Corinthian orders can run round the entire building at the same levels. Visually this unifying effect is lost; intellectually it is extremely satisfying.

His success at Blois established Mansart's reputation at court, and when Anne d'Autriche wanted a monumental church built to celebrate the long-delayed arrival of a son, she gave him the commission for the Val-de-Grâce. In order to create an effect of dignity and grandeur, Mansart borrowed a great deal from Palladio's church of Il Redentore in Venice, and designed a central domed space above the crossing, with the choir and the two transepts treated as three equal apses. The lofty line of the nave was strongly emphasised by great Corinthian pilasters, rising to a severe, unadorned entablature which encircled the whole interior of the church, unifying and knitting it together. Externally the dome was the most dramatic feature, and so, to give the façade greater force, Mansart brought the central section forward in a portico supported by two pairs of columns and approached by a wide flight of steps. His ultimate intentions, however, are unknown because, having designed the church so far, he was dismissed by Anne who found him intolerably arrogant. This ended his connection with the court. A brief meeting with Colbert in 1664 to discuss plans for the Louvre came to nothing, and the rest of his work (see chapter 5) including the Château de Maisons, a superb example of French classicism at its best, was done for the prosperous bourgeoisie of Paris.

The completion of the Val-de-Grâce was left to Le Mercier, mainly because he had already designed and successfully completed a domed church of his own. Richelieu, as Principal of the Sorbonne, had begun to pull down many of the old, dilapidated buildings of the university, despite the protests of a professorial body which

abominated change of any kind as vigorously as it detested paying
for it, and Le Mercier had been commissioned to design the new
church. Completed in 1635, it was altogether different from his
other buildings. His style in general hovered between mannerism
and classicism, proficient, as we have seen, in the techniques of
classical architecture but lacking its essential spirit. At the Sorbonne,
the Roman influence is paramount, not because Le Mercier had
succeeded in synthesising it with his own tradition but because, very
simply, he had imported it wholesale from the churches being
built in Rome during his years of apprenticeship there; and, in
particular, from Rosati's church of San Carlo ai Catarini and della
Porta's Santa Maria dei Monti.

The Roman design is apparent in the ground plan, which is
virtually that of a Greek cross, since the nave and choir are of equal
length on either side of the domed crossing. The treatment of the
west front was derived from della Porta. Two orders are superimposed on the façade but, as the lower storey extends across the nave
and aisles while the upper storey covers the upper half of the nave
alone, the awkward transition between the two is concealed by a
massive volute on each side of the upper section. Le Mercier's treatment of the north front, however, where a courtyard gives access
from the Sorbonne, was more original. He introduced the classic
use of the peristyle, a freestanding portico with classical columns
which, at the head of a broad flight of stairs from the courtyard,
makes a most impressive entrance. The dome itself, the crowning
glory derived from Rosati, terminates, not in a gentle cupola at
the lantern, but in a short spire which succeeds in drawing vigorously
upward the ribs of the dome to point at the heavens. At the Val-de-
Grâce he went further by using twice as many piers and ribs to
accentuate the upward thrust; moreover, the loftier line was achieved
by building a false timber dome above the masonry of the inner
shell.

Le Mercier's other churches at Rueil and at Richelieu have many
features in common with the Sorbonne, and so far as church architecture is concerned his influence in directing French taste towards
classicism was important. The style he introduced was the one current

in Italy shortly before the baroque was fully established, and was therefore acceptable to those who were dissatisfied with mannerism but who would have been overpowered by the baroque. It is an interesting point, developed by Blunt, that Simon Vouet, who was almost as much Richelieu's painter as Le Mercier was his architect, did exactly the same thing in the field of painting.

Vouet was the son of a painter employed by Henri IV. Born in 1590, he left France in 1611 in the household of the French ambassador to Constantinople, was in Vienna in 1612 and in Rome a year later. There he stayed for 14 years, enjoying the patronage of the influential Cardinal Barberini, later Pope Urban VIII, and winning the respect of Roman artists, to such an extent that in 1624 they elected him director of their academy of St Luke. At last, in 1627 Louis XIII and Richelieu persuaded him to return home, made him *premier peintre du roi* with rooms in the Louvre and a regular pension, and loaded him with commissions.

His work caused something of a sensation since he brought to France a style of painting hitherto unknown, which blended the dignity and clarity of the classical school with some of the drama and emotion of early baroque. For all the popularity he enjoyed he was not a great artist; his deliberately eclectic style could, on occasion, be too contrived, too suave and too pedantic. Vouet and his school 'tried to persuade their patrons that an anthology of quotations from Raphael and Titian can pass as an original work of art' (Newton), and his tremendous success was perhaps a measure of his patrons' lack of taste. While this is true in one sense we must also remember that these patrons had no comparative studies of European art to guide them. When Vouet is set against the great Italian and Dutch painters he does indeed seem formal, lifeless and derivative, but in comparison with the Second School of Fontainebleau, which was all that France had yet produced in the seventeenth century, his qualities as a painter are seen to be outstanding. Not surprisingly he attracted to his workshop a generation of talented pupils who derived from him a tradition of craftsmanship, of style and of professionalism which had been lacking in France. With his new ideas from Italy and his own solid competence as an artist, it is not surprising that

Vouet's work stood 'at the root of nearly all the Parisian ecclesiastical and decorative painting of the first half of the century' (Wilenski).

Richelieu could not persuade him to decorate his château at Richelieu, since Vouet was too happily occupied to leave Paris for Poitou, but he did a great deal of work at Rueil and at the Palais Cardinal where he painted the Chapel and shared with Philippe de Champaigne the Galerie des Hommes Illustres. None of this survives, but some work for Richelieu's protégé and assistant at the Hôtel Séguier reveals a new trend in his style, combining a degree of illusionism by perspective and *trompe l'œil* with the introduction of architectural features, a style which anticipates Versailles—which is not surprising when we notice that Le Brun was first apprenticed to Vouet while he was working for Séguier. 'Theoretically Poussin represented the ideal which the Academy set itself to follow in the later seventeenth century, but all its members, starting with Le Brun, sacrificed as often, though with less ostentation, at the altar of Vouet' (Blunt).

Vouet was swamped with commissions for religious works and did several altar pieces at Richelieu's request, including a 'Martyrdom of Saint Eustache' for the church of that name and, in 1641, a 'Presentation in the Temple' for the novitiate church of the Jesuits. This proved to be his most popular and most influential genre. It was far superior to anything that had yet been produced in France, and it gave satisfaction and reassurance to patrons who would have been horrified by the naturalism of Caravaggio, and whose religious enthusiasm was too restrained, too intellectual, to accept the fervid intensity and emotionalism of baroque religious painting. Vouet offered a nicely balanced compromise of baroque qualified by classicism, of devotion interpreted by reason. The longer he stayed in Paris, however, the more the balance moved from baroque to classicism. His 1641 'Presentation', for example, has the flights of angels and the air of religious emotion we associate with baroque, but the mood is brought down to earth by the vigorous vertical lines of the columns around the main group which anchor the picture firmly to the temple floor. In the structure, cohesion and restraint of this painting we can see that Vouet has come much closer, independently of

Poussin, to the mood of classicism. It is a progress paralleled by Corneille in drama, for example, and in both cases we have creative artists who, without perverting their genius or mutilating their personality, were nonetheless encouraged to follow one course rather than another because of the expectations and tastes of their public.

Another influential artist supported and encouraged by Richelieu was Philippe de Champaigne. He came from Brussels at the age of 19 in 1621 to work at the Luxembourg and, as a foreigner, was given special protection by Marie de' Medici against the Maîtrise, the Parisian gild of artists which was jealous of foreign labour. In 1628 he celebrated the fall of La Rochelle, as we have mentioned, and became one of Richelieu's chief painters. He painted the four great doctors of the church on the four pendentives within the dome of the Sorbonne, he decorated the little theatre at the Palais Cardinal, produced a series of allegories of Justice, Piety and other virtues accompanying Richelieu in the Galerie des Objets d'Art, and shared with Vouet the Galerie des Hommes Illustres. In this last commission his ability as a portrait painter was more in demand, for among his subjects were Louis XIII, Anne d'Autriche, Gaston d'Orléans and Richelieu himself. Richelieu valued him highly as a portraitist and commissioned at least four full-length studies, such as the one now in the National Gallery.

Like Vouet, Champaigne had arrived in France from a baroque environment, except that his masters were not Italian but Flemish. Rubens had passed unnoticed in Paris because his style was too emotive and indeed too alien for the French to appreciate; Champaigne, whose overall grasp of composition and whose use of colour and light reveal his debt to Rubens, was nonetheless able to achieve fame in Paris by moderating his style to satisfy the taste of the court and in particular of Richelieu. His style changed considerably after 1643, when he became associated with the Jansenists of Port-Royal (see chapter 6), but well before this date a shift towards classicism can be discerned. In the National Gallery portrait, for example, 'the modelling of the robes is much more classical and even sculpturesque, a fact which suggests that Champaigne had been studying Roman statues and that he was moving towards the imitation of them at the same time as Poussin, but independently of him' (Blunt).

One aspect of Richelieu's patronage recalls Père Arcère's comment on his 'over-keen desire' to instruct posterity. Certainly the desire to perpetuate his memory explains the great number of commissions for portraits, painted or engraved, by Philippe de Champaigne, Matthieu Le Nain, Nanteuil and many others, including the shrewd sketch by Claude Mellon. We have referred already to the Galerie des Hommes Illustres at the Palais Cardinal, but at Richelieu, where perhaps he felt freer in private to indulge a mood of self-glorification, he commissioned Nicolas Prévost to record his personal achievements. Prévost not only painted the great events of his patron's career but, with unsubtle flattery, found parallels to them in the great deeds of antiquity; so that the siege of La Rochelle is set against the siege of Tyre, and the French army's crossing of the Alps is compared to Hannibal's. Also at Richelieu, Deruet, mentioned earlier for the popularity he enjoyed among the salons by his allegorical studies, did a special allegory of the four elements in which Richelieu is featured with the royal family. Jean Warin, a sculptor and the most brilliant medallist of the century, produced a series of medals to commemorate his features, as did Guillaume Dupré. Medals were one thing, busts were another for these might well have been construed as too blatant an act of self-deification. Instead, he employed sculptors to exalt his own king, and, thanks to his patronage, we have Warin's brilliant bust of Louis in old age, several by Pierre Biard and Berthelot, and an equestrian statue by Biard the Younger for the Place Royale. It is possible, however, that Philippe de Champaigne's triple study of him, like Van Dyck's study of Charles I, was intended for a sculptural purpose, and we know that Richelieu approached Van Dyck to make sketches for a statue to be executed by Bernini, yet the fact remains that the only bust ever to be made of Richelieu was one by Jean Warin.

Though Richelieu had a great deal to do with artists in general, he was, if anything, on even closer terms with writers, and significantly he was most in touch with those who were continuing the process of refinement and self-discipline begun by Malherbe and the

Hôtel de Rambouillet. Malherbe welcomed his accession to power as the signal for a return to order, and one of his last odes, in 1628, was in his praise; but it was with the next generation of writers that Richelieu was most concerned. Among these was Guez de Balzac who tried to do for prose what Malherbe had done for poetry. He was greatly admired for faultless vocabulary and clear exposition, and was the first to exploit the supple advantages enjoyed in French by the free use of the subjunctive, whereby—avoiding the clumsy inflexions of the verb *to be*—a mood is changed by merely changing a letter. This also encourages the clearer exposition of abstract themes, since there is no danger of hypothetical statements of opinion being taken for assertions of categoric fact.

Clarity was not all, however, and Balzac's title of '*le plus éloquent homme*' was earned by meticulous attention to the art of sentence construction. He knew the importance of assumed nonchalance, calling it '*un génie secret*', which is lost by too much seeking, but he stressed above all the necessity for constant revision. He once wrote of 'an author who was said to have written a long book because he did not have enough time to make it shorter', and his ninth *Entretien* defended the thesis 'that it is impossible to write much and to write well'. He invented a distinction between Asiatic and Attic eloquence: the one resembling a vast countryside covered with great fields of black corn, the other a cultivated garden of simple, exquisite and rare plants, and there was no doubt where his preference lay. Ronsard, of course, was an obvious target for his criticism: '*peu d'ordre, peu d'économie, point de choix soit pour les paroles, soit pour les choses; une audace insupportable à changer et à innover, une licence prodigieuse à former de mauvais mots et de mauvaises locutions*'—the elegant periods flow on in condemnation of Ronsard's disorderly vigour.

Superior form demands a quality of content if it is not to appear ridiculous, and Balzac did not always achieve it. His *Dissertations Politiques*, for example, dedicated to the memory of classical Rome for which he had a great enthusiasm, written from his estates in the manner of the Younger Pliny and constructed according to the canons of Ciceronian rhetoric, are self-conscious, lifeless and unread.

His *Lettres*, however, won him perpetual fame. He spent some time as secretary to the duc d'Épernon who once left him in Rome for 18 months with instructions 'to let nothing happen in society without writing to him about it and to make public business the subject-matter of his letters'. In an age without newspapers this was a practical task of some importance, but Balzac's style became so popular that, even after his return to semi-retirement on his estates at Charenton, his *Lettres* were published in series, and each publication anxiously awaited. So much so that he complained of being pestered by correspondents, 'most of whom only write in order to publish my replies'.

One correspondent who much admired his work was Richelieu, and when Balzac had congratulated him on his cardinal's hat in 1622, he promised to find him a benefice: 'If, in the service of the Church and of those to whom I owe this dignity, I find any opportunity to show how much I esteem both your goodwill towards me and your merit, you may rest assured that I am a man of deeds not words.' But nothing came of it. Balzac's patron, the duc d'Épernon, belonged to Marie de' Medici's party, and Balzac himself was implicated by association with some of the Libertins; so that when the bishopric of Grasse fell vacant it was given to another literary figure, Antoine Godeau. Godeau had been a favourite of the Hôtel de Rambouillet, and had dedicated to Richelieu a political paraphrase of the Benedictus. With a typical salon pun Richelieu wrote to inform him of his preferment: 'You have offered me *Bénédicité*, I give you *Grasse*'.

In his patronage of letters Richelieu had a political axe to grind. To him it was wholly unacceptable to hear the Hôtel de Rambouillet described as 'a select court, less crowded and more refined than that at the Louvre', not merely for the overt slight, but because independent cultural centres were in his view intolerable, equivalent to the overmighty subjects whose power he was diminishing. Just as the royal council and its *officiers* were taking over the administration of France, so Richelieu wanted to establish a formal organisation capable of mobilising men of letters in the service of the State. The Hôtel de Rambouillet could not be taken over for this purpose, but

14. Miracle at Port-Royal, by Philippe de Champaigne (see pages 200–1)

15. Louis Le Nain's portrait of peasant life (see page 144)

an unofficial literary club, which met under the leadership of Valentin Conrart, offered a distinct possibility.

It was Conrart who had piqued Richelieu by his remark about the Hôtel de Rambouillet. He was a famous habitué of the salons, attending not only Mme de Rambouillet but Mme de Sablé and Mlle Scudéry, and he preserved a meticulous record of salon news— to the extent of 50 manuscript volumes at present in the Bibliothèque de l'Arsenal. As a *secrétaire du roi* he held a useful position, made more agreeable by a considerable private fortune. He had little formal education, but was a keen bibliophile, and where he lacked the classical languages in which others were proficient he built up a library of translations. A dozen or so men of similar interests began to meet on Saturday mornings at his house in the rue Saint-Martin. It was not so much a salon as a club, and authors who were aware, even at the Hôtel de Rambouillet, of a measure of condescension towards them welcomed the chance to meet professional colleagues on terms of equality. 'They just chatted with each other', wrote Pellison who became their historian, 'as they would have done on an ordinary social occasion, but if one of them had written anything, as often happened, he would read it freely to the others who would just as freely give him their opinions'.

Collectively they were distinguished more for their ideas about literature and language than for their own performance. Jean Chapelain, for example, had little ability as a poet but was very knowledgeable about literature. He spent most of his life preparing *La Pucelle*, one of the longest and most tedious epics of the century, which was received by most people with derision.

> *Après une vie éclatante*
> *La Pucelle fut autrefois*
> *Condamnée au feu par l'Anglois,*
> *Quoy qu'elle fust très innocente;*
> *Mais celle qu'on voit depuis peu*
> *Mérite justement le feu.* *

* After a brilliant life the Maid was long ago condemned to the fire by the English, although she was entirely innocent, but the Maid we have seen lately justly deserves to be burnt.

As a critic, however, Chapelain did a great deal to establish classicism by acclaiming the sovereignty of reason, *le père des règles*. More talented as a poet, though less influential as a critic, was Honorat de Bueil, seigneur de Racan, regarded by Malherbe as his most gifted disciple despite a genuine lyrical quality which disconcerted him by its easy nonchalance. As a pious duty, Racan published his *Mémoires pour servir à la vie de Malherbe*. His fellow disciple, François Mainard, was absent for 17 years as a magistrate in Aurillac, but he returned to the salons, and to Conrart's Saturday mornings, in 1628.

There were nine original members of the group and they kept their meetings secret, but as their numbers increased their reputation spread abroad. Nicolas Faret, whose *L'honnête homme* made a great impression on salon society in 1632, was invited to discuss his book at Conrart's house, and so excited was he by the quality of the discussion that he could not restrain himself from speaking of it to the abbé Boisrobert, one of Richelieu's protégés. Just as he had appointed a staff to supervise his building programme, so Richelieu had set up a team of literary advisers. These included the comte de Bautru who introduced writers to the cardinal, Jean des Marests, a writer himself with whom Richelieu liked to engage in literary contests of subtlety and invention, and Boisrobert, a picaresque rogue who had entered the Church after a libertine youth. At Richelieu's hands he enjoyed appointments worth 10,000 livres a year, acted as the agent of his patronage and stole his books. He was often in disgrace, but Richelieu found life dull without him and restored him to favour—until in 1641 he was expelled to a canonry at Rouen for hiring notorious prostitutes to act in a play which Richelieu had specially written for performance before Louis XIII.

Once Richelieu learned of Conrart's informal society he invited the members to form an official academy under his direction, an exclusive literary club, a permanent and better-organised salon. To give it official tone he proposed to add several of his *conseillers d'état*, men like Hay du Chastelet and Sirmond who acted as his publicists, and Jean Silhon who had prefaced the 1627 edition of Balzac's *Lettres* with a long dedication to Richelieu. The offer was received with dismay. Apart from the loss of informality, privacy and free-dom, there were other serious objections; Conrart was a Huguenot, Mallevilles's patron, the maréchal de Bassompierre, was in the Bas-tille for opposing Richelieu, and Balzac wrote to warn them that any academy run by Richelieu would be merely an instrument for his propaganda: 'I would rather ruin all my small hopes [of pre-ferment] than renounce my liberty and act like Sirmond and Chastelet.' But Richelieu was too powerful to be denied. With great reluctance his proposal was accepted, and after debating the rival attractions of Académie des beaux esprits, Académie des polis, and Académie de l'éloquence, the members settled for Académie Française. They agreed to meet on Mondays, Conrart was appointed secretary, membership was established at 27 (subsequently 40), and the first session took place on 13 March 1634.

There was opposition too from the Paris Parlement, which had vetoed a similar proposal in the sixteenth century for fear of juris-dictional rivalry, and which suspected the purposes of any new institution manipulated by Richelieu. Its grievance was already being voiced against the establishment of special tribunals, and Chastelet was one of the men appointed to serve on them, but finally it registered the edict of incorporation after securing a limit-ing clause that 'the Academy can only take cognisance of the French language, and of books written in this language which are exposed to it for its judgment'.

Certainly the Académie Française had political work to under-take. Chapelain and Godeau prepared Richelieu's speeches, pole-mical tracts of the kind Balzac had anticipated were produced as a necessary feature for the propaganda war with Spain, and the praises of Louis XIII had to be dutifully hymned by his loyal academicians. In 1635, a year ironically when victories were out of fashion and Paris nearly fell to the Spanish troops, the Académie published its *Parnasse Royale* in honour 'of the immortal actions of the most Christian and most victorious monarch, Louis XIII', and a parallel volume entitled the *Sacrifice des Muses* eulogised Richelieu. But all this was in fact kept to a minimum. Richelieu had always intended that the prime function of the Académie should be to establish and maintain by legislation and adjudication the standards of the French language. Its role was therefore very similar to that of Malherbe and the salons, although the political intent was frankly recognised. The royal speech to the Parlement at the Académie's registration referred to the crown's success in remedying the disorders of civil war, and went on to state that it was now time for the language to be similarly regulated, 'to make it not merely elegant but capable of dealing with all the arts and all the sciences'. For Richelieu this became all the more vital as French influence grew in Europe. He referred to 'this language which we speak and which our neighbours will soon be speaking if our conquests continue as successfully as they have begun', and hoped that 'French would succeed Latin as Latin had succeeded Greek as the language of civilisation'. He had his reward, posthumously, when in 1745 the Berlin Academy of Science and Literature announced in words that echoed his own; 'We have substituted French for Latin in order to extend the usefulness of our *Mémoires*; for the boundaries of the empire of Latin are visibly receding, while the French language now occupies the place that Greek occupied at the time of Cicero—everyone learns it.'

In pursuit of its aims the Académie decided to regulate the language by producing 'a comprehensive dictionary and a most precise grammar'; it also planned to draw up the rules of rhetoric and of verse so that no one in the future need write poetry or prose unaided. In fact only the *Dictionnaire* was published, and that slowly. Letter A was completed in October 1639, to provoke the ironic couplet:

> *Et le destin m'aurait fort obligé*
> *S'il m'avait dit: tu vivras jusqu'au* G.

It was finally published in two volumes in 1687 and 1691.

The informing spirit behind the *Dictionnaire* was essentially that of Malherbe and the salons: it robbed poetry to pay prose, it played down the colourful, the concrete and the picaresque, it stressed what was rational, abstract and prosaic. At the same time it enabled men like Conrart, Mainard and Chapelain to continue formally what they had been doing informally in furnishing an undiscriminating society with the weapons of criticism and, by using the Académie's authority as an official lever, to secure the removal from the language of all words scorned by polite society. The preface to the *Dictionnaire* was quite explicit: 'The Académie has decided that it will not include archaic terms, nor the technical words of the arts and the sciences which rarely enter into normal conversation. It bases itself in common speech, in so far as it is used in the day-to-day business of *honnêtes gens* and by orators.' With a reference to the growing demand for the *bienséances* it adds, 'as for words used in fits of passion or which are wounding to modesty, we shall refuse them admission because *honnêtes gens* take care not to use them in their conversation'.

The work of the Académie Française owed a great deal to the ideas of Claude Favre, seigneur de Vaugelas. The son of a Savoyard magistrate, he was yet desperately poor and eked out a living by denouncing Richelieu's enemies in order to claim as his reward a quarter of their confiscated goods. This was before the publication in 1647 of his *Remarques sur la langue française*, which served so well as a guide to his colleagues in compiling the *Dictionnaire* that Richelieu awarded him a pension of 2,000 livres. His declared object was to 'purify the language of all the filth it had picked up', his criterion being the speech of the *honnêtes gens*. It was pedantry of a new kind, and not without its problems. *Poitrine*, for example, was abhorred in the salons for its association with the butcher's shop and the sale of *poitrine de veau*: Vaugelas objected that they might as well eliminate *tête* for the same reason but added, 'nevertheless, though these are scarcely good reasons for eliminating a word, this does not stop the word going out of use, and when it goes out of use it slowly dies since usage is the life and soul of a word' provided the usage was of the right kind. On this Vaugelas had no doubts: *bon usage* is 'the manner of speech of the most sensible men at court consistent with the manner of writing of the soundest authors of the time'. It was an attitude which went unchallenged in the Académie, and survived the satirical attack of Saint-Évremond who parodied the new preoccupation with usage in his *Comédie des Académistes*.

*Je dis que la coutume, assez souvent trop forte,*
*Fait dire improprement que l'on ferme la porte.*
*L'usage tous les jours utilise des mots*
*Dont on se sert pourtant assez mal à propos;*
*Pour avoir moins froid à la fin de décembre*
*On va* pousser sa porte *et* l'on ferme sa chambre*

To a great extent the Académie Française was saved from the worst features of *préciosité* parodied by Saint-Évremond, from the fantasy and frivolity of poets dressing up as shepherds and so on, by its official connection with the government and by the heavy programme of work it had to undertake. Yet its members not only reflected the standards of the salons but, as habitués themselves, helped to establish these in the first place. In consequence the Académie became a kind of official salon, holding a mirror to the tastes and prejudices of a social élite. Unfortunately this meant that the principles of good usage, once analysed, tended to become rigid, and there was no room for innovators of genius like Molière. The Académie, indeed, never represented literary excellence, but literary authority, which is quite another matter. As an association of critics reflecting the rigid divisions of its own society, it was dangerously susceptible to sterility and conservatism.

On the credit side, however, the letters patent of the Académie Française have been justly called 'French literature's letters of nobility'. The very existence of a body of writers and critics, officially recognised and established by the authority of the State, undoubtedly gave a peculiar prestige to the profession of letters in France. It was not immediate, of course. The writer's position in French society, though rapidly improving, was not yet assured. We must not forget the ease with which noblemen were accustomed to take a stick to writers, and that a common expression for beating someone up was *traiter en poète*. There were indeed scores of ragged *poètes crottés* who thronged the streets and taverns of Paris, and aristocratic disdain for the breed in general could not be immediately

---

* I say that custom, which is often too powerful, makes us say improperly that one *closes the door*. Everyday usage employs words which are yet used improperly; to get rid of cold at the end of December one *pushes the door* and *closes the room*.

dispelled by the elevation of a few to polite society. For the few, however, it was galling. 'Poet, singer, mountebank, beggar, buffoon and parasite', wrote Chapelain bitterly, 'are all held to be synonymous and interchangeable'. Even in the Hôtel de Rambouillet the young Condé could remark, 'If Voiture was one of our own kind he would be quite insufferable', and the best that Saint-Simon could say of Racine at Versailles was that 'there was nothing of the poet about him'. Visconti summarised the attitude in his *Mémoires*: 'In France they only esteem titles of war; those of letters and of any other profession are despised, and a man of quality who actually writes is considered to be worthless'.

This is to show the worst side of the medal; in fact, as the century progressed, the nobility in general showed much less disdain and a great deal more respect for the writer, partly because of the Académie but even more because in the salons, as we have seen, the writer made his entry on terms acceptable to the noble. This, of course, is what the writer was only too happy to do. The intense social ambition which drove the bourgeoisie to dream of attaining *la vie noble* affected writers as urgently as merchants, *financiers* and *parlementaires*. In practical terms this meant that the writer had to subscribe to the conventions of classical culture and medieval chivalry in which the noble was educated, and this explains why 'the themes as well as the style of so many seventeenth-century works appear so remote to the modern reader. On the one hand we have the prestige of certain genres, the fondness for mythology and allegory, and the characteristic attempt to rival or surpass the masterpieces of antiquity; on the other hand, the survival of the soldier as hero, and of military prowess as a favourite theme' (Howarth). Real life could not be described objectively but had to be idealised in terms of these conventions—as in tragedy where the story can be constructed only around noble characters—or else travestied in satire and burlesque. Even the life of the bourgeois, which most writers knew intimately, had to be seen from the false vantage point of the salon window. This compelled him to repudiate his own background and to pour scorn on bourgeois solecisms and pretensions. 'It is a pity', writes Furetière of a young girl in his novel, *Le Roman Bourgeois*, 'that she had not been nurtured at court or with people of quality since that would have cured her of the bourgeois airs and graces which mar her wit and which make it obvious where she was brought up'.

The writers were fully conscious of what they did. Writing was no longer undertaken by a leisured class as an incident in a life of action and adventure, as it had been by d'Urfé; most seventeenth-century writers were desperately eager to make a living and a reputation for themselves, and the patronage of both was largely controlled by the fashionable world of the court and the salons. Few of them originally wrote to make a living in the sense of warding off starvation. Conrart had a private fortune in inherited *rentes* and an office in the royal household; Baro was a *conseiller du parlement*, Corneille an *avocat* in Rouen, and Malherbe secretary to a provincial governor. Like most of their colleagues and rivals, who with very few exceptions came from the comfortable environment of the *officier* class, they wrote in order to win greater fame and to secure a better living than that afforded by employment in an office.

> *Un rare écrivain comme toi*
> *Devrait enricher sa famille*
> *D'autant argent que le feu roi*
> *En avait mis en la bastille,** *

wrote Mainard to Malherbe. Mainard himself was less fortunate, and was reduced to selling his own cutlery before being rescued by appointment to a magistracy in Aurillac. Others who abandoned a safe if modest career in order to write were driven into poverty—the *poètes crottes* who eked out a living with scurrilous verse, political libels and petty theft. Furetière, in the *Dictionnaire* of his own making, illustrated the word *état* by the mournful sentence, 'Celibacy is for men of letters a more fitting *état* than that of marriage'. Writers, of course, always bemoan their lack of income, when very often it is lack of recognition which really galls them, and we must be chary of taking too seriously their accounts of their own predicament. Yet it remains clear that many gambled on the chance of

* An exceptional writer like you ought to enrich his family with as much wealth as the late king left in the Bastille.

literary success and failed. The market was too limited to satisfy all who beseiged it, no matter how carefully they adapted themselves to its conventions. 'Only when the eighteenth century is well along do we find any considerable group whom we may call professional authors, men who depended solely upon what they could earn by the sale of their manuscripts' (Pottinger).

Molière was envied by many for what he earned in the theatre but most of it came from acting rather than play-writing. Any play written by him was only too likely to be pirated by another publisher, and by Jean Ribou in particular. Ribou had pirated *Les Précieuses Ridicules*; consequently, when *Le Cocu Imaginaire* seemed to be going well, Molière took out a *privilège* from the censors, not because he wanted to publish it himself but as a device to prevent Ribou doing so. Ribou, however, bribed a member of the company to show him the script, and published it as a text with commentary under the title of *La Comédie Seganorelle (sic)*—with a dedication to Molière! The edition was finally confiscated after an appeal to the civic authorities, but the incident reveals how uncertain were the rewards to be gained from writing plays. Molière, like Alexandre Hardy at the Hôtel de Bourgogne, was paid more by his own company than he ever received from the booksellers, except in the case of *Tartuffe*, a quite exceptional *succès de scandale* which brought him 2,000 livres. Rewards for novelists and poets were better, but still meagre. By the end of the century the average novel would earn 300 livres, and run to 500 copies. Anything more than this was reckoned a great success, and when Boileau's *Lutrin* was well received his publisher was so delighted that he wrote in great glee, 'our success far exceeds my wildest hopes, and I think we shall be able to sell up to 1,200 copies'. Even greater successes were recorded by a popular burlesque writer like Scarron; the second half of the *Roman Comique* earned him 1,000 livres, and *Virgile Travesti*, an exceptional bestseller in the year of the Fronde, produced 11,000 livres. Chapelain's *Pucelle*, despite its indifferent quality, had been publicly prepared and advertised for nearly 30 years and ran through six editions in 18 months, earning him 3,000 livres, but successful second editions were rare. If a book was as popular as that, another publisher was likely to pirate it, and some publishers even pirated their own works to avoid paying their author a second royalty.

Although every author wrote deliberately to make money, none was allowed to admit it. Writers, unlike artists, had to affect an amateur status if they were to admit to the company of *honnêtes gens*, and when Mairet out of jealousy accused Corneille of writing for money he was obviously anticipating that this would turn the public against him.

> *Travailler pour la gloire, et qu'un sordide gain*
> *Ne soit jamais l'objet d'un illustre écrivain.*

Boileau no doubt choked on his own fine sentiments, but the convention persisted throughout the century.

Nonetheless there were loopholes. Hawking your wares in public was one thing; winning the private patronage of the wealthy—preferably of the noble, ideally of the king—was quite another. It was considered legitimate practice to invoke such patronage by means of fulsome dedications. Corneille, who was well looked after by Richelieu, wasted no time after the cardinal's death in dedicating *Cinna* in 1643 to a wealthy bourgeois, Montoron. He left nothing to chance. Montoron was compared to no less a Maecenas than the Emperor Augustus, and Corneille was rewarded with 2,000 livres. Racine did better still. At a time when he was known only as a minor poet he won 2,400 livres by dedicating his first tragedy to the duc de Saint-Aignan. Lesser mortals earned, or gave, lesser amounts. Mazarin was never worth more than 50 livres for a dedication, nor was Gaston's daughter, La Grande Mademoiselle, and authors became ingenious by reprinting their works with dedications to different patrons. D'Assouci dedicated his *Poésies et Lettres* in 1653 to a M. Bordier. The book sold well and a second edition appeared in the same year, with the same dedicatory epistle, but addressed on this occasion to the comte d'Harcourt. One obscure writer, Rangouze, went even better. By not paginating his book he enabled the binder to slip a different dedicatory letter into each copy, and his gullible patrons rewarded him with 15,000 livres in all.

Voiture pretended to be above such practices: 'I am not one of those who set out to convert their eulogies into special favours by treating all the cardinal's deeds as miracles'. But the tone of lofty disdain was pitched too high, since Voiture was being looked after very generously by the cardinal's enemy, Gaston.

All writers in fact were in desperate need of protection. They posed as amateurs and attacked each other viciously for fawning upon the great, but the system permitted them no other way to make a living. With only a limited market to write for they could not survive without the private patronage of the noble and the wealthy, and on them they depended for gifts, for pensions, for lodging or for preferment to sinecures. Voiture depended on Gaston, on the comte d'Avaux and on Mme de Rambouillet; La Bruyère on Condé; Saint-Amant on the duc de Retz; Balzac on the duc d'Épernon; Chapelain on the duc de Longueville, and so on. Richelieu was perhaps the most consistently generous of patrons; he maintained as many as 26 writers at one time and is reckoned to have spent 40,000 livres a year in gifts and pensions. When he died there were many who must have echoed the serious plaint behind the irony of Benserade's mock epitaph:

> Ci-gît par la morbleu
> Le Cardinal de Richelieu
> Et ce qui cause mon ennui
> Ma pension avec lui.*

* Here lies, dammit, Cardinal Richelieu and, what vexes me, my pension with him.

# four

# Richelieu and Mazarin

## II

Richelieu's intense interest in the theatre prompted him to employ his own team of authors to write plays at his direction. Among these, for a short time, was Pierre Corneille, who became one of the greatest dramatists of the century. His father, a *maître des eaux et forêts* in Rouen, had given him the kind of education best suited for a career in the administration by sending him first to the local Jesuit College and then for two years of training in law. From the Jesuits Corneille derived an abiding interest in the Stoics and in the rational eloquence of Seneca and Lucan; he was also greatly influenced by the dramatic productions which were a feature of Jesuit education. This did not deter him from becoming an *avocat* in the local *parlement* in 1624 but it left him with a passionate desire to write for the stage. In 1628 the Troupe de Monsieur le Prince d'Orange came to Rouen on tour, and Montdory not only met Corneille but urged him to write for them. The result was the comedy *Mélite* with which Montdory opened at the Marais in 1629, and Corneille became the company's *poète à gages*—but on rather better terms than most. One of the company, Mlle de Beaupré, complained that Corneille was ruining them: 'We used to get our plays for three *écus*, which we could make in one night; we were accustomed to this and we made quite a lot of money; but now we pay much more for Corneille's plays and we make very little out of it'.

In Paris Corneille was drawn into the circle of the Cinq Auteurs, including Boisrobert and Rotrou, who worked for Richelieu. They produced *La comédie des Tuileries* in 1635 and were preparing *La Grande Pastorale*, to which Richelieu himself contributed 500 lines, when Corneille tired of his position as the cardinal's hack and returned to Rouen to work independently. Late in 1636 he reappeared with a new play, *Le Cid*, which delighted the public by its powerful and passionate treatment of a dramatic Spanish story. The detail of the plot is worth relating since it was relevant to the public dispute which this play provoked. The Cid himself is Don Roderigo, a champion of the Spanish wars against the Moors, and suitor for Chimène, daughter of Don Gomez. His father, however, is insulted by Don Gomez, calls upon the Cid to avenge him, and Don Gomez is killed in a duel. Chimène appeals to the King to punish the Cid but he disappears to win further triumphs against the Moors and returns to claim from the King her hand in marriage. Chimène meanwhile has come to recognise that in fact she still loves him, and the play ends with the King's decision to impose a year's delay while Chimène makes up her mind between marriage and vengeance.

It was indeed a story full of incident and excitement, yet Corneille succeeded in reducing to order the separate episodes by subordinating them to the central theme of the issues of love and duty. Moreover, though the final outcome is not necessarily tragic, his play is one of the first of the French classical tragedies in that it transforms a recital of mere misfortune into a study of the agonies of inner conflict. Why then was it so severely criticised? In the first place its success with the public merely aroused the worst type of professional jealousy. Mairet, for example, began by attempting to discredit Corneille for writing for money, and compared his visits from Rouen to Paris to trading expeditions. He then made much of the fact that Corneille had dispensed with the unities, and claimed that the very idea of Chimène marrying her father's murderer was a gross affront to propriety.

Richelieu did not conceal his dislike for the play. He had already declared himself in favour of the rules in drama, since he found in the civilised treatment of emotion, and the restrained use of language, a welcome parallel to the good order he was seeking to establish throughout France. *Le Cid*, no matter how much Corneille had refined the original, remained a turbulent, passionate play which flouted the unities and the growing taste for *bienséance* and *vraisemblance*. Its popularity only aggravated the issue. Richelieu resented Corneille's independent success, particularly as the latest play by his own authors, *L'Aveugle de Smyrne*, had been a dismal failure, but there were political factors which carried greater weight than personal resentment. He felt bitterly about the glorification of a Spanish theme in the very year that Spanish troops had nearly entered Paris; but what angered him still more was that while he was struggling against tremendous opposition to enforce the laws against duelling, Corneille not only made a duel the central incident in his plot but used language throughout which justified the practice of private vengeance.

> *Ce que le comte a fait semble avoir mérité*
> Ce digne châtiment *de sa témérité.*\*

Aggrieved patron or outraged politician, Richelieu nonetheless kept his silence, mainly because of Mme de Combalet, his niece, who pointed out that whatever his motives he would only be taken in public as a jealous playwright, like Mairet himself. The matter might have ended there but for the action of another jealous rival, Scudéry, who lodged a formal complaint against *Le Cid* with the newly constituted Académie Française. Balzac was extremely angry with him: 'You may carry the day in committee', he wrote, 'but Corneille has triumphed in the theatre', and he added, 'Corneille has a secret which succeeds far better than art itself'. But the appeal to the Académie Française had to be met if it was ever to function as the public arbiter of French literature, and since this was its first case, Richelieu demanded a verdict from the members.

It had been laid down by the Paris Parlement that no judgment could be made of any book without its author's consent. Boisrobert was therefore despatched by Richelieu to win Corneille's. '*Mes-*

---

\* What the count has done seems to have merited *this just chastisement of his rashness.*

*sieurs de l'Académie'*, he replied grudgingly, 'can do what they please, and as you tell me that Monseigneur would be most happy to see a verdict made, and that this would very much interest his Eminence, I have nothing further to say.' Richelieu now put the pressure on Chapelain to mobilise a verdict. Chapelain, pedantic though he was about the rules, had originally agreed with Balzac's good opinion of the play, but when we consider that the Académie's culture was that of the salons and its function to establish rules for literature, it is difficult to imagine how else Chapelain could have decided but in defence of *vraisemblance*, *bienséance* and the unities. He did his best to satisfy the conflicting demands upon him, and in 1637 the *Sentiment de l'Académie sur Le Cid* was made known. 'Finally, we conclude that although the subject matter of *Le Cid* is not good, that it is at fault in the *dénouement*, that it is burdened with irrelevant episodes, that propriety and theatrical good taste are lacking in several places and that there are many poor verses and much impure speech; nevertheless, the candour and violence of its emotions, the powerful effect and the delicacy of several of its sentences, and that inexplicable pleasure to be found mingled with its errors, have won for it a place of high repute among other similar works of French literature which have given the greatest satisfaction.'

The comment was indeed so fair that it annoyed all the parties concerned; it was too mild for Mairet and Scudéry, too harsh for Corneille and too independent for Richelieu, who would have liked to have seen the verdict drafted with greater solicitude for his own view. It was unfair that Corneille was given no official right of reply, but we must remember that the Académie's powers were those of censure, not of censorship, and the ill effects of its action against *Le Cid* must not be exaggerated. Corneille in fact lost nothing. He retired to Rouen in high dudgeon, digested the *Sentiments* in private and finally applied them in his subsequent plays. In these he combined the consciously artistic intent of Jodelle with the boundless vitality of Hardy. In different circumstances Corneille might have preferred to have emphasised the Hardy tradition and made an art form of it but, in a society which was just discovering, and therefore valued all the more, the qualities of form, order, reason and good taste, he chose instead to develop the consciously literary tradition of Jodelle and bring it to life.

The other plays upon which Corneille's reputation rests are the Roman plays—*Horace, Cinna, Polyeucte, La Mort de Pompée* and *Rodogune*—written between 1640 and 1645. In considering them it is worth bearing in mind not only the *Sentiments* but also Corneille's own *Discours* and *Examens* published after 1660 in which he rationalised what he had done in the theatre since 1640. Tragedy, he said, 'must have some serious, illustrious and extraordinary actions for its subject matter', and he explained that extraordinary themes were necessary because it was only in an abnormal situation that the true courage of the tragic hero could be demonstrated. But since abnormal situations were likely to be so incredible as to be ridiculous, *vraisemblance* was to some extent preserved by taking the plot directly from history, and from the classical history with which society was wholly familiar. In the *Discours de l'utilité et des parties du poème dramatique* he wrote: 'It is not *vraisemblable* that Medusa kills her own children, that Clytemnestra murders her own husband, that Orestes stabs his mother to death, but history tells us that this is so, and the re-enactment of these great crimes does not provoke incredulity.'

Having established a credible context such as Rome, Corneille was free to develop the conflict necessary for the drama. Physical violence was severely held in check, and instead he became preoccupied by the conflict of the passions, of the intellect and of the will. Love itself he reduced to secondary importance: 'I have always held that love was too feeble a passion to be the dominant theme in a tragedy.' The tragic hero is motivated by will and overcomes his emotions and inclinations in the name of honour and duty.

Some modern writers have seen in this emphasis upon the will the influence of Descartes's *Traité des Passions* (see chapter 5) but, apart from the fact that the *Traité* did not appear until 1649, there is a much simpler and more straightforward connection with the Stoic authors by whom Corneille was enthralled as a boy at the Jesuit College. His audiences, too, were aware of Stoicism since it had been widely publicised at the start of the century by Guillaume du Vair.

16. Molière (see pages 170–4, 258–61)

17. Molière as Sganarelle

18. Jean Racine (see pages 261–7)

'THE SCHOOL OF 1660'

19. Nicolas Boileau (see pages 215–18)

Du Vair and his followers were not *libertins*: he, indeed, was Bishop of Lisieux, *garde des sceaux* (1610–20) and highly respected, but he wrote against the theological dogmatism of the clergy in order to persuade reasonable men, including the *libertins*, that Christianity could be reconciled with both nature and reason. In the outcome he offered a purely natural religion, set out in language which owed more to the Stoics than to the Gospels. Hence the tremendous determination of Corneille's characters to base their actions upon reason where possible but also, by an effort of the will, to rise above the passions and emotions and to defy if necessary mankind, the elements and even destiny itself—as we see in a spirited *tirade* by Cléopâtre in *Rodogune*:

> *Tombe sur moi le ciel pourvu que je me venge!*
> *J'en recevrai le coup d'un visage remis:*
> *Il est doux de périr après ses ennemis;*
> *Et, de quelque rigueur que le destin me traite,*
> *Je perds moins à mourir qu'à vivre leur sujette.**

This preoccupation with the struggle of the human will was warmly received. The stricter observance of the unities had accustomed audiences to take a greater interest in the minds of the characters rather than in their actions, and the taste for psychological analysis, the staple of French classical tragedy, had already been well established in the salons since the first discussions of *L'Astrée*. But we must not imagine that Corneille wrote to satisfy conventions for their own sake, nor even to demonstrate the principles of Stoic philosophy. The object of dramatic poetry as Corneille described it 'is to give pleasure, and the rules are merely instructions to make it easier for a poet to do so and cannot serve as reasons to persuade an audience that a thing is good when they actually dislike it'. To please an audience meant to move it emotionally, and this was Corneille's prime object. If the conventions of the day discouraged the violence of physical conflict, then he would give them the violence of mental

---

* May I be avenged, and though the heavens fall upon me, I shall receive the blow with a composed countenance. It is sweet to perish after one's enemies, and, whatever rigours fate decrees for me, I shall lose less by dying than by living as their subject.

and spiritual conflict, and this he achieved less by his powers of psychological insight than by his ability as a rhetorician. 'It is the poetry of Malherbe multiplied a thousand fold in vigour and in genius' ( Lytton Strachey), and it was at its most effective in the great *tirades*. Given the right performers these *tirades* were not merely literary set-pieces; they awoke the most passionate responses from the audience, carrying it forward on a full-flowing tide of language. To quote them out of context is, therefore, misleading, but if we take one from *Le Cid* we can not only experience some of its emotional power but also realise why its sentiments were so abhorrent to Richelieu. It embodies the kernel of the plot, the pleading of Don Diego to the King to justify the action of his son in fighting a duel on his behalf, and with great economy the point is made, the tension heightened and the drama established.

> *Moi, dont les longs travaux ont acquis tant de gloire,*
> *Moi, que jadis partout a suivi la victoire,*
> *Je me vois aujourd'hui, pour avoir trop vécu,*
> *Recevoir un affront et demeurer vaincu.*
> *Ce que n'a pu jamais combat, siège, ambuscade,*
> *Ce que n'a pu jamais Aragon ni Grenade,*
> *Ni tous vos ennemis, ni tous mes envieux,*
> *Le comte en votre cour l'a fait presque à vos yeux,*
> *Jaloux de votre choix, et fier de l'avantage*
> *Que lui donnait sur moi l'impuissance de l'âge.*
> *Sire, ainsi ces cheveux blanchis sous le harnois,*
> *Ce sang, pour vous servir, prodigué tant de fois,*
> *Ce bras, jadis l'effroi d'une armée ennemie,*
> *Descendaient au tombeau tout chargés d'infamie,*
> *Si je n'eusse produit un fils digne de moi,*
> *Digne de son pays et digne de son roi:*
> *Il m'a prêté sa main, il a tué le comte;*
> *Il m'a rendu honneur, il a lavé ma honte.**

---

* I, whose lifetime's labours have won such glory, whom victory accompanied everywhere, now see myself, because I am too old, receive an insult and stay silent. Something which combat, siege and ambush could never do, which Aragon and Granada and all your enemies and all my rivals could never do, has now been done

So different in quality are the tragedies of Corneille from the plays of 1600 that many have found it difficult to accept that they were all written for the same audience. Thus, to explain a revolution in taste from Hardy to Corneille, a plebeian rabble had to be postulated for the one, an aristocratic élite for the other. The problem is aggravated by a lack of accurate statistics. Even after 1680, when figures are available for the Comédie Française, we only know how many tickets were sold, and not to whom they were sold. Lancaster has argued that by the end of the century 100,000 people would visit the theatre in a year; Lough suggests a much smaller group of, say, 35,000 who went to more than one play in the year. This on the face of it seems the more likely, especially as even the successful plays had only a short run, indicating that there was a limited pool of theatregoers. This limited group was indeed an aristocratic élite, composed of royalty, courtiers, army officers, *officiers* and merchants. Moreover, it was a constant group: it attended in 1600, in 1640 and in 1680, and the changes wrought in the theatre were the consequence of changes in this group's tastes. The Hôtel de Bourgogne, for example, recognised this; it abandoned the multiple settings for the single unadorned *palais à volontiers* or the *chambre à quatre portes*, and staged the reformed type of tragedy epitomised by the plays of Corneille.

We must not assume, however, that because Corneille and the Hôtel de Bourgogne conformed to the principles demanded by the salons and the Académie Française, the rest of the Parisian theatre went the same way. Much of what was written, and enjoyed, is not included among the selections now made by historians who seek to generalise about the age. Tragi-comedy, which was the dominant genre for a decade after Hardy's death, ceased to be so after 1640, but it still remained significantly popular: 80 tragi-comedies were

---

within your very court, almost before your eyes, by the count who resented your favour to me and who boasted in the advantage which my impotent old age conferred upon him. Thus, Sire, these hairs grown grey in harness, this blood so freely spent for you so many times, this arm once the terror of your enemies, would have descended to the grave covered in infamy, if I had not produced a son, worthy of me, of his country and of his king. He lent me his hand; he killed the count. He has restored my honour and washed away my shame.

produced between 1630 and 1640 as opposed to 40 tragedies, but in the following decade there were still 67 as against 69 tragedies. We might take, for example, the play by Baro on the life of Saint Eustache. Performed in 1639 and published ten years later, it was treated as a robust melodrama, the unities were ignored, and storms, shipwrecks and divine thunderbolts all succeeded each other in a tumultuous series of episodes leading up to the final martyrdom. Its popularity was not surprising. Baro was already well known, as d'Urfé's secretary and the author of the final volume of *L'Astrée*. Moreover, he could satisfy a popular demand for simple entertainment and spectacle which Corneille could never meet; tragedy at the Hôtel de Bourgogne might appeal to the cultivated intelligence and stir the heart, but there were also large audiences who as always were eager to be regaled and excited by pageantry, pantomime and extravaganza.

If tragedy made a living for the Hôtel de Bourgogne, it was spectacle which saved the Marais. Corneille had given it a new lease of life, and Montdory had been an excellent leader of the company, but he retired in 1637 and his two immediate successors were swiftly lured away to the Hôtel de Bourgogne. In 1644 the theatre was burnt down, but the new one which opened in 1648 began a new line of theatrical entertainment by offering the *pièces à machines*, the fascinating spectacles with their staggering scene changes which are described below.

> *Des machines d'abord le surprenant spectacle*
> *Éblouit le bourgeois et fit crier miracle,*★

was an unkind jibe: in fact, the same audience which rose to the *tirades* of Corneille and was thrilled by the Stoic sentiments of his heroes crowded also to the Marais to gaze with rapturous wonder at the exotic triumphs of its stage manager.

One of the things for which the Palais Cardinal was famous was the special theatre which opened in January 1641 with a production of Richelieu's own play *Mirame*. Apart from the general magnifi-

---

★ At first the astonishing spectacle produced by the machines dazzled the bourgeois and made them acclaim it a miracle.

cence of the decoration there were two unusual features about the stage: it had a proscenium arch to emphasise the separation of the actors from the audience; and 100,000 livres worth of stage machinery, capable of engineering transformation scenes and a dozen other effects, rapturously recalled by the *Gazette de France*— 'delightful gardens, decorated with grottoes, fountains, statues and flowerbeds, along a terrace by the sea, which had the most natural-looking waves, and two great fleets, one seemingly two leagues off shore, which both passed in full view of the spectators'. Yet, at the very moment when the classical theatre was dispensing with scenery, and certainly with scene-changing, why should Richelieu have so equipped his theatre? The answer was not revealed until February 1641 when, with the production of *La Prospérité des armes de la France*, presented with music and dance and numerous transformation scenes, it became clear that Richelieu had designed his theatre not so much for conventional drama but for the wholly different genre of the *ballet de cour*.

The *ballet de cour* in the sixteenth century had been an attempt to revive classical tragedies with the aid of music and dance, but the declamation of the words to music proved unpopular and was abandoned. In 1581 Catherine de' Medici staged *Le Ballet Comique de la Reyne*, an impressive union of music, dance, poetry and spectacle, which also united performers and spectators since everyone participated. Three points of décor were set up in the hall, with the dancers moving between them, and the audience joining in the set-pieces, such as the processions and the courtly dances. Performances could go on all night since there was no set pattern or form. Indeed, the *ballet de cour* became very much a *bonne à tout faire* with elements of pantomime, ballet, spectacle, masquerade and tournament; a performance of 1695, for example, made excellent use of a pair of camels which happened by chance to have been brought to Paris, and the Carrousel of 1612 in the Place Royale was essentially an outdoor *ballet de cour*.

There were several contrasting developments in the form and content of the *ballet de cour* in the seventeenth century. One trend emphasised a literary or allegorical theme, rather like the painters of the Second School of Fontainebleau; another, exemplified by *La Délivrance de Renaud* (1617), combined satire with burlesque; and both of these gave more importance to the words than to the music and dance. But as the theatre too adopted these themes, the *ballet de cour* became more of a spectacle, a trend encouraged by Louis XIII's director of ballets, the duc de Nemours, whose particular enthusiasm was for masquerades and processions in which spectators and performers took part. Quite different again were the attempts to import the complex stage machinery invented by the Italians which encouraged a complete indifference to the plot provided the transformation scenes were sufficiently ingenious—as when the sky opened in the *Ballet de Tancrède* (1619) to allow the descent of musicians and dancers on a cloud. Dancing, of course, was common to all types of *ballet de cour* but the incoherence of the form in general was reflected in the great variety of dance forms. Figure dances, for example, were carefully rehearsed formation dances performed across the hall floor and designed to be seen from the gallery; burlesque dances were platform performances to raise laughter, but a development of this led to a form of ballet in which the dancer, with serious or with comic intent, attempted to reveal an inward mood by stylised movements; and finally there were the courtly or society dances in which everyone could join.

This, therefore, was an art form which, by its very lack of form and by its wholly emotional appeal, ran counter to all the cultural concepts of the Académie. It is true of course that spectacle was enjoyed by everyone as a legitimate contrast to the tragedies of Corneille, and that Richelieu was particularly fond of music, but it was primarily for political reasons that he interested himself in the *ballet de cour*. It seemed to him to be an admirable means of propaganda, as indeed it had seemed to Henri IV's illegitimate son, the duc de Vendôme, who presented in 1610 an allegorical version of his father's defeat of disorder in the *Ballet de Monsieur de Vendôme*. In 1641, therefore, the *Ballet de la Prospérité des armes de la France* reunited the elements of spectacle, dance and music in order, by allegorical and historical examples, to represent the glory of the monarchy in as stunning a way as possible.

From all accounts, and not merely from those in the *Gazette de France* which he controlled, Richelieu succeeded. The curtain rose on a pastoral scene; Harmony, borne aloft in the clouds, proclaims her establishment by Louis XIII and his minister; the screens part to reveal the depths of hell where the champions of disorder are attacked by an eagle bursting from the skies and two lions from their caverns; the screens close to let the Gallic Hercules restore the peace and order of the pastoral scene. This was merely the first act. Act Two included the siege of Casale, the siege of Arras and seven other victories over Spain, each celebrated by an appropriate ballet, and Act Five returned to the theme of mythological allegory in which Concord and Abundance return to France. For the finale, the curtain rose on a gilded hall, with crystal chandeliers and the luxurious appointments, where a loyal and astonished audience was overwhelmed to see its own King Louis XIII seated in person by his Queen.

The *ballet de cour* was thus given its characteristic form by Richelieu. The unifying theme of royal propaganda put an end to the indiscriminate staging of tournaments and circuses, the *mise en scène* became all-important and poetry and music served only to accompany the general spectacle and the dances. The form of the dances themselves was determined by the raised platform stage which was unsuitable for figure dances, and by the proscenium arch, which prevented any participation by the audience, so that the courtly dances had to be reserved for the balls which followed the conclusion of the performances. The dancers, therefore, concentrated upon the expression of mood and in this way prepared the foundations for the classical ballet of the eighteenth century. This of course was incidental to Richelieu's purpose. What mattered most to him was the spectacle of monarchy triumphant observed through the proscenium arch.

The equivalent of this outside the theatre was the Royal Entry with its stately procession under triumphal arches. Such an Entry was staged by Mazarin, for example, in August 1660 to celebrate the triumph of his foreign policy and to welcome the return of Louis XIV with his Spanish bride, Marie-Thérèse. Throughout the morning a massive review was held outside the city walls near Vincennes when members of the university, officers of the gilds, magistrates, *parlementaires* and clergy paraded before the king. At 2 p.m. the entire procession began to move towards the Louvre via the Île de la Cité, passing beneath a series of triumphal arches. The first of these was in the Faubourg Saint-Antoine, made by a master carpenter, Fleurant le Noir, for the sum of 1,400 livres and the right to take away the timber for his own use afterwards. Disguised to look like stone, it stood 48 feet high and 60 feet wide with triple arches, pediments and entablature—and an internal staircase by which a small woodwind orchestra climbed up to serenade the king as he passed. The next, the Porte Saint-Antoine, was a genuine archway but it had been specially embellished for the occasion. The keystone was concealed by a bust of Louis XIV, and at the top stood Hymen, appropriately enough, accompanied by Hope of France and Public Safety. The inscription on the archway was tactfully and comprehensively composed: 'To the peace gained by the victorious arms of Louis XIV, the wise counsels of Anne, the august marriage of Marie-Thérèse, the diligent help of Jules, Cardinal Mazarin, obtained, founded and forever confirmed, this arch is consecrated by the Provost of the Merchants, Guilds and Counsellors of Paris in the year 1660.' Other arches were constructed on the route across to the Cité, but none could compare in magnificence with the final *pièce de résistance*, a triumphal arch of colossal size which stood in the Place Dauphine. Designed by Le Brun with tremendous skill and ingenuity, the fantasy of its decoration and the splendour of its overall design beggar description.

The propaganda value of the *ballet de cour* was recognised by Mazarin, and he set out to go one better than Richelieu. The hall of the Petit-Bourbon palace was altered to accommodate the most impressive stage in Paris, and its deep apse was used to house the massive machines, flats and backcloths which he imported from Italy. But Mazarin was not content to stun the French with spectacle; he planned also to seduce them with opera. The distraction of *il popolo* from the embarrassments of the government by a judicious programme of bread and circuses was no novelty, and according to *Der*

*musikalische Quack-Salber*, by the seventeenth-century composer
Kuhnau, 'Music diverts the thoughts of the people . . . as in Italy,
where the princes and their ministers have so infected the people with
music that they are no longer troubled in their affairs'. The fact that
Mazarin so signally failed to persuade the French to love Italians or to
distract them from rebellion does not mean that he did not hope,
by the introduction of opera, to stem the strong current of hostility
directed against him as an Italian and as Richelieu's successor. Nevertheless, it is evident that he was so great an enthusiast for opera that in
any event he could not bear to be deprived of it.

Italian composers had diverged widely from the narrow paths
followed by the rest of Europe, and their creation of a style analogous
to the baroque in painting and architecture was the most exciting
musical achievement of the century. As with art, so in music, the new
style was a development of techniques, concepts and attitudes established in the Renaissance and influenced in Italy by the special
circumstances of the Counter-Reformation.

In the Renaissance tradition of *a cappella*, that is unaccompanied,
singing, the several voices were given their own evenly flowing
rhythms to pursue independently, and the production of chords was,
as it were, a by-product of the composer's handling of the independent parts. This linear and polyphonic style was both austere
and controlled. Though the emotional impact of Palestrina's music
sung *a cappella* can be considerable, it yet remains a controlled
emotion, and this is apparent from the cautious use of dissonance,
the carefully balanced harmonic progressions, and the restraint in
representing the meaning or mood of the words. By 1590 the style
was under attack. A group of Roman poets and patrons, the
Camerata, reacted violently against what it termed '*il laceramento
della poesia*', the tearing to shreds of the verse and its meaning by
singers who, in pursuing their autonomous parts, were frequently
singing different words from each other. Palestrina had already laid
down that if a composition had two or more parts, each with an
independent melody of its own, then the musical rendering should
not be allowed to obscure the text; but this was not enough for the
Camerata which demanded that greater emphasis be given to the

words and that their meaning should be reflected more directly and expressively in the music.

Initially the demand was met by Monteverdi in a manner which in self-conscious contrast to *il stilo antico* of Palestrina he termed '*la seconda prattica musicale*'. In this new style the words of the verse were given clearer exposition, their mood was evoked more dramatically and, to achieve this, the independence and equal weight of the separate voices was ended. Instead, greater emphasis was given to the outermost voices and instruments so that attention was virtually monopolised by the melody-carrying treble and the fundamental basis, the *basso continuo*. An important consequence followed: 'Melody itself now became conditioned by harmony and, what is of great importance, people have listened to it ever since by applying mentally a harmonic foundation or "accompaniment" even if such was not provided. Every tone becomes now the representative of a harmony, a principle which is the complete antithesis of linear-polyphonic conceptions' (Lang).

The middle voices and instruments, instead of following their own melodic lines, were reduced to filling in the chordal harmonies. For the performer this presented new problems since frequently the treble and the *basso continuo* were the only parts to be scored, the rest being left to the imagination, initiative and skill of the players. Thus challenged, they acquired, and rushed to demonstrate, new skills of elaboration and ornamentation, among them that of diminution, a most popular and overworked device in which a long note, instead of being sustained, is resolved and broken into many other shorter, quicker ones. So eager were instrumentalists to make their mark that they had to be restrained from poaching. In the aptly titled *Del Suonare sopra il Basso con Tutti Stromenti et Uso Loro nel Concerto*, Agostino Agazzari tried to legislate accordingly: 'Everyone should listen to the others and for his turn to apply his runs, trills and accents.'

This type of playing, with the supporting instrumentalists providing impromptu embellishments of the melody and its harmonies, had already spread to France and became a characteristic feature of Louis XIII's Vingt-Quatre Violons, but this alone was not the full measure of the baroque. As the Italians continued to develop it, excitement came with the invention of richer harmonies, with the expressive use of dissonance and sensuous chromatic alterations and with the musical equivalent of chiaroscuro—emotional qualities which the champions of the Counter-Reformation could not fail to exploit in their passionate crusade to recover and confirm the allegiance of the masses. A more resonant musical sound was needed to complement the sumptuous décor of the baroque church. To this end the richer harmonies were enriched still more in presentation by means of multiple choirs and orchestras and by the development of that superb instrument of baroque splendour, the organ. Palestrina's *Missa Papae Marcelli*, no longer sung *a cappella*, was performed with a full orchestral accompaniment which exploited the newly discovered techniques of dissonance and chromaticism.

A new type of impassioned declamation was demanded from the singers, a degree of pathos and emotional violence calling for qualities of volume and endurance which were deemed beyond the province of boys and women. Hence the castrati; combining the clear and sexless voice of the boy with the powerful larynx and lungs of the man, they became the virtuosi of the world of oratorio and opera. Opera indeed was the baroque form *par excellence*, stirring the emotions by the combination of drama, spectacle, voice and music. It was this which had enslaved Mazarin as a boy at the Jesuit College in Rome so deeply that as a young man he returned to sing the title role in an opera written by the Fathers on the life of St Ignatius. Subsequently, in the service of Cardinal Antonio Barberini, one of the great patrons of opera in Rome, he met the finest musicians and singers of the day. One of these, Leonora Baroni, became, if not his temporary mistress, then a permanent ally in his diplomatic career. She also played an important role in 1644 when Mazarin brought her to Paris to arouse the Queen's interest in Italian singing. Her considerable charm and her powerful soprano, though deemed a degree too forceful for French ears, won her immediate success, and she left for Rome with gifts worth 40,000 livres.

One singer alone could not establish opera in France, but heartened by her success, Mazarin enlisted the aid of Giacomo Torelli, at that time the most brilliant stage manager in Italy, whose scenic effects and transformation scenes were calculated to astound the eyes of a Parisian audience while the unaccustomed music assailed its ears. The piece selected for production in November 1645 was *La Finta Pazza*, neither an opera in the true sense nor a *ballet de cour* but a kind of musical *festa* with transformation scenes and spectacular *entrées*. Written by Strozzi and set to music by Sacrati, it had been first performed in Venice in 1641. Torelli adapted it for the French court by introducing one scene set against Henri IV's Pont Neuf, and another, designed to captivate the very young Louis XIV, with a ballet of ostriches. Mazarin was agog to make a success of the production. He begged the duke of Parma to lend him his most experienced stage-hands, musicians and singers, and Leonora Baroni again crossed the Alps to set her own mark upon the performance. Paris was captivated. The combination of poetry, music and spectacle was lifted altogether out of the ordinary by 'Torelli's dextrous skill with his machines and by the wonderful changes of scene, the like of which we have not seen in France before' (*Gazette de France*, December 1645).

Voiture, in competition with nearly every other poet in Paris, hastened to celebrate Torelli's success, adding a few judicious lines in honour of the Cardinal.

> *Dedans un mesme temps nous voions mille lieux,*
> *Des ports, des ponts, des tours, des jardins spacieux,*
> *Et dans un mesme lieu, cent scènes différentes.*
>
> *Quels honneurs te sont dûs, grand et divin Prélat,*
> *Qui fais que désormais tant de faces changeantes*
> *Sont dessus le théâtre, et non pas dans l'Estat?*\*

By the early months of 1647 the courtiers were in a state of feverish excitement, their anticipation whetted daily by the stream of new arrivals from Italy to take part in the production, and by the rumours

---

\* In one same time we see 1,000 places, ports, bridges, towers and spacious gardens, and in one same place 100 different scenes. What honours are due to you, great and divine prelate, who has so contrived that henceforth the variety of change is confined to the theatre and not to the State?

of the great expense—the gossips said half a million *écus*—which Mazarin was incurring. The struggle for tickets was almost more intense than the struggle for power; and those senior officers of the army who had contrived to secure them watched with mounting tension as the start of the spring campaign against Spain drew nearer and as rehearsals continued without apparent end. In the event the first performance was given on Saturday, 3 March 1647. So great was the crush that those with tickets were instructed to come unattended, whatever their rank, and foreign diplomats were asked to dispense with protocol. Despite these precautions the scrum outside, as those without tickets blocked the entrances and attempted to bribe their way in, delayed the performance by more than an hour. Anne d'Autriche was furious. She had promised her confessor to retire before midnight in order to attend mass the next morning but, since she knew that the performance was expected to last six hours, it quickly became evident that, after months of anticipation, she would have to miss the last act.

The success of *La Finta Pazza* coincided with a sudden influx of Italians fleeing into France on the death of Pope Urban VIII, to escape imprisonment or death at the hands of his former enemy and successor, Innocent X. Among these were the two Barberini cardinals and the Prince of Palestrina, passionate enthusiasts for opera. In their eyes *La Finta Pazza* was a mere curtain-raiser, nor were they satisfied by the performance in February 1647 of Cavalli's opera *à soli* —*Egisto*. Thus, with the agreement of Anne d'Autriche who was fast becoming something of an enthusiast too, it was agreed that within a year Mazarin should undertake the production of a fullscale Italian opera in Paris. The choice fell on *Orfeo ed Euridice*, perhaps because the librettist, the abbé Buti, had accompanied the Barberini to France. Luigi Rossi, the composer, was summoned to join him to direct the orchestra, Torelli was engaged to create his inimitable effects, and Charles Errard, a court painter of some distinction, to paint the scenery.

After all the months of expectation there was no anticlimax. *Orfeo* was an immediate success. Though a few purists were antagonised by the total disregard for the unities, the audience was enthralled by the variety and colour of the scenes, the richness of the orchestration and the emotional power of the arias. The emotive qualities of the opera caused some concern. It was both novel and disturbing to find music treated no longer as a sonorous or sentimental decoration but rather as a vehicle for the unruly passions, and many shared Anne's personal uneasiness at her unabashed delight in such sensuous enjoyment. It was this which prompted the *Gazette* to cock a wary eye at the puritanical Catholics of the Compagnie du Saint Sacrement by lamely adding to its eulogy of *Orfeo*: 'What gives this work its importance and has caused the most outspoken critics of the theatre to approve it is that virtue throughout always triumphs over vice.' A further criticism was voiced by Ormesson. He hated Mazarin but had struggled for one-and-a-half hours to secure a ticket, and though he echoed grudgingly the general shout of praise he also added; 'the voices are beautiful, but the Italian language is annoying as one cannot easily understand it'. In this he revealed an important problem. Painters and architects could adopt or adapt Italian forms without obvious difficulty, but opera involved language and music in so intimate a relationship that one could not be taken across national frontiers without the other.

*Orfeo* ran with three performances a week for two months, but there was no immediate sequel. The Fronde made opera impossible, not because Mazarin was unable to stage performances but because all the factions hostile to him combined to condemn everything that was Italian. The cost of producing *Orfeo* was made a public scandal; that it should have given money into the hands of Italians made it a national disgrace. Rossi went into hiding for several months before making his escape to Italy, and one of his company was only saved from lynching because an astute bystander convinced the mob that their intended victim was not an Italian at all but a Florentine!

Opera as such was not restored after the Treaty of Rueil. Instead there were two developments in public entertainment which were patently influenced by memories of *Orfeo* and *La Finta Pazza*. The *ballet de cour* laid greater emphasis on the music, and it became profitable to stage plays at the Marais which owed much of their success to the elaborate scenic effects introduced by Torelli. Corneille's *Andromède*, produced in 1650, derived its theme from Ovid's *Metamorphoses* and its setting from the very scenery which had been used for Act III of *Orfeo*. Torelli was paid 12,000 livres to operate his machines and pay his stage-hands and Corneille received 2,400 livres though his expenses were slight in comparison. There was music too by d'Assouci, who was influenced by Italian practice but discreet in his borrowing; for *Andromède* he composed nothing but ornamental background music, and there was no singing. 'I have been careful', wrote Corneille, 'to have nothing sung that is essential to the understanding of the play because the words are generally badly understood in music.'

In the same year d'Assouci produced a pastoral, *Amours d'Apollon et de Daphné*, in which spoken verses and sung airs alternated as in the older type of *ballet de cour*. This was a genre attractive to the young Louis XIV and at his command *Le Ballet de la Nuit* was staged in the Salle du Petit-Bourbon in 1653. Cambefort, his *surintendant de la musique*, composed it, Louis himself took part in the *entrées*, and Torelli, apart from bringing a whole choir down from heaven on a cloud, excelled himself by producing a house bursting into flames. During the next two years, however, two significant if inconclusive attempts were made to revive at least something of Italian opera. In his *Ballet du Temps* Cambefort tried his hand at recitatives, making great use of the anapaestic patterns suggested by the French language instead of using Italian; and an opera by Caproli, *Le Nozze di Peleo e di Theti*, was produced in 1655 in such a way as to reconcile French ears to Italian music by letting the stage effects dwarf everything. Since clouds descending with their choirs was becoming a cliché, Torelli devised nothing less than a moving mountain from which appeared Louis XIV as Apollo, in the midst of the young nobles of his court.

It was during the rehearsal of Louis's entrance that Gianbattista Lully (1632–87) made his appearance. A native of Florence, he had refused to follow his father as a flour miller. He haunted the streets and sideshows where he picked up tricks of buffoonery, made a name as a singer and even acquired some rudimentary skill as a violinist.

Here he was noticed in 1646 by Roger de Lorraine on his way back to his duchy from Rome. The duke, a close friend of Gaston, had promised to find his daughter a companion for her Italian lessons to aid her in her conversation, and Lully was quick to accept the offer of service in France. Roger delivered him to the Tuileries where he was made a *garçon de la chambre* to Mlle d'Orléans with an income of 150 livres—but since La Grande Mademoiselle had meanwhile lost all enthusiasm for her Italian lessons, the young boy was left entirely to his own devices.

This left him free to do much as he pleased and, since rehearsals were beginning for *Orfeo*, he spent most of his time in haunting the Italian musicians who had been brought over for the occasion. A chance meeting with one of them, Francesca Costa, who had herself employed Lully to sing for her in Florence, secured him introductions to the rest of the company, and he sat in at rehearsals, listening with an acquisitive ear to the novel dissonances and chromatic progressions of the score. He also fell in with Lazarin, a fellow exile who had been admitted to the Vingt-Quatre Violons and who taught him the dance rhythms of the *ballets de cour*. In this way his musical education continued informally, until an impromptu violin solo in Mademoiselle's kitchen led to his talents being reported to his mistress. She gave him a special position in the household thereafter and sent him for instruction to Nicolas Métru, a talented composer of *airs de cour*, to François Roberdet, *valet de chambre* to Anne d'Autriche and organist of the church of the Petits-Pères, and to Gigault, the most talented of the three, who played the organ for several Paris churches. For special occasions in her household, Mademoiselle would borrow the Vingt-Quatre Violons, but at other times she would leave it to Lully to round up and rehearse a scratch orchestra of his own.

It was now that Lully began to learn that the Italian music which so excited him was not altogether acceptable to French taste. Lazarin was a most helpful guide in this respect, but he also learnt much from Mademoiselle and her friends who complained of the recitatives in *Orfeo* and of the dissonance in the orchestration. From this he realised that, for the time being, French taste was unlikely to go

20. Self-portrait by Nicolas Poussin (see pages 209–14)

21. The Ashes of Phocion. One of Poussin's finest paintings in the French classical manner (see page 214)

much beyond the combination of song, dance and spectacle established in the *ballet de cour*.

With the outbreak of the Fronde, Lully was safe from the angry mobs who hunted Italians so long as he wore Mademoiselle's colours, but it was Mademoiselle herself who almost terminated his career. Determined to play a dominant role in both the intrigues and the campaigns of those troubled years, she sought no less a prize than the hand of Louis XIV; her failure led to the humiliation of mockery and satire, and also to exile on her estates at Saint-Fargeau. Lully followed her with great reluctance since it was only in Paris that he could achieve his ambitions, but Mademoiselle took pity on him. 'He did not want to live in the country', she wrote later. 'He asked for permission to leave, which I gave, and since then he has made his fortune, for he is a good trouper.' He arrived back in Paris on Christmas Eve, 1652, with only 15 *écus* and his violin, but he soon had the great good fortune to be presented to Louis XIV at a rehearsal for the *Ballet de la Nuit*. Seizing the opportunity of the confused circumstances of the rehearsal, Lully, with great finesse and self-assurance, took over the direction of the *entrées* with such success, and coached the King in his own moves with such a blend of frankness and respect, that his fortune was made.

Thereafter Lully played an important part in developing the *ballet de cour*, either by directing the *entrées*, as he did for Cambefort's *Ballet du Temps*, or by writing his own dance tunes. In collaboration with the poet Benserade he tried to go beyond the disconnected *ballet à entrées* by establishing a more coherent dramatic theme. At the same time he began to strengthen the role of vocal music by introducing choral ensembles, and even by introducing interludes for solos in a recitative manner. In this sense he was moving away from the *ballet de cour* towards opera, although his instrumental music was becoming much more obviously French. This was clear from the attention he gave to the development of dance forms—the *passepied* in lively 3/8 time, the gavotte in graceful duple time—and it was this which led him into conflict with the Vingt-Quatre Violons du Roi. He disliked their improvised ornaments and virtuoso tricks which in his view concealed the melody, and their tempo seemed both clumsy and inaccurate. They were, however, strongly entrenched in royal favour, and so Lully, in 1656, won permission from the King to establish his own Petits Violons, 16 strong. With them he created a technically simple style of playing, most of it in the first position, with none of the multiple stops being used in Italy and Germany and with no improvised diminutions. Because of his experience as a dancer, he demanded a high degree of rhythmical precision with emphatic downstrokes in the bowing. In this way, 'he combined the unornamented, straight playing of the Venetian opera orchestra with the emphatically rhythmic style of French music' (Bukofzer).

In 1657 Lully wrote the music for the abbé Buti's *Amor Malato*, but the combination of two Italians in an Italian-inspired genre produced a chauvinistic reaction. The duc de Guise staged a rival production, *Les Plaisirs Troublés*, in which all the participants were French. 'The duc has been put up to it', recorded the Florentine Resident, 'by several jealous people who cannot suffer the King to employ Italians for the production of his ballets, and who thereby hope by staging their own to draw his attention to their own talents.' But it was a vain hope. *Amor Malato* triumphed over its rival, and Lully was fast becoming indispensable. He wrote the music for the *Ballet Alcidiane* in the following year, produced the ballet, danced in three of the *entrées* and played the guitar disguised as a Moor. Nevertheless, he was shrewd enough to mark the danger signals of national prejudice. He was beginning not only to identify himself less with the Italians in Paris, but also to tackle the problem of presenting Italian opera in a manner acceptable to French taste.

He was not alone in his search for a compromise. The abbé Perrin, who produced the *Pastorale d'Issy* in collaboration with Robert Cambert in 1659, made every effort to introduce a more melodious recitative, and wrote in the preface: 'Our language is capable of expressing the most beautiful passions and the most tender sentiments, and if one mixes the Italian style of music a little with our manner of singing one may achieve something in between the two, more agreeable than either.' Lully, in the same year, exposed the problem of the two styles by including in his *Ballet de la Raillerie* this masterly dialogue between two styles, in which the French voice claims its power to express delicate sentiment while the Italian demonstrates its greater variety and vehemence.

·ti che languen — — — — —·— ti    e

mes - ti    la - i.

Et   crois tu qu'on ai - me   mieux tes longs

fre — — — — — dons en - nu-yeux tes longs

Qual ra-

fre — — — — — dons en - nu - yeux.

gion vuol che tu deggi del tuo gusto altrui far leggi?

Je n'ordonne point du tien.

Mais je veux chanter au mien.    Mais je veux chanter au mien. Mais je

Io di te    canto più for-te  perchè a - mo più di

veux chanter au mien.:

te   per - chè a - mo  più   di te, Chi risente un mal di morte più che

può grida mercè grida mercè più che può gri - - - da mer-

cè. La manière dont je chante ex-prime mieux ma langueur

exprime mieux ma lan - gueur gueur quand ce

mal tou - che le cœur, la voix est moins é-cla - tan -

te          la voix      est   moins é - cla - tan - - te.

The French voice represents most accurately the tradition of the *air de cour*; the Italian, however, has been modified. It has little of the operatic about it, and represents what Lully imagined was acceptable to the French. He moved further still to the French view in 1660 when Mazarin staged a magnificent performance of Cavalli's opera *Xerxes* to celebrate the Treaty of the Pyrenees and the victory over Spain. Louis XIV, horrified by the prospect of an evening of Italian opera, insisted upon as many as six *entr'actes entrées*, despite their irrelevance to the opera, and commissioned Lully to write the music for them. Lully exploited Louis's anticipation of boredom by deliberately making his ballets as lively, as charming and as French as he could, and achieved his reward by winning universal admiration for his *entr'actes* while the opera was indifferently received. He did the same thing again in 1662 for the performance of Cavalli's *Ercole Amante*, and his role was becoming much more clearly defined. In words which echo what Blunt has written about Vouet's relation to the Italian painters, Prunières says of Lully: 'The Parisian public greatly preferred Lully's Italianate music, with its concessions to French sensibility, to Cavalli's original and essentially Italian work, whose boldness and vehemence of expression seemed to be an affront to good taste and to reason.'

From now on Lully was assured of respectability and fortune. He married the daughter of another musician, Lambert, partly to enjoy her dowry of 20,000 livres, but even more to reassure the King who had expressed a touching concern over the notorious promiscuity of his private life. He then confirmed his repudiation of Italian connections by taking out naturalisation papers in 1662, and was rewarded by Louis with the succession to Cambefort as *surintendant de la musique* at 30,000 livres a year.

Lully's decision to become naturalised was mainly provoked by the general hostility to Italians which was an unfortunate consequence of the Fronde. The Fronde, too, had abruptly terminated the warm enthusiasm for Italian opera which *Orfeo* had kindled in 1647. Nonetheless, there were many other difficulties to be overcome before Italian music could be generally accepted in France, and we must not attribute them to the Fronde itself. Indeed, there has been too great a tendency to read too much cultural significance into the Fronde, to term it the *dérèglement* and to identify it with the overthrow of the rules of classicism. Lavisse, of course, has a valid point to make about memoir-writers, indicating that they are rarely found in periods of strong government but abound in periods of anarchy, 'when the strongest personalities emancipate themselves', but this relates only to a small field of literature. What is not so acceptable are such statements about the chequered political history of the years 1600–60 of which the following is typical: 'the more tranquil phases of these vicissitudes were of a nature to encourage the idea of literary discipline, while the agitated ones were an effective stimulus to the free impulses of writers' (Cazaman). In the first place it is hard to identify the 'tranquil phases'. There were very few years in this period without the threat or the reality of conspiracy or rebellion, and the Fronde, for all its violence, was simply the last of a long series of eruptions against royal authority going back to the sixteenth century. It was, of course, a crisis of great magnitude, but it failed to change the general direction of French history in the seventeenth century, and it is a fruitless task to seek its cultural equivalent.

For every classical writer or artist, there were others who represented alternative styles; Malherbe had his enemies, tragi-comedy and *pièces à machines* played to packed houses during the greatest days of Corneille's ascendancy, and we can find trends contrary to classicism in any given year. 1648 is not therefore particularly significant. There was a mass of *Mazarinades*—a series of pamphlets hostile to the cardinal which we can adjudge to have been a political not a cultural manifestation—and a glut of burlesques, which more directly reflected the current mood of repudiating all authority. Pellisson records the craze for them in the bookshops: 'Everyone thought they could write them, be they men or women, from the lords and ladies of the court to serving-women and valets. This rage for burlesque became so great that the bookshops would not accept anything which was not of this genre.' It is also true that the salon of a notorious *Frondeuse* such as La Grande Mademoiselle did not reflect the taste of the court. Her father indeed reproached her for reading too many romantic novels which, he said, only encouraged her to play the role of a romantic heroine in French affairs. Her reply epitomised the arrogance of the nobility: 'I have no need to play the heroine, as you put it. I am of such exalted birth that I have only to follow my own desires and take my own course: I was born to do no other.' Bucolic verse and notions of pastoral simplicity derived from *L'Astrée* were in vogue in her salon, and her poet Segrais exalted the imagined charms and innocence of bygone days before a corrupt court 'had destroyed our habits of candour and sincerity'.

Nonetheless, it is not possible to discern any serious reversal of established trends, nor to discover any permanent cultural manifestation of the political crisis. All those who postulate a direct cultural parallel to the Fronde ignore the fact that the years of rebellion and civil war were the very years in which the public taste for the Roman plays of Corneille, the classical works of Poussin and the buildings of Mansart and Le Vau continued undiminished and unchecked. Perversely, we might go one stage further and claim that the only disruptive tendency of the period was the introduction of baroque music, not by the *Frondeurs*, of course, but by Mazarin himself.

Mazarin's private patronage was not unlike Richelieu's. He inherited the services of Alphonse Lopez who helped him to build up a collection of over 500 pictures for which one man was employed full time to clean, restore and preserve them. Mazarin loved his collection, and not merely for its value, despite his reputation as a miser, and his death-bed farewell was genuine enough: 'Goodbye, beloved pictures which I loved so dearly and which cost me so much money.' In addition, he had scores of marble antiques, and it was as much to house his collection as to enjoy the formal accoutrements of splendour that he decided to build his own palace. He bought the Hôtel Duret de Chevry and called in Mansart to enlarge it by adding two great galleries. The interior was left to Giovanni Francesco Romanelli, the ablest pupil of Pietro da Cortona, who painted mythological scenes on wall panels framed in heavy stucco, an Italian motif which was later to influence Le Brun at Versailles.

The fact that the Palais Mazarin is today the Bibliothèque Nationale is not without significance, since Mazarin was a keen bibliophile and employed Gabriel Naudé to superintend his collection. Naudé was a scholar of exceptionally wide reading and taste; he knew his classics well and the Doctors of the Church, but he was also well-read in the great heresies of the past and was a close friend of the scientists of his own day. In 1627 he had published *Avis pour dresser une Bibliothèque*, which throughout the century remained the most authoritative guide to the subject, and in Mazarin's service he followed his own precepts, building up a collection of 40,000 books, the richest in Europe. When Mazarin was exiled in 1651 much of the collection was pillaged, but once order had been restored Naudé painstakingly recovered many of the books. The collection survived Mazarin's death and was subsequently shared between the Bibliothèque Nationale and the Bibliothèque Mazarine. Librarianship was indeed becoming a profession. The Du Puy brothers, keen scientists like Naudé, looked after Louis XIII's library, patiently cataloguing it and generously mingling their own superior collection with the King's until the latter numbered about 10,000. Another famous bibliophile was Théodore Godefroy, who worked in the royal cartulary as an archivist, 'more skilled than anyone else in the laws and statutes of the realm', wrote Chapelain. His collection, naturally enough, included over 500 manuscripts, and his son followed a similar path as librarian to the President Harlay.

The Palais Mazarin was not the last of Mazarin's buildings, since the desire to perpetuate his memory was as strong with him as with Richelieu. In 1654, for example, he was appointed Governor of Vincennes and decided to commemorate his term of office by commissioning Le Vau to rebuild some of the great medieval castle. Louis Le Vau was the son of a Parisian master mason, born in 1620. His earliest work was in the du Cerceau decorative tradition, with ingeniously carved entrances, rich ornamentation and heavy rustication, but, as he developed, his designs became increasingly classical though he never achieved the full mastery, the overwhelming sense of mass, attained by Mansart, his closest rival. Mansart, so unreliable as a man, so scrupulous as an architect and designer, stands in sharp contrast to Le Vau, a meticulous and successful businessman, whose treatment of detail was often slipshod, and who made his fame as a kind of project manager or *metteur-en-scène*. He had already built several *hôtels*, including his own, on the Île Saint-Louis where, characteristically, he had had the foresight to buy up property just before the area became fashionable, but no major commissions had come his way before Vincennes. Not that Vincennes was important in itself: he had only to redesign and complete the Pavillon du Roi begun by Louis XIII, but he did it soberly and well, and a colossal order of pilasters went well against the great buttresses of the medieval towers. The importance lay in the commissions which followed, not only from Mazarin but subsequently from Colbert and from Louis XIV.

After Vincennes, he did the hospital of the Salpêtrière in 1660, and finally, for Mazarin again, a posthumous commission. Mazarin was jealous of Richelieu's rebuilding of the Sorbonne and in his will he planned his own Collège Mazarin, which was to accommodate students from the provinces acquired by France in the treaties of Westphalia and the Pyrenees—an astute act of self-advertisement. (Subsequently it was known as the Collège des Quatre Nations, housing 60 students each from the four provinces of Artois, Roussillon, Pignerol and Franche Comté, this last acquired in 1678.) The project had therefore to be realised in the grand manner, and Le Vau's achievement was as monumental as his late patron could have wished. On a difficult site—a narrow strip along the south bank of the Seine, facing across to the Square Court of the Louvre—Le Vau proposed a bold solution. In the centre, facing the river, he built the college chapel, complete with dome and portico to rival the Sorbonne, flanked by the two great wings of the façade which curved gently forward to the line of the embankment. It was impressive, and would have been seen to even better advantage had it been possible to complete Le Vau's plan by linking the college to the Louvre by a new bridge.

Le Vau, son of a mason, and Mansart, son of a carpenter and trained by his brother-in-law as an architect, illustrate an interesting point about the painters, architects and sculptors of seventeenth-century France. Unlike the writers, who ranged from a tradesman's son such as Voiture, to a noble like La Rochefoucauld, they were a remarkably homogeneous group. The occasional noble, such as Gaston d'Orléans, dabbled in painting perhaps, but the professionals all came from the lower middle and upper working classes. (Crozet provides long lists of names to illustrate all the generalisations which follow.) Poussin was the son of a peasant, Georges de la Tour of a baker, and the Le Nains of a *sergent au baillage*. Having come from the same social milieu they also remained a closely knit community, with many examples of intermarriage: Philippe de Champaigne and Eustache Le Sueur married painters' daughters and Jacques du Cerceau married the daughter of an architect. Du Cerceau, of course, founded a famous dynasty of architects, and there are many examples of sons following their fathers: Salomon de Brosse, the son of one architect, was father of another; Le Mercier had a father and two brothers in the same occupation; Le Vau a father and a brother; and Vouet three sons. The Mansarts were so proud of their long dynasty that they even invented a genealogical table going back to a Michele Mansarto, a Roman knight who built an abbey for Hugh Capet.

The family connection was strong for other reasons. Painters, sculptors and architects were still regarded as tradesmen. Talent was less in demand than training, and all of them were apprenticed to their trade like any furrier or baker. To be apprenticed within the family therefore saved the payment of premiums to another master. Premiums were generally of 200 livres or more, depending on the length of the apprenticeship—from three to five years—and on the reputation of the master. Vouet, for example, was paid 600 livres to take on Pierre Mignard for five years in 1659. When the formal period of training was complete, at some time between the ages of 15 and 20, the young apprentices would then make their way to Italy. Le Sueur and the Le Nains never went, nor did Salomon de Brosse, but the majority regarded the journey, whatever the problems of expense and even of danger, as an indispensable stage in their professional training. It was to make this stage less indispensable that Mazarin generously arranged to make public his collection of antique busts and statues in the Palais Mazarin, 'in order to save French youth from the need to make long journeys to Italy to make themselves perfect in the art of sculpture'. In fact, his gesture made very little difference to the number who went, and the provincial cities of the Rhône valley owed much to this perpetual progression of artists, disseminating the ideas of Paris and Rome.

Some young artists found sponsors not only for the journey but also for their accommodation in Italy. Le Brun, for example, had his expenses paid for by the Chancellor Séguier who was impressed by his talents, and the city of Paris backed Louis Boullongne for the same reason. Other artists would canvass support among the nobility and members of the royal family. Alternatively they might offer, in return for a contribution to their expenses, to carry out commissions in Rome and to arrange for the collection and delivery of pictures, statues and other works of art. Some made a virtue out of necessity and went as pilgrims to the Holy City, and François Perrier, a foundation member in 1648 of the Académie de Peinture et de Sculpture, hired himself as a guide to a blind pilgrim. For most of them, however, there was nothing for it but to earn what they could on the way in order to support themselves over the three years or more of their absence.

In Italy these apprentices must have been intoxicated not only by the wonders of architecture and painting to be seen but also by the high esteem in which artists were held. It is true that the vaunted freedom of the Renaissance artist was severely curtailed by the strict terms of his commissions, often couched in legal terms, but the liberal arts had won for themselves a special status. The painter, no longer an artisan, had become an artist. In France no such development had taken place. Architects had somehow escaped control, but the masons had a guild and the painters belonged to the Guild of St Luke, better known as the Maîtrise. This protected and regulated every stage of the painter's life; his apprenticeship, his work as a *compagnon* and his *chef d'œuvre* to become *maître*. Its rules were strict, confirmed by royal charters, and no painter could sell or exhibit his work unless he had first secured admission to the Maîtrise. Not surprisingly, Poussin, the greatest French artist of the century and the only Frenchman to share the exalted notions of Leonardo and Michelangelo about the artist's position, chose to spend his life in Italy.

We should not assume, however, that the French practice was necessarily inimical to the interests of art and artists since, as Samuel Butler once wrote, 'An art can only be learned in the workshop of those who are winning their bread by it'. Because of the craft guilds, moreover, with their limitations on numbers, painters, engravers, masons and sculptors, unlike poets, novelists and playwrights, could generally make a living by their skills. The seventeenth century was a period of reconstruction and conspicuous expenditure by nobles compensating for their loss of power, by bourgeois rivalling the nobility, by churchmen maintaining the impetus of the Counter-Reformation and, above all, by the court and the great ministers of state; there was therefore plenty of work for skilled craftsmen and artists, but it is not easy to assess their income. Frequently their fee had to cover the cost of materials used, including expensive items such as gold leaf, and many were paid less than others but received accommodation while they completed their contract. Those in royal service might receive anything from 30 livres a year for artisan decorators to 1,200 for the best artists, while sculptors averaged 400 livres. This salary, however, was sometimes nothing more than a kind of retainer, and artists could undertake private commissions as well.

On the open market there was obviously great variety in the fees to be earned. Richelieu paid Philippe de Champaigne 150 livres for the famous triple portrait of himelf, Le Sueur received 4,000 for six scenes from the life and martyrdom of Saints Gervais and Protais, and Sebastian Bourdon, the least talented of the three, earned 1,000 livres for only one such scene. De Champaigne, however, was employed at Vincennes for 35,000 livres. Le Brun was always well rewarded. Fouquet paid him 12,000 livres for his work at Vaux-le-Vicomte, and he received 14,000 for decorating the ceiling and ten wall panels in the church of Saint-Sulpice. Generally speaking, the best-paid men were the architects, especially if, like Jacques Androuet du Cerceau, they supplied their own materials from their own quarries. *L'architecte du roi* or *l'architecte ordinaire du roi* were paid on a casual basis, and were quite distinct from *l'architecte des bâtiments du roi* who exercised a long-term supervision over royal building projects. Salomon de Brosse earned 300 livres a year in 1608 as *architecte et conducteur des bâtiments du roi et de la reine*; in 1614 he succeeded one of the du Cerceaus as *architecte général des bâtiments du roi et de la reine* at 1,200 livres a year, and ended up with total emoluments worth 2,700. Le Vau and Le Mercier, when in royal service, averaged 3,000 livres.

Artists in royal service enjoyed a particular privilege of great importance for, in addition to board and lodging in the Louvre, they were exempted from the jurisdiction of the Maîtrise. From the earliest times artists had been attached to the Lord Chamberlain's department at court with the title of, say, *valet de chambre*. In addition, by special licence or *brevet*, artists could be appointed *peintre du roi*, *peintre de la reine*, or *peintre ordinaire*, and granted the same privileges. Other craftsmen and artists had become by-appointment tradesmen, as *fournisseurs du roi* or, as with Molière's father, *valet-tapissier du roi*, and Henri IV had formally recognised a distinction between the arts and crafts by releasing as many as 480 master craftsmen and apprentices from the control of their craft guilds and bringing them into his own service.

All those under royal protection, in whatever form, were thus entitled to sell their work publicly, and it was this which aroused the indignation of the Maîtrise, especially when the practice developed in the seventeenth century of granting or selling the title of *maître* to men who had not complied with guild regulations, and who then became *maîtres de lettres* as opposed to *maîtres des chefs d'œuvres*. Worse still, the *maîtres de lettres* and the *breveté* artists were allowed to transmit their privileges to their pupils, and the ateliers of guild masters were becoming deserted as their pupils rushed to enrol with masters whose regimen of training would be less strict than the guilds. This was an issue which came to a head, as we shall see, in 1648.

Meanwhile, there were 'master-less' men across the river by the abbey of Saint-Germain, where the abbé's jurisdiction protected them from the Maîtrise. Living there in itself meant nothing, but the annual fair in February afforded a necessary occasion to sell their works. It was a popular quarter with Netherlanders and those from the northern provinces of France, and the Dutch element was strong in the work of the engraver Abraham Bosse. His prints are used unendingly to illustrate histories of seventeenth-century life, and their real talent is sometimes overlooked for their historical importance. In such plates as the 'Mariage à la Ville', and the 'Mariage à la Campagne', Bosse observes with great skill the life of the well-to-do bourgeoisie. There is nothing romantic in these scenes; they are records of a business transaction more than a page from L'Astrée, but they were in great demand among the owners of the new hôtels springing up in Saint-Germain and around the Luxembourg.

Chief among the residents were the Le Nains—Antoine, Louis and Mathieu—from Laon. Much of their life remains the subject of controversy: did Louis go to Rome, did the brothers paint in collaboration, and why, in an age which idealised the noble hero and the honnête homme and could only regard the peasantry as contemptible or comic, did they produce such beautifully observed scenes of peasant life? Possibly they were influenced by the Netherlanders of their quarter who brought with them the descriptive genre and the passion for close observation which so characterised Dutch art in the seventeenth century. Yet their techniques were not those of the Dutch. Louis, the most gifted and whose works most resemble the finest achievements of Dutch art, laid his paints on thickly, where the Dutch worked with light touch to create transparent effects, and selected his colours from a narrow range of cool greys, grey-browns and grey-greens. Within these subdued tones he observed the peasantry with accuracy and sympathy, without mockery or satire and without idealising or romanticising his subjects. The com-

22. Colbert, engraved by Nanteuil

23. Statute of Louis XIV at Versailles

24. Colbert hoped to make the Louvre the principal royal residence by means of Bernini's baroque designs (see pages 240–8)

25. Instead, Louis XIV extended Versailles. The engraving illustrates the Rampe de Latone by Le Nôtre, and Le Vau's garden front (see pages 248–54)

position, the observation and the rendering are so skilfully organised, the manner so grave and dignified, that we cannot deny the essential classicism of Louis's art. 'Here we find again that recurrent phenomenon in French art of this period, a classicism which does not use the outward forms of Greek or Roman formulas, but attains to the clarity and calm which are the more fundamental qualities of the style' (Blunt).

Antoine became *premier peintre* to the abbé, painting very much in Louis's style, and it is difficult to imagine how either of them could have made a living from their scenes of peasant life. There is no recorded vogue for them until the age of Rousseau, and it is certain that few peasants could have bought them. The only explanation to carry weight is that many serious-minded bourgeois admired the classic composition of their work, independently of the subject-matter. Whatever the explanation there was clearly a market since the Le Nains were not alone. Van Laer from the Netherlands, known as Bamboche, specialised in peasant scenes, giving to the genre the name of '*bambochades*', and Sebastian Bourdon and Jean Michelin made a living by passing off their own *bambochades* at the Saint-Germain fair as genuine Le Nains. Mathieu Le Nain, by contrast, worked more directly in the popular tradition of Dutch painting, and became a specialist in civic groups, such as his '*Corps de Garde*'. For this he had to cross over the river into Paris, but this was made possible after 1648 by his election to the newly formed Académie de Peinture et de Sculpture, and he finally became *premier peintre* to the city.

The new Académie owed its origin in part to the conflict between the Maîtrise and the artists in royal service. The complaint of the Maîtrise has been described; what the royal artists complained of was the restrictive policy of the guild, and of the implied degradation for an artist to be made subject to a system properly applicable only to tradesmen and artisans. This social attitude was well expressed by Henri Testelin, writing in 1680, of the importance of the Académie: 'Until that time painters and sculptors were lumped together with daubers, marble cutters and polishers of marble in a mechanic society known as the Maîtrise.' While such a state was continued, they argued, French painters would continue to be regarded not as creative artists but as mere *fournisseurs* of decorative and ecclesiastical pictures.

Everything came to a head in Mazarin's day, mainly through the ambition of Charles Le Brun. Le Brun's career as a painter could not have gone more smoothly. He was first apprenticed to François Perrier, but his father, a sculptor employed by the Chancellor Séguier, persuaded Séguier to take an interest in his son and have him bound to Vouet, the greatest painter in Paris. Le Brun profited well from his apprenticeship for he had considerable talent, though it was not until later that he revealed a degree of genius by his organising ability as a decorator on the grand scale. He also had an eye to the main chance, and, at the age of 19, presented Richelieu with a tactful allegory of the cardinal's political achievements. In consequence, he was *breveté* as a *peintre du roi* and was thus released from the Maîtrise.

Three years later, in 1642, he observed the tremendous respect accorded to Poussin on his brief visit to Paris, and arranged to accompany him on his return, his expenses being paid by Séguier. In Rome he completed his education and returned in 1646, impatient for fame and glory, and all the more convinced that artists could never enjoy their rightful place in society while they remained bound to the Maîtrise. He had observed the Italian academies, and noticed that these did not merely disassociate the artisan from the artist, but also the wealthy and successful from the less talented and less fortunate. Indeed, membership was confined to an élite of the best artists in company with the most sophisticated laymen, and this, as Arnold Hauser indicates, created 'a solidarity between the cultured circles of the general public and the artists which is without precedent in the history of art'. It was also clear to Le Brun that if he could bring about the foundation of such an academy in France—and ideally a royal academy at that—he himself might be accorded some place of honour within its portals. At 26 this was no mean ambition.

Séguier at any rate agreed to the idea, and by 1648 had carried the day in the council of regency. The Académie de Peinture et de Sculpture was therefore established with 20 members, most of them coming from the quartier de Saint-Germain where hostility to the Maîtrise was greatest. Le Brun, of course, was a member—along with the three Le Nains and François Perrier—but not Vouet. Vouet chose to champion the cause of the Maîtrise against his pupil, and he was a formidable opponent, but his death in 1649 left a vacancy that none could fill. For several years the Paris Parlement delayed the ratification of the Académie's charter, but once the Fronde was over it could delay no longer. By this time, however, a more serious problem had arisen. To Le Brun's great chagrin, few of the members would do anything. Their role was to protect all artists in royal service, educate pupils and establish doctrine, but their sessions to fulfil this last objective had to be abandoned time and time again for lack of a quorum. The Académie in fact seemed doomed to sterility until in 1661, with the appointment of Colbert as its vice-protector, a new lease of life was assured.

*five*

# Paris and the
# Bourgeoisie

By the time of Richelieu's death, Parisian society had produced a host of women in earnest imitation of Mme de
Rambouillet, though none as successful. Mme des Loges, her principal rival for a time, succeeded in striking the same healthy balance
of aristocratic tone and literary enthusiasm, but the presence of many
Huguenot leaders made the government suspicious of her salon,
and when Gaston d'Orléans, of all people, gave her a pension of
4,000 livres, Richelieu hastily compelled her to rejoin her family in
the Limousin. Other salons were to suffer by their connection with
religious or political groups out of favour at court—as, for example,
the Jansenist salons described in chapter 6—but it was for quite a
different reason that Mme d'Auchy had to close her salon in 1624.
Her literary lion was Malherbe, but his extravagant and repeated
eulogies of her beauty, coupled with his well-deserved reputation
for lechery, so alarmed the lady's husband that he summoned her
to his side in Saint-Quentin where he was governor. After his death
in 1628, Mme d'Auchy returned to Paris but her salon acquired an
exclusively bookish air. Chapelain, pedant though he was, in-
dignantly repudiated the charge that he belonged to the '*Académie
féminine*', as he called it, and Balzac, who had corresponded happily
with both Mme de Rambouillet and Mme des Loges, recoiled in
horror from their rival: 'I would as lief endure a woman with a
beard as one of these women who try to be *savante.*'
What was new and totally unexpected was the interest in science

which began to sweep many of the salons, an interest inspired principally by the writings of René Descartes (1596–1650), the son of a *conseiller* of the Brittany Parlement. He had been educated by the Jesuits at the Collège de la Flèche in Anjou and then qualified in law at Poitiers. Subsequently he went, in his own words, to study '*le livre du monde*' by enlisting in the service of Maurice of Nassau, a Dutch Protestant and one of the most imaginative and most scientifically minded commanders of the Thirty Years War. Two years later, in 1619, he transferred to the Catholic army of the Duke of Bavaria and served until 1621. His brief military experience produced a treatise on the mathematical basis of harmony, and an emotional experience in 1619 when, in the loneliness of his winter quarters, he discovered with great excitement his own novel method for testing the nature of truth (see page 150). For a few years he travelled across Europe, settled in Paris in 1625 where he established a following in the salons, and then, in 1629, left for Holland where he felt freer to develop and to publish his ideas.

Though Descartes is remembered as a philosopher, it was as a physicist that he first made his mark. The *Discours de la Méthode* was originally important only as the introduction to the three treatises—*La Dioptrique*; *Les Météores*; *La Géométrie*—which established his reputation among contemporaries and which he wrote in French deliberately to catch the attention of the Parisian public. His contribution to the remarkable revolution which was taking place in the natural sciences was an important one. He discovered the principles of co-ordinate geometry, which allowed the motion of planets and projectiles to be expressed in terms of an algebraic equation, and made a substantial contribution to Galileo's theory of motion. The Aristotelian assumption that bodies remain in motion only if they are driven or propelled by a constant force had been discredited by Galileo who had shown how the moon, for example, could remain perpetually in orbit around the Earth under the impetus of its initial propulsion. Descartes developed this further by asking why the moon remained in orbit instead of flying off at a tangent to the Earth.

The question was most significant—it exposed the fact that natural motion in an ideal Euclidean sense was straight-line motion—but the answer was unsatisfactory. Descartes believed, on *a priori* grounds alone, that a vacuum was impossible. Space, therefore, was packed continuously and throughout with tiny particles, motion being imparted by one to another just as the jostling of one individual in a crowd causes the movement of those nearest to him. Moreover, as eddies form in the course of a river, trapping and carrying around a passing leaf, so in the universe the particles of matter form vortices whose circular motion carries the planets in their orbits. Suction towards the centre of the vortex was thus proposed as the cause of deviation from a straight-line path.

This image of a mechanical universe with particle interacting upon particle in one massive continuum was both intelligible and satisfying to many in the seventeenth century, and long withstood the rival theories of Isaac Newton, but the influence that Descartes finally exerted upon his contemporaries owed more to the method he evolved than to the scientific results achieved by it. Initially the method was derived from the logical systems of geometry. 'The long chains of simple and easy reasonings by means of which geometers are accustomed to reach the conclusions of their most difficult demonstrations, had led me to imagine that all things which are open for man to know are mutually connected in the same way, and that there is nothing so far removed from us as to be beyond our reach ... provided only we abstain from accepting the false for the true.' This last he proposed to do by relying upon common sense, the common prerogative of humanity—'*la chose du monde le mieux partagée*'—in order to distinguish truth from falsehood.

The 'long chains of simple and easy reasonings' must, however, have a beginning, and it was Descartes's programme of systematic doubt in order to establish a bedrock of indubitable and self-evident truth which made him famous. It is most clearly expressed in his own words. He decided, he tells us, 'that I ought to reject as absolutely false all opinions in regard to which I could suppose the least ground for doubt, in order to ascertain whether after that there remained anything in my belief which was indubitable'. Accordingly he dismissed everything he knew as unreliable as a delusion of the mind or of the senses, 'and finally, when I considered that the very same thoughts which we experience when awake may also be experienced when we sleep, while there is at that time not one of them true, I supposed that all the objects that had ever entered into my mind when awake had in them no more truth than the illusions of my dreams. But immediately upon this I observed that while I thus wished to think that all was false, it was absolutely necessary that I who thus thought should somehow exist; and as I observed that this truth, *I think, hence I am*, was so certain and of such evidence that no ground of doubt could be alleged by the sceptics capable of shaking it, I concluded that I might, without scruple, accept it as the first principle of the philosophy of which I was in search.'

*I think, hence I am* was a purely intuitive maxim, whose very clarity and distinctness made it indubitable; and another innate conviction, as certain for Descartes as the fact that the points on a sphere are equidistant from its centre, was that God existed. But God and the human personality seemed so distinct from the material world that Descartes was forced into a dualist philosophy. The material world, the body, the *res extensa*, was one extended substance, varying in density but never discontinuous, subject utterly to the laws of physics; the mind, the *res cogitans*, 'this Me, that is to say the soul which makes me what I am', was wholly distinct. This merely solved one problem to create fresh ones, and the nature of the interaction of mind and body became his chief concern. It runs through the Latin works, the *Meditationes* (1641) and the *Principia* (1644), but the most influential proposals for a solution were made in 1649 in his *Traité des Passions de l' Âme*.

In this treatise Descartes maintained that physiologically men and animals are machines, whose sense organs and muscles are linked to the brain by nerves in which circulate minute particles of blood, *les esprits animaux*. These react spontaneously whenever the sense organs touch anything and thereby cause the movement of the appropriate muscles. Man, however, has a soul located in the pineal gland, and the movement of the *esprits animaux* causes movements in this gland so that the soul is given knowledge of the body's sensations. Within the gland are the *passions de l' âme*, such emotions as fear, joy, sadness, love or admiration, and these serve generally to reinforce the action of the *esprits animaux*, as when fear or love stimulates the muscles to move with greater vigour. Feeble men are those who fall prey to the *passions de l'âme*, are ruled by them and are inconstant as one passion succeeds the other in the ascendancy. But the soul of stronger men has a will-power capable of mastering the passions. By will-power, for example, the soul can countermand the instructions to the legs to run away when danger approaches and, having achieved this stay of action, the soul can then reason with the passions that 'the danger is not so great as imagined, that there is greater security in defence than in flight, that one can win the glory and the joy of victory in place of the shame and sorrow of running away, and similar arguments of this sort'. This closely resembles the Stoic philosophy current both among many Parisian bourgeois and in the plays of Corneille, and though chronological difficulties prevent a causal chain between the philosopher and the playwright, the audiences of the subsequent generation nevertheless found a special satisfaction in Corneille's drama as a result of the *Traité des Passions*.

One of Descartes's most influential disciples, nicknamed Le Résident de M. Descartes à Paris, was Père Mersenne, whose scientific studies of music have been referred to already. From his cell with the Minims of the Place Royale he exercised tremendous influence over Parisian sociey, and around him there developed an informal group of men like the Du Puy brothers, Naudé and Étienne Pascal, who discussed new experiments and laws and maintained constant correspondence with the great Peiresc who dominated the society of learned magistrates in Provence. After Mersenne's death in 1648, the group began to meet at the *hôtel* of M. de Montmar, a *maître des requêtes*—and thereafter developed in much the same way as the literary club which had once met at Conrart's house on Saturday mornings, and with ultimately the same result since Colbert at length made them the nucleus of the Académie des Sciences.

The *officier* class seems to have been particularly responsive to the new developments in science, partly of course because they were generally well educated and the subject was intrinsically interesting, but also perhaps because these new developments were so revolutionary in their nature that the guardians of tradition in the universities and in the Church were being proved wrong—a source of great satisfaction to a class of ambitious laymen who resented clerical assumptions of superiority. The demand for information was great, and it was for this public that Descartes and others wrote deliberately in French. M. Jourdain, the ambitious bourgeois of Molière's play, found it expedient to employ tutors to teach him the rudiments of science, and in real life Théophraste Renaudot, who edited the *Gazette de France* for Richelieu, arranged weekly lectures on Monday afternoons at the Grand Coq on the Cité.

The Jesuits very quickly took up the new sciences in their schools and in society at large, and it was one of their number, Jean Leurichon, whose *Récréations Mathématiques*, a collection of ingenious problems in arithmetic, geometry, optics, telescopes, mechanics and chemistry, published in 1624, ran quickly through 17 editions. The ladies of the salons showed much interest in the new ideas, and Molière was a little slow off the mark in satirising their new enthusiasms; he had ridiculed their literary *préciosité* in 1658 but did not reveal the telescope in the attic until *Les Femmes Savantes* in 1672. The ladies no doubt preferred to have their science diluted with a little fable and gallantry and the Jesuit Jacques Lambert met their wishes in his *Philosophie de la Cour Sainte*, written for them in 1656. He greatly simplified the subject while tactfully asserting that he would never so insult the intelligence of the fair sex since 'it would be wholly lacking in respect for that liveliness of mind with which that sex is favoured by birth and education, to confine the most virtuous to the lives of the saints and the most inquisitive to the reading of novels'.

For all the excitement of the new philosophy and the new science, novels were still of course very much the rage in the salons, and the genre established by Honoré d'Urfé had been developed and expanded by several worthy successors. *Polexandre*, by Marin le Roy de Gomberville, for example, added a further dimension to the tradition by exploiting the new interest in geography. The hero travels the regions of the New World, though his motive is traditional enough since he seeks the whereabouts of his Princess Alcidiane, and of those presumptuous rivals who dared to sigh for her love. Even more popular were the cloak-and-dagger romances of

Gauthier de Costes de la Calprenède, who spun out *Cassandre* to ten volumes by 1642, and *Cléopâtre* to 12 by 1647. Mme de Sévigné recorded her pleasure in rereading La Calprenède in 1671, adding that it was all very shaming but she was totally unable to put it down unfinished.

The most remarkable and the most successful author of this genre was Madeleine Scudéry (1607–1701). Intelligent and intellectual, ugly but with great vivacity, she was a close friend of Conrart who described her as a walking encyclopædia and, at the age of 64, she won the *prix d'éloquence* of the Académie Française for an essay on *La Gloire*. She nevertheless disclaimed the charge of being a bluestocking and, perhaps a shade too self-consciously, distinguished in her novels between women who were well read and those who were bookish. There was no doubt in which category she saw herself and in *Cyrus* she wrote: 'There is nothing more attractive than a woman who has gone to the trouble to embellish her mind with any amount of knowledge provided she knows how to make proper use of it, but there is nothing so ridiculous as an unintelligent but learned woman.'

Her novels, published under her brother's name, were best-selling historical romances, *Ibrahim* (1647), *Artamène ou Le Grand Cyrus* in ten volumes (1648–53) and *Clélie*, also in ten volumes (1654–61). Each volume was anxiously awaited in the salons, for what gave a special interest to her novels was not just the general portrayal of salon society as practised by La Calprenède but the particular identification of the characters with prominent individuals of the day. The great Condé, for example, was none other than Cyrus, the hero of ten volumes, and not only were his features and his personality implanted on the conqueror of Asia, but also his victory at Rocroi. His sister, the duchesse de Longueville, appeared in the novel as Mandane, the object of Cyrus's passion; Mme de Rambouillet as Cléomire, Voiture as Callicrate and Mlle de Scudéry herself as no less a personage than Sappho.

From this was derived a new game in the salons, the *jeu des portraits*, in which one of the party composed portraits for the others to identify. It became at one and the same time a literary vogue, a psychological study and an art form, and secured a distinguished place in seventeenth-century literature. Nowhere was the game more popular than in the salon of Mlle de Montpensier—La Grande Mademoiselle—whose infectious enthusiasm for the genre inspired the habitués of her salon to produce a mammoth collection of portraits, published in 1659 as *La Galerie des Portraits de Mlle de Montpensier*. Characteristically she claimed the credit for inventing the game, but her poet Segrais admitted in the preface that 'we are very indebted to *Cyrus* and *Clélie* which have furnished us with our models'.

In all her novels Mlle de Scudéry devoted much space to the analysis of love, a subject in which, if her self-portrait is to be believed, she considered herself remarkably expert. 'Sappho', she wrote, 'expresses so delicately those sentiments which are so difficult to express, and she understands so well how to anatomise, if one may use the word, a loving heart that she knows how to describe in exact detail all its jealousy, all its anxiety, all its impatience, all its joys, all its loathings, all its grumblings, all its griefs, all its hope, all its indignation and all those tumultuous sentiments which are never understood but by those who feel them or have felt them.' This, in short, is what she did in *Cyrus* as volume succeeded volume, analysing here the 12 types of sigh and there the nine grades of esteem, and reaching a veritable climax in *Clélie* with an allegorical landscape, the '*Carte du Tendre*', which revealed the degrees and nature of love itself.

The *Carte*, which became the talking point of the salons, began as a light-hearted affair in her own salon where her literary lion, Paul Pellisson, wooed her for *la tendre amitié*. When she replied that she distinguished between '*les particuliers et les tendres amis*', he then demanded to know how far it was from *Particulier* to *Tendre*, and from this was derived the notion of a map. From the town of Nouvelle Amitié three routes led to Tendre-sur-Estime, Tendre-sur-Reconnaissance and Tendre-sur-Inclination, and dangerous by-ways led tragically to the Lake of Indifference, the Sea of Hatred and the Sea of Danger. Love, for example, which springs from Inclination moves swiftly to its journey's end, 'but to go to Tendre-sur-Estime, Clélie has ingeniously put as many villages along the route as there are things both great and small which help to bring about love based on esteem. In fact you can see that from Nouvelle Amitié one passes through a place called Grand Esprit, because this is what usually gives rise to esteem; then you see the pleasant villages of Jolis-vers, Billet-galant and Billet-doux, which are the most usual undertakings of great minds at the beginning of a friendship. Thereafter, to go further along this road, you see Sincérité, Grand Cœur, Probité, Générosité, Respect, Exactitude and Bonté, which is right next to Tendre to show that one cannot have true esteem without goodness and that one cannot arrive at Tendre from this side without this precious quality.'

Mlle de Scudéry maintained that the 'Carte du Tendre' was nothing but a private joke, 'written only for a handful of intelligent people to read, and not for the 2,000 who have scarcely understood it or misunderstood it altogether'. Nonetheless it was she who published it in the first volume of Clélie, and though it can be taken at a superficial level, symbolising the complex refinements of the salon code of gallantry, it is also clear that it reflected her own immature concept of love, a concept lacking both passion and consummation. Of herself as Sappho she wrote: 'I want not a husband but a lover who will content himself with possessing my heart alone, and who will love me until death.' Not only is this unnaturally passionless, it soon becomes both silly and selfish: 'I want a lover, moreover, who will be faithful and sincere, who will tell no one else of his love for me and who will lock up in his heart all his sentiments of love so successfully that I alone shall boast of knowing them.'

To write so exclusively in praise of love without sex was to carry a civilising trend to excess. L'Astrée had served an excellent function in putting forward ideals of social behaviour other than those of the soldier and the camp follower, but Clélie, by removing all trace of physical passion, by reducing love to a set of intellectualised images, made love itself unreal. This was merely to substitute one excess for another—and an unnatural for a natural one at that. It was this préciosité d'amour which Adam now suggests is the true essential nature of préciosité itself. 'La Précieuse is a woman or a girl who mistrusts those who woo her and who has no wish to imitate the coquette and the profligate'—the sort described more brilliantly in the seventeenth century by the notoriously passionate Ninon de Lenclos as the 'Jansenists of love'.

But this is to restrict too closely the meaning of *précisoité*. Following Mornet and others we have already allowed its use in a non-pejorative sense to describe certain features of the salon of Mme de Rambouillet, where the dangers of excessive refinement were generally avoided by the good sense and humour of the hostess and by the aristocratic self-assurance of her guests. In Mlle de Scudéry's salon, however, *précisoité* became a fault. It was not merely a matter of *précisoité d'amour* but of a self-conscious coterie whose members vied too obviously with each other to demonstrate their refinement by their speech and manners. Such deliberate affectation with its attendant exaggeration and bad taste was quite unlike the Hôtel de Rambouillet and came nearer to reflecting the pages of the abbé Somaize's *Dictionnaire des Précieuses* (1660) where chairs are *les commodités de la conversation* and teeth *l'ameublement de la bouche*. For this there is a simple social explanation, since a taste for salon life had been acquired by the lower ranks of Parisian society, and Mlle de Scudéry's salon was one of many whose tone was predominantly bourgeois. It was a matter of degree and balance. Bourgeois, especially literary men, had called upon Mme de Rambouillet, but the tone had been established by the guests of noble birth. Several nobles, too, attended Mlle de Scudéry—including a few Frondeurs to whom she remained unfashionably loyal after their disgrace—but not enough to dominate the bourgeois. Moreover, the interest in poetry, novels and letters in general which had been one among many valuable features of social life at the Hôtel de Rambouillet became an almost exclusive interest among the habitués at Mlle de Scudéry's Saturdays.

The great nobles had not had to model themselves upon anyone, and were therefore secure from affectation. The bourgeois who imitated them were all too often exposed to the danger of exaggeration, of excessive refinement and thus of bad taste. This lack of self-confidence in bourgeois society was an unhappy consequence of the social structure of seventeenth-century France. Administratively and economically the bourgeoisie was a most valuable and necessary class, and its patronage of the arts was of greater cultural importance, especially in the middle decades of the century, than that of any other, but in social terms it remained a derided class for whom salvation could only be achieved by learning to live like the nobility.

Into the medieval hierarchy of king, noble and peasant, a hierarchy mirrored in the organisation of the Church, had intruded the bourgeoisie, which made its living from the non-agrarian crafts of industry and commerce, and in this sense the term applied to most town-dwellers. Socially, however, it was soon reserved for those who, though engaged in trade and manufacture, were sufficiently successful to employ others to labour on their behalf, and the sharp division between such masters and their artisan employees was confirmed in the constitution of the civic guilds and corporations. The aristocrats of Parisian society were the masters of the six great corporations, the haberdashers, the drapers, the furriers, the hosiers, the goldsmiths and the grocers, and those among them who were wholesalers were indeed ennobled by an edict of 1627. Membership of these corporations was a jealously guarded privilege, and when Louis XIV, as a fiscal expedient to avert bankruptcy in 1691, opened the corporations to all who were ready to purchase membership from him, the existing members raised sufficient capital to buy up the places for themselves—an operation which cost the haberdashers, for example, 300,000 livres.

Unlike the merchants of Holland and England, few French merchants had an exclusive interest in commerce and industry for its own rewards. On the contrary they were enthralled by the grandeur of aristocratic life, and as the younger sons of noble families did not, as in England, look to trade to supplement their family incomes, the gulf between the classes was made at once more real and more recognisable. The acquisition of wealth was therefore a necessary means by which to cross this gulf, a universal trend recorded in an official report on trade in 1701: 'We know that the great contempt for trade and traders which reigns in France has for many years prompted them to retire from it as soon as they have gained sufficient wealth to assume a social position in which they enjoy more pleasure and approbation, greater eminence and distinction.' Traditionally the easiest step towards this goal was to sell out their business and to purchase an office from the crown.

The *officiers*, the bureaucracy of France, had grown in numbers as the kings had extended their power. Moreover, since the *officiers* were the agents of the royal courts and tribunals, any extension of royal jurisdiction at the expense of that of the nobles or of the Church was also an extension of their own power and prestige. It also increased their opportunities for profit, along more socially acceptable channels. Their salaries were relatively unimportant; it was the payments made by the public for every act of justice or administration carried out for them which made the offices valuable—and all *officiers* were exempted from taxation. Equally important was the fact that the purchaser of an office had security of tenure and, since 1604, in return for an annual payment to the crown of one-sixtieth of the value of his office, he not only insured against dismissal but also secured the right to pass on his office to his heir or sell it to the highest bidder. Not surprisingly the demand for offices was insatiable.

The *officiers* had their own hierarchy. The lowest were little more than clerks and bailiffs, the middle ranks included notaries and procurators, while the coveted posts were those within the *parlements* —and especially in the *parlement* of Paris. *Parlementaires* were men of influence and social standing, and a *premier président* was accorded dignities and precedence which ranked him among the greatest nobles. Such a man was Achille de Harlay who leased from Henri IV the building plots of the Place Dauphine. Another group with close connections with the *parlementaires*, but of necessity of a rather different cast of mind, were the *financiers*, the agents of tax collection who staked everything on making a fortune from the antiquated system of revenue collection. Those who failed, provided they avoided imprisonment, looked elsewhere for less vulnerable positions, but the successful ones acquired not only wealth but influence at court and the opportunity to become a minister of the crown. This hierarchy is best reflected in the pedigree of Nicolas Fouquet whose grandfather was a merchant of Nantes, whose father secured a post in the Paris Parlement and who himself became not only *procureur-général* in it but also a *financier*. Here he found his true *métier*, rising to become *surintendant des finances* and, for a short period, the chief minister of Louis XIV.

The higher ranks of the *officier* class claimed for themselves a particular status of nobility, *la noblesse de la robe*, which they asserted to be the equal of *la noblesse de l'épée*: 'There is only one kind of nobility: it is acquired in different ways by fighting for the king or by serving him in his law courts, but its rights and prerogatives are the same for all.' These were brave words but they fooled no one, least of all the *officiers* themselves who, whatever their wealth or rank, struggled endlessly to secure a place among the true nobility of France. Nothing less could resolve the predicament of the bourgeoisie —and until that day arrived the only thing to do was to demonstrate as obviously as possible by one's appearance and behaviour that one had at least learned to live like a nobleman. 'You are mad, my lord', says Mme Jourdain in *Le Bourgeois Gentilhomme*. 'All this nonsense has gone to your head. It all comes of hanging around the gentry.' 'If I hang around the gentry', replies her husband, 'I show my good taste. It's better than hanging around your shop-keeping crowd.'

In general, the *officiers* were men of simple tastes, avaricious rather than opulent, given to caution and carefulness, but as they reached the higher grades of their profession their social ambitions grew apace, prompting a new style of living. *Vivre noblement* was thus the height of bourgeois ambition. Since noblemen of any consequence—and this could only mean those who were seen in Paris and at court—did not work for a living it was something of an asset to have no visible means of financial support. Many bourgeois accordingly sold their businesses and invested in government bonds, the *rentes* on the Hôtel de Ville, issued against the surety of future taxes. The interest was not always paid in full, but the status of *rentier* was much envied. Alternatively, since the nobility ruined themselves to make a good appearance in public, the bourgeois forced themselves to break the ingrained habit of thrift and undertook the path of conspicuous expenditure. This they did in remarkable numbers, and the growth in the production of luxury goods during the century is explained by the middle-class demand for the mirrors, the glassware, the porcelain and the silverware and the cloth of gold, which had formerly been confined to the homes of the great nobles. A few with more acumen perceived that it was not enough to buy what the nobles bought but that their new possessions had somehow to acquire the patina of age; and Tallement writes of a *conseiller*, Sevin, who rolled his silver pots and dishes up and down stairs so that dents of noble antiquity could be acquired.

As men of education the *officiers* had a measure of interest in literature, and it was from this class that most of the great writers of the age appeared, but it was not until the second or third generation of a successful family that the arts in general became an object of interest. Those who rose swiftly, however, soon discovered the social value of patronising the arts. Great ministers like Richelieu and Mazarin, great princes like Gaston, had set a pattern of behaviour which others were quick to imitate, especially in the collection of works of art, an activity which had the additional advantage of satisfying the innate traditions of avarice and investment. Between 1640 and 1660 private collectors began to vie with each other, and Pierre Crozat, a wealthy banker, was supposed to have acquired the wholly improbable number of 200 by Rubens, 100 Titians and 100 by Veronese. Another banker, Everard Jaibach, who moved to Paris from Cologne, transformed his *hôtel* into a museum and art gallery and bought up scores of paintings in England at the end of the Civil War. Mme de Longuet, wife of a *trésorier* in the war department, had a gallery famous for its comprehensive collection of seventeenth-century masters; Pointel, a banker from Lyons, was the friend of Poussin and of de Chanteloup and collected Poussins in great numbers; Passard, a *maître des comptes*, sought out the works of both Claude and Poussin; the *conseiller* Poucet, those of Le Brun and Le Sueur; and the *président* Nicolas Pomponne de Bellièvre, those of Poussin and Le Brun. For the many who could not afford the originals, the collection of prints became the vogue, and in this field the palm went to Michel Marolles, abbé de Villeloin, who by 1666 had amassed 123,000 prints by over 6,000 artists. Zigrosser has uncovered evidence of at least 85 large collections of prints in Paris by 1673, and of more than 130 by the end of the century.

But it was building which most appealed to the bourgeoisie and, outside the narrow circle of the royal family and the two cardinals, every single commission of importance in the period 1630–60 came from this class. The nobility it is true lived in fashionable areas like the Place Royale, but only in rented accommodation; the building of houses there and elsewhere was undertaken only by *financiers* and *parlementaires*. To dignify their residences still further, they appropriated for them the name of *hôtel*: this was a medieval term to denote the town house of the king or of a great lord, and therefore applied to an administrative centre, such as the Hôtel de Ville, but it had since become a general term for the town houses of the nobility. In the seventeenth century the wealthier bourgeois followed the example of the chancellor Séguier who, as Tallement recorded, 'has baptised his house a *hôtel*'. Pierre d'Alméras, a *surintendant général des postes*, built his private mansion in the Faubourg Saint-Germain; Catalan, a *fermier général*, in the rue Vivienne; Antoine Scasson, *contrôleur des ponts et chaussées*, in the rue de Jouy; Claude de Guénégaud, Bertrand de la Bazinière and Gaspard de Fieubet, all three *trésoriers de l'Épargne*, in the rue Saint-Louis, the quai Malaquais and the rue des Lions respectively.

In general the *parlementaires* and *financiers* moved into the Pré-aux-clercs along the right bank of the Seine, and also into the Île Saint-Louis where they built their splendid houses along the quays, oblivious to the teeming community of shopkeepers and artisans behind them. Those of more modest means would build in the Place Dauphine or in the Marais, a region which became increasingly fashionable after the construction of the Place Royale. Costs varied according to the period. Marguerite de Valois, for example, purchased a house on the left bank in 1606, paying one livre for each *toise* (3·8 metres) of frontage; in 1620 she sold it for 20 livres per *toise*, and a similar house in the rue de Richelieu went for 70 livres per *toise* in 1634. The rise in prices was reflected in the increase in rents: one house in the Faubourg Saint-Honoré cost 300 livres a year in 1608, 410 in 1620, 500 in 1632 and 1,000 in 1651.

In all expenditure on building, however, the proportion of costs remained more or less constant, with one half spent on masonry, a quarter on timbering and a quarter on joinery, tiling and the rest.

There was plenty of information and advice available. Jacques Androuet du Cerceau's *Livre d'Architecture*, 'containing plans and designs for 50 houses, all different, for the instruction of those who desire to build', was adapted and brought up to date in 1623, and again in 1647, by Pierre Le Muet under the title, *Manière de bien bâtir pour toutes sortes de personnes*. Where du Cerceau's plans had been on the generous side, Le Muet added plans for houses from 850 square metres in ground plan down to 27. His smallest houses had a street frontage of only 12 feet, and comprised one small room with a passage to a backyard and staircase. The surface decoration of his houses was very much in the brick and stone manner of the Place Dauphine, though in the 1647 edition he added rather larger houses with rustication and bas-relief in what he took to be the grand manner, using the mannerist motifs of du Cerceau. Louis Savot's *Architecture Françoise* was one of the most practical and helpful books, designed in the words of the 1673 edition expressly 'to rescue honest men from the clutches of middlemen and builders'. First published in 1624, it provided exhaustive details about the cost of materials, and summarised the complex web of bye-laws and building regulations. Two books of particular value were the *Grand Marot* and the *Petit Marot* by Jean Marot, a designer of *hôtels* who made a comprehensive series of engravings of his contemporaries' work. From these delightful studies we derive much valuable information about ground plans and elevations.

Jean du Cerceau, one of the famous family of architects, made his own reputation as a designer of *hôtels* in the early seventeenth century. Commissioned by Mesme Gallet du Petit-Thouars, a *contrôleur des finances*, to build a *hôtel*—now the Hôtel de Sully—in the rue Saint-Antoine, he developed a plan which was becoming more or less traditional. The *corps de logis* was set well back from the road, two wings led forwards to two pavilions on the road itself and these were linked by a screen containing the gateway. The wings, containing stables, kitchens and outhouses, enclosed a courtyard, and the garden was laid out on the other side of the main *appartements*. The surface was heavily decorated in the du Cerceau manner with friezes above the doorways, allegorical figures in niches along the first floor and elaborate scrollwork on the dormer windows. Another famous *hôtel* by the same architect was designed for Claude le Ragois, sieur de Bretonvilliers, a *financier* who had made his fortune as secretary to the *conseil des finances* and who had bought up the eastern point of the Île Saint-Louis. This gave him a superb site with the garden open to the river, and du Cerceau showed great ingenuity in exploiting the situation. Instead of placing the main staircase in the centre of the main building he put it at the angle of the courtyard between the *corps de logis* and the left wing, and therefore left himself free to establish on the first floor a continuous row of interconnecting reception rooms overlooking the garden and the river. The originality of the device has recently been questioned by Babelon who finds late-sixteenth-century examples of it, but its essential rightness at the Hôtel de Bretonvilliers cannot be denied.

Ingenuity in making best use of the site was a necessary quality. When the duc de Liancourt acquired the Hôtel de Bouillon, built by Salomon de Brosse on conventional lines, he also purchased the site adjacent to it and employed Le Mercier to merge the two. Using de Brosse's courtyard as the principal entry to the hotel, he left the other, separated from it by one of the original projecting wings, as a base court and a small garden. Within this dividing wing he placed the main staircase and entrance lobby so that he could run the *corps de logis* in an uninterrupted line right across the two sites. This not only created a splendid series of rooms overlooking the enlarged garden, but allowed him, because of the great length of the main building, to add projecting pavilions at each end of the garden façade with a portico entrance in the middle.

A much more complex problem was that posed to Antoine Le Pautre by Mme de Beauvais. She was a woman of great self-importance, having been *femme de chambre* to Anne d'Autriche, and had married an old but extremely rich haberdasher. With his wealth she bought two contiguous sites, one facing the rue Saint-Antoine, the other the rue de Jouy. Since none of the sides were parallel, and most

of the angles re-entrant, Le Pautre's ingenuity was tested to the full.
He put the main gateway between a row of shops on the rue Saint-
Antoine, leading through to an apse-ended courtyard with coach
houses around the apse. From the courtyard to the right of the apse
a passage way with stables and other offices on each side gave access
to the rue de Jouy. The main *corps de logis* was built over the shops
and the main gateway with the rooms more or less corresponding
to those on the ground floor, but above the stables and the stable
entry he totally ignored the disposition of the ground floor, creating
a long gallery overlooking the central courtyard on one side and a
hanging garden, of all things, on the other, with an *appartement*
beyond the garden, overlooking the rue de Jouy. Above the coach
houses he laid out a terrace and a small chapel.

One architect in great demand among the wealthy officers of the
Treasury was Mansart, whose work at the Château de Berny for
Nicolas Brulart de Sillery led to many commissions to build *hôtels*
for Sillery's colleagues, including La Bazinière, Guénégaud and
Fieubet (see page 162). In 1635 he built the Hôtel de la Vrillière for
yet another *trésorier*, and we can see from the Marot engraving the
same simplicity, regularity and balance we have already noticed in
his work. The overall design, conventional enough in plan, is extremely satisfying, and the firm disposition of the masses is not
compromised by too much surface decoration. The windows have
the simplest moulding possible, there are no scrolls, few pediments
and very little rustication. Even the enclosing screen and gateway,
which many architects sought to make as imposing as possible in
order to impress passers-by with their patron's magnificence, has
only a simple square moulding and a balustrade. Behind the *corps de
logis*, La Vrillière had wanted to enclose the garden with two galleries to house his collections, but he was deprived of one of them by
the building of a new road which cut across the site.

For men of extraordinary wealth such as these, a *hôtel* in Paris,
no matter how fashionable the quarter, was not enough. They had
come to realise that *vivre noblement* meant to escape the city from
time to time, and the notion of 'a little place in the country' suddenly became overwhelmingly attractive. From 1630 masons were

at work in the forest belt encircling Paris and in the open fields of the Île de France. Claude de Guénégaud, in addition to the *hôtel* built for him by Mansart in the rue Saint-Louis, bought a house at Le Plessis-Belleville and demonstrated his landed status by hyphenating Du Plessis with his surname. Duret de Chevry, one of Richelieu's men and a *président aux comptes*, who had several *hôtels* in Paris and one dutifully erected in the Grande Rue at Richelieu, built himself a country seat at La Grange; Barthélemy Hervart, a German banker in Mazarin's service, settled at Saint-Cloud, and Henri Clausse, *grand-maître des eaux et forêts*, followed suit at Courances.

But the most spectacularly successful of these country houses was the Château Maisons, built by Mansart between 1642 and 1646 for the *président* René de Longueil. Since the seventeenth century, roads and other houses have cut into the spacious garden setting which Mansart created for this château, but it remains nonetheless a masterpiece. It consists very simply of a free-standing block as at Berny, crowned with a lofty mansard roof and decorated by an imposing central frontispiece which combines both splendour and elegance without fuss. It is is flanked by two short wings of the same height as the main block, each with a short projection one storey high. But it is not the features so much as the total composition which marks this as a great work of art; and one which epitomises the definition of classical beauty given by the Renaissance architect Alberti as 'the harmony and concord of all the parts achieved in such a way that nothing could be added or taken away or altered except for the worse'. No other building demonstrates so well the satisfying balance of order, simplicity, mass, harmony and intelligence which characterises French classicism in the seventeenth century.

Mansart's most talented rival, Le Vau, was also in great demand among the wealthy bourgeois, but curiously, when we consider the contrast between their styles, it was Mansart who worked for the flamboyant *financiers* and great officers of state while Le Vau was patronised for many years by the more serious-minded *parlementaires*, until he was finally carried off by Fouquet, Colbert and Louis XIV. Earlier, as at the Hôtel de Bautru, completed in 1637, he revealed a preoccupation with surface decoration in the mannerist tradition, but at the Hôtel Tambonneau, built in the rue de l'Université for a rich and debauched *président de la cour des comptes*, he was clearly beginning to evince a greater feeling for mass. It was nonetheless characteristic of the difference between himself and Mansart that he could still regard a building as a series of separate façades rather than a solid block whose surface was to be carefully and consistently articulated by the correct orders. Mansart's meticulous care in this respect we have noted at Blois, but Le Vau at the Hôtel Tambonneau used a colossal order of Ionic pilasters along the façade of the garden front without any on the courtyard side, save for two small orders at the main entrance.

*Metteur-en-scène* and entrepreneur, Le Vau's success sprang directly from his ability to create splendid settings without too scrupulous a regard for stylistic detail, and to organise a team of talented artists who stayed with him for most of his career. This team included painters of the quality of Le Sueur, Bourdon and Le Brun, and such sculptors as Sarrazin, Guérin and van Obstal. Much of their work was done initially on the Île Saint-Louis where Le Vau had shrewdly invested in land, building and decorating the Hôtel Hesselin and the Hôtel Sainctot side by side on the quay, and then undertaking a commission of great importance at the eastern tip of the island, opposite to the Hôtel de Bretonvilliers, for Jean-Baptiste Lambert. What made the *hôtel* so famous was the quality, profusion and splendour of the interior decoration. At this Le Vau excelled, and Le Brun who worked closely with him learned much of the skill which he in turn was to employ at Versailles. Contemporaries were amazed by the Cabinet de l'Amour and the Cabinet des Muses, most of whose contents are now in the Louvre, but the gallery was perhaps the finest room of all. It was built on the first floor at right angles to the main block, overlooking the garden on one side and ending in a bow window from where the spectator had a magnificent view upstream. On the walls van Obstal produced a series of stucco reliefs in gold and bronze to represent the labours of Hercules and the same theme was taken up by Le Brun on the ceiling.

Of all the wealthy bourgeois who employed Le Vau the wealthiest and most influential was Nicolas Fouquet. Grandson of a merchant, son of a *parlementaire* and himself *surintendant des finances*, his career was the envy of his class. By nature ostentatious and fond of luxury, he spent his fortune freely, recognising the value of cutting a figure in the world and at the same time delighting in the patronage of arts and letters. He very much enjoyed salon society, and his wife, greatly assisted by a cousin who had married into the nobility, organised a successful salon of her own. The death of her parrot was an occasion for a symposium of verse to rival the *Guirlande de Julie*, but her interests extended to the fine arts in general and she was given lessons in painting by Le Brun. Fouquet's tastes were extraordinarily wide, ranging over music and drama, poetry, painting and architecture, and he possessed an uncanny gift of recognising and securing for his own service the finest exponents of every art form.

For years he had wanted to establish himself in the country like any great aristocrat; in 1641, when he was only a *maître des requêtes*, he had bought up the village of Maincy, conveniently near to Paris, and had added to it as his fortune grew until in 1657 his estate, under its proud name of Vaux-le-Vicomte, had become a sufficiently splendid setting for the great château he had dreamed of building. The commission went to Le Vau who decided to abandon the traditional plan of the quadrangle enclosed by *corps de logis*, projecting wings and entrance screen, in favour of an open free-standing block. In this he was probably influenced by Mansart's work, and also by the Roman architect Carlo Maderna, whose Palazzo Barberini was built on this plan and who had incorporated as his central feature a domed oval salon. Le Vau had already experimented successfully with an oval room at Le Raincy when he built a country house for Jacques Bordier, an *intendant des finances*, and at Vaux-le-Vicomte he made the central feature of the château a rectangular vestibule on the courtyard side adjoining a vast oval salon on the garden side. To east and west of this were two great *appartements*, one for Fouquet, the other reserved for the king.

The *appartements* are in effect the wings of the château, and since they do not advance beyond the line of the entrance portico, except for one room at each end which projects about 15 feet, there is therefore no courtyard in the traditional sense. The visitor dismounts alongside the château rather than within it, advances through a triple-arched portico into the vestibule, through another triple opening into the oval salon, and from there, by a third triple doorway, he gains access to the garden. The total effect, both inside and out, is most impressive. The wings in particular are given great power by their high-pitched roofs, and by the colossal, though delicate, Ionic orders which rise up the whole façade. The weakness is that they bear no relation to the central block of the salon and the vestibule where, instead of the one colossal order, the two floors are most clearly articulated, and where the dome and cupola can do nothing more than coexist with the high-pitched roofs to either side. Nonetheless, the château illustrates that individual genius of Le Vau to bring off a superb appearance without too much attention to details of style.

Vaux-le-Vicomte, designed so that a bourgeois minister might astound not only the nobility but the king himself, was a brilliant success, and it was typical of Le Vau's skill as a *metteur-en-scène* and of his concern with the overall setting that a measure of the success was due to the landscaping of the estate. For this he brought in André Le Nôtre (see chapter 7). Variations in level, as the ground fell slightly across the estate from west to east, were skilfully masked by laying out groves of trees in the dips, balanced by terraces cut into the higher ground.

To the south stretched an enormous parterre with a magnificent *pièce d'eau* at its centre. Beyond it a central alley stretched ahead, flanked by two streams and along which a line of fountains created the illusion, recorded by Mme de Sévigné, of a crystal balustrade. Another ingenious illusion was created where a cascade of water, a *théâtre d'eau*, fell down a steep slope into a pond; the pond, however, was invisible from the house, and so a sheet of water was laid out just before it, so that from a distance the cascade might appear to tumble down on to its smooth mirror-like surface. To either side of the central alley stretched parterres of flowers and of water, and the line of the garden was finally closed by the water of the grand canal running across it at the horizon.

Within the château, Le Vau's team of painters and sculptors was led with greater self-assurance than ever by Charles Le Brun, who also established the manufacture of tapestries for the château in the village of Maincy. The decoration reflected the current taste for legend, allegory and self-glorification. In the king's *appartement* the rooms were devoted to representations of the triumph of Truth, of the labours of Hercules, allegories of Peace and War, of the Seasons and of Louis XIV, aided by Love, enchaining Rebellion. Throughout Fouquet's rooms his own device of a *fouquet*, a squirrel, was to be seen everywhere along with its dangerously aspiring motto, '*Quo non ascendam*', and, as if to give a clue, the crenellated towers of the royal blazon of Spain, appropriated in some mysterious way by the family of lawyers into which he had married, were given due prominence. Finally, in the very centre of the château, on the dome of the salon, Le Brun was about to record the apotheosis of his patron, a new star taking its place in the firmament, when he was forestalled by Fouquet's sudden downfall.

Though it is unfair to Vaux-Le-Vicomte not to study it in its own right, it is inevitably seen merely as the forerunner of Versailles, the practice-ground where Le Vau, Le Nôtre and Le Brun tried out their skills in their first large-scale commission. The connection is made all the closer by the patronage which Fouquet, advised by Pellisson, offered there to musicians, poets and playwrights. Lully was summoned to write the music for his entertainments; La Fontaine was pensioned at 1,000 livres to provide four poems each quarter; Corneille, encouraged by Fouquet, returned to the theatre to write *Oedipe*, his last success; and for the greatest night in Fouquet's life when, on 17 August 1661, he entertained the royal family and 6,000 guests at Vaux, Molière was commissioned to write a new play.

For Molière too it was an occasion of great importance as his previous career had taken some very bad turns. His father, Jean Poquelin, was an upholsterer who secured a post in royal service as *tapissier du roi* and could then afford to educate his son at the Jesuit Collège de Clermont—a fashionable school where Molière became a close friend of the prince de Conti. Molière, as was expected of him, joined his father's business in 1642, but within a year had met Madeleine Béjart, the daughter of an *officier* who, with her brothers and sisters, had broken away from her family to take up acting. Such a career was generally considered to be at best penurious, at worst immoral, and in any case liable to excommunication by the Church, but Molière was so fascinated both by Madeleine and by the life of the theatre that he resolved to abandon his own safe career for the stage. His father, despite the expensive education he had provided, and the ambitions he had justifiably entertained for his son in the royal service, surprisingly gave his consent. In 1643, Molière and the Béjarts took a three-year lease of a Parisian tennis court and called themselves the Illustre Théâtre. It was a brave beginning, but the annual charge of 1,900 livres was too heavy for them to bear. Though the burning of the Marais gave them an unlooked-for spell of business, they failed to rival the tragedies of the Hôtel de Bourgogne or the *pièces à machines* at the new Marais. By 1645 the company was in debt, and Molière had been thrown into prison by his creditors.

In the eyes of conventional bourgeois the whole episode was an object lesson in the wasted opportunity of a good education and the perils of a theatrical career, but Molière's father generously rescued his son and even agreed to his making a second attempt. To do so in Paris was of course out of the question and the company set out in 1646 for the provinces. This was the stark solution for all who failed in Paris, and though it appeared at first to be something of a sojourn in the wilderness, the company was nonetheless able to make a living for 12 years. At first they teamed up with another troupe led by du Fresne, who had secured the protection of the duc d'Épernon, governor of Guyenne, without which travelling actors were liable to arrest as vagabonds and rogues. Until Épernon left Guyenne in 1650 they enjoyed a successful tour throughout his jurisdiction, playing mainly at Narbonne, Toulouse and Carcassonne. Molière then moved the company to Languedoc where his former school friend, Conti, was governor. Conti willingly gave him a pension and official protection and it was as the Troupe de Monsieur le Prince de Conti that Molière's company based itself at Lyon and made periodic forays across Languedoc. In 1657, however, Conti with remarkable speed abandoned his former mode of life, his atheism, his mistress—and his players—to undertake a life of penitence under the spiritual direction of the Jansenists of Port-Royal. Worse still, he joined the Compagnie du Saint-Sacrement which regarded the theatre as a principal source of moral infection, and Molière in consequence was forced to move hastily to Rouen in 1658, and then, in the same year, to Paris.

The company's tour of the provinces had not consigned it to total oblivion. During its seven years at Lyon, for example, it had established a local reputation which was spread by those who passed through on their way to or from Paris. Gaston d'Orléans, for one, had heard something of Molière and agreed to let him stage a production at the Louvre in October 1658. The company played Corneille's *Nicomède* with little success, but scored heavily with Molière's own play *Le Docteur Amoureux*. Louis XIV granted them permission not only to perform in Paris as the Troupe de Monsieur but also to share the Petit-Bourbon theatre with the Italians. By arrangement with Scaramouche, therefore, Molière paid 1,500 livres to play on Mondays, Tuesdays, Thursdays and Saturdays, and once again set out to make his fortune in Paris.

This time, however, he could exploit the experience of 12 years work both as actor-manager and as playwright. In the former capacity he had created a well-drilled troupe of performers. Himself apart, none of them was particularly talented, but the Béjarts provided the nucleus of an extremely professional team. Madeleine and Geneviève were experienced and versatile, Armande had great charm, and their brothers Joseph and Louis played the lovers and comic valets respectively. Their secret lay in teamwork and timing. 'Never was comedy so well-performed or with so much art', wrote Donneau de Visé after a performance of *L'École des Femmes* in 1662. 'Every actor knows how many steps he has to take and his every glance is counted.'

This same expert professionalism is evident in Molière's writings for the stage. When, for example, he makes Harpagon in *L'Avare* scrutinise the audience and say, 'They're all looking at me and beginning to laugh'—a dangerous line indeed for a poor actor—we have an obvious instance of his constant preoccupation with direct communication across the footlights. In Paris he had watched Tabarin and Gros-Guillaume and though he avoided their gross indecencies he learned much from them of knock-about clowning, of stumbling drunks and bewildered cuckolds. Even more formative an influence was that of the *Commedia dell'Arte* which frequently performed in Lyon on its way between Italy and Paris. From the Italians he learned how to improvise on stock situations according to the nature of each audience; like them he often performed with a mask or floured face in order to enhance the significance of the gestures which had thus to convey their meaning unaided by facial expression. 'Every phrase of his dialogue has its implicit movement and gesture; every dramatic effort is calculated and virtue is even made of necessities—his own cough and his brother-in-law's limp in *L'Avare*, Mlle Beauval's gift for infectious laughter in the part of Nicole, the permanent sets of the Italians which he had to make the best of when he shared their theatre with them' (Wood).

In short, after barn-storming across the south of France for 12 years Molière had learned at first hand how to make audiences laugh by gesture, mimicry, exaggeration, asides and repetition, and all his writing was based upon his experience of what a good actor could make of a phrase or a situation. To understand his plays it is more valuable to understand this practical apprenticeship than to study the social environment from which he derived his comic situations. It is misleading to take his plays as though they represented comments of tremendous significance about seventeenth-century France by Molière, social satirist extraordinary; it is much wiser to remember that as a professional comedian he was too experienced not to miss a trick and that he always found out first what any particular audience might find amusing.

In November 1659, for example, he was commissioned by friends of La Grande Mademoiselle to do a skit on people like Pellisson and Mlle de Scudéry who belonged to a rival coterie associated with Fouquet and his friends. To please them, therefore, he wrote *Les Précieuses Ridicules* to caricature the over-refined sensibilities of Sappho and her circle—and with Somaize's *Dictionnaire* as a lead there was nothing too ridiculous which could not be invented as the

very latest thing in salon conversation. There were of course many
telling points which revealed the skill of Molière as a commentator
on human foibles but his play was not the nicely observed satire of
the salons which many have taken it to be. Not only was it expressly
written for the habitués of one salon, but it was played as a boisterous
farce in which Jodelet appeared with floured face like any pantomime
comic. So boisterously offensive was it—and so successful—that its
victims soon complained to Fouquet of its comic savagery. Molière
was then induced by Fouquet to tone it down a little, and to present
it to Fouquet's friends at the Hôtel de Nevers.

Whatever its value as a presentation of *préciosité*, *Les Précieuses
Ridicules* established Molière as a master of comic invention. Another
farce followed, *Sganarelle*, in 1660, and the failure of a tragedy, *Don
Garcie de Navarre*, prompted a swift return to comedy with the
successful *L'École des Femmes*. It was then that he was called to
Vaux-le-Vicomte in August 1661, to enter a new phase in his development, for he now had to work in collaboration with Lully. The
outcome was *Les Fâcheux* which combined a series of satirical
caricatures with the type of ballet which Lully had made popular
at court, with colossal transformation scenes engineered by Torelli.
The night of the fête was indeed a memorable one, with 6,000 guests
entertained at a cost of over 120,000 livres, against a background of
splendour and beauty created by the joint efforts of the finest artists
of the day. Not even Richelieu had been able to entertain his
sovereign with the collective skills of such men as Le Vau, Le Brun,
Le Nôtre, Molière and Lully.

But Louis xiv thought it too much of a good thing. Not only did
it far surpass anything he himself could provide but it angered him
that his *surintendant des finances* should be so prodigiously rich when
the royal finances were strained to breaking point. Worse still,
Fouquet did not take sufficiently seriously Louis's determination to
be his own first minister: tactlessly he had made advances to the
current royal mistress, and he had fortified another residence at
Belle-Île in a manner which revived in Louis's mind memories of the
overmighty subjects of his childhood. Colbert, eager to succeed to
Fouquet's title, supplied the evidence of his peculation. Three weeks

after *Les Fâcheux* he was arrested and committed to life imprisonment at Pignerol.

The apotheosis of Fouquet was abruptly abandoned by Le Brun, and on the day after the arrest he begged Mme Colbert to accept the present of a drawing.

# six

# Port-Royal

The restoration of order by Henri IV gave the Catholic Church an opportunity to establish a similar degree of order in its own affairs. When weapons have failed, conversion can only be achieved by spiritual example, and the end of the Wars of Religion inaugurated a period of intense religious fervour which lost nothing for being contained within a stricter framework of discipline. The Tridentine decrees, issued by the series of councils called at Trent in the sixteenth century to meet the challenge of the Reformation, were at last taken seriously in France, and obvious reforms of discipline and organisation were introduced. Less obvious but of great importance were the liturgical reforms which imparted greater order to the Mass, and made worship more hieratic. The service was shortened, the haphazard conditions in which the sacrament had been reserved were terminated, and the role of the congregation was reduced to that of making restrained and well-defined responses.

Against the background of this remarkably disciplined and widespread enthusiasm, the behaviour of the most fervent Catholics, the *dévots*, can be put into perspective. The more extreme forms of their devotion become intelligible when we recognise that the whole membership of the Church was more universally devout than it had been for centuries and, though the *dévots* were accused of excess, the majority maintained a degree of intellectualism and restraint in sharp contrast to the torrid romanticism and spiritual anarchy which characterised much of the Catholic revival in Spain and Italy. In France a combination of mystical enthusiasm with much practical common sense and organising ability led not to passive contemplation but to active service, epitomised by the life of Pierre de Bérulle. Though his vocation had been rejected by the Jesuits, Bérulle had become a cardinal and a leading figure of the Counter-Reformation. He was not afraid of emotional warmth in religion and assisted the introduction of the reformed Carmelites into France, an order founded in honour of the Spanish saint, Teresa of Avila, the record of whose visions and ecstasies served frequently to provide excesses of emotional hysteria among her followers. On the other hand, and to greater practical advantage, he introduced the Oratory, a Roman foundation which existed not for withdrawal and contemplation but for the re-invigoration of pastoral work. We have noted the social consequences of the academies established by the Oratory (see chapter 2), but of greater importance was the establishment of 50 houses in France for training a more intelligent and a more devout priesthood.

This characteristic blend of fervent devotion and practical action was maintained by his two most famous disciples. Saint Vincent de Paul, after seven years as a Turkish galley slave, founded the essentially practical order of the Filles de la Charité who tried to alleviate the suffering of the rural areas—most notably during the campaigns of the Fronde. Like Bérulle he knew the perils of ignorance and set up the Collège des Bons-Enfants which specialised in providing much-needed education and advice to country curés, the weakest ranks of the Church militant. Saint Francis de Sales produced two classic works of devotion, an *Introduction à la vie dévote* and a *Traité de l'amour de Dieu*, but he did not ignore the practical needs of the world around him. He founded the Visitandines, who left their convents to teach and to care for the sick, until his superior, the archbishop of Lyon, suppressed such unconventional action. More acceptable was his plan to take the system of spiritual direction as practised in the cloister and adapt it to the needs of laymen, who he realised were as much in need of guidance as the clergy. Only such a man combining such devout faith with such practical energy could have succeeded, as he did against enormous odds, in recovering the inhabitants of the Chablais from Calvinism.

Among laymen one of the most extreme and influential manifestations of Catholic fervour was the Compagnie du Saint-Sacrement. It was founded by an extreme fanatic, the duc de Ventadour, who razed to the ground every Huguenot village or house on his estates and who was equally outraged by the apparent indifference of many Catholics. Neither the Pope nor the archbishop of Paris paid him much attention, so the Compagnie, formed to combat both heresy and indifference, became a secret body more or less independent of the Church. With the aid of Suffren, Louis XIII's confessor, and of Condren, Bérulle's successor at the Oratory, the Compagnie established 51 local groups across France during the period 1630–60, each one remaining largely autonomous, but all of them sharing the same special features. It never acted publicly through its leaders but exercised its influence by a process of secret collective lobbying which gave it an exaggerated aura of strength and mystery.

Infamous in many eyes for its relentless persecution of Molière and the suppression of *Tartuffe*, it was also given to genuinely pious works, helping alike prisoners, prostitutes, galley slaves and victims of the Fronde. But these activities, as was the attack on *Tartuffe*, were merely means to an end, the conversion of souls and the strengthening of Catholicism. The Compagnie was at its most influential in enforcing the practice of religious observances by its members, by insisting upon a puritanical code of behaviour and by encouraging laymen to admit spiritual directors into their households. Its influence was profound over Anne d'Autriche and over many of the bourgeois, but it was disliked by the nobles who resented the principle of spiritual direction all the more for being coupled with a strict code of behaviour which condemned duelling as well as adultery. Moreover, it was too obviously a formidable secret society, and on these grounds alone fell foul of Mazarin and Colbert. *Tartuffe* proved to be a Pyrrhic victory and the Compagnie was closed by Louis XIV in 1666.

But though the mystics, the saints and the Compagnie, too, represented the more extreme forms of devotion in France, we must not forget that French society as a whole was much more devout and more intense in its religion than in the previous generation. The practice of spiritual direction was widely adopted, laymen increasingly went into retreat, charities and educational foundations were better supported, Mass was attended with greater regularity, the Bible was studied more thoroughly, and there was a greater interest in, and devotion to, the human personality of Christ. It was this blend of spirituality, intellect and practicality which was to be found especially among those who settled to a semi-monastic life at Les Granges, near the convent of Port-Royal des Champs.

Port-Royal des Champs, 18 miles south-west of Paris, was a former Cistercian monastery which in 1602 housed 13 nuns. Angélique Arnauld, their superior, was a girl in her teens with little interest in religion but content to enjoy the comfortable sinecure which family influence had secured. A visiting preacher, however, achieved her conversion to religion, and on 25 September 1609—the Journée des Guichets as it became known—she astounded her parents by refusing to meet them except for a short conversation through the conventional grille. The incident demonstrated her decision to take her calling seriously; it also revealed a tendency to over-dramatise her experience and to accentuate its unique nature. This was indeed to be a failing of many who became associated with Port-Royal. Self-consciously aware of a special vocation and often extremely self-willed, they were guilty, as de Sales warned Angélique, of intransigence and secret pride. If this was indeed the stuff of martyrs, the denizens of Port-Royal were all too aware of it.

In 1626 the nuns suffered badly from ague which they attributed to the unhealthiness of their location, and Mme Arnauld, Angélique's mother, bought them a house for 24,000 livres in the Faubourg Saint-Jacques. Soon after their move to the new Port-Royal the nuns fell under the influence of Duvergier de Hauranne, abbé de Saint-Cyran, a man of extreme piety and severity. His views were largely influenced by his friendship with a Flemish bishop, Jansen of Ypres, who condemned church ceremonial on the ground that it merely disguised the unalterable fact that man could only be saved by God's grace. Since he derived much of this from St Augustine, the

saint most drawn upon by sixteenth-century Protestants, it was not
surprising that Jansen's ideas were similar to those of Calvin on
matters of predestination and social behaviour.

Jansen was cautious—his views were published posthumously in
1640—but Saint-Cyran was impetuous and enthusiastic: 'He is a
Basque', said Richelieu, *'ainsi il a les entrailles chaudes.'* He openly
embraced the harsh doctrine that the majority of mankind was condemned to perdition and he taught that the few who were privileged
to receive God's grace should immediately renounce the world that
their salvation be not impaired. His sermons electrified the nuns who
were already more than half-convinced of their status among the
elect, but his influence extended beyond the convent walls to include
many noblemen of Parisian society. These did not become monks,
nor were they technically Jansenists, but a dozen of them abandoned
the pleasure-seeking capital at his direction and, in conscious imitation of the Desert Fathers, went out to the lonely site of Port-
Royal des Champs. There they undertook a life of self-discipline,
study and practical devotion, draining the marshland of the valley
and setting up their own school. In 1648, when some of the nuns
returned from the Paris house, the Solitaires, as they were called,
moved up the slope of the valley to settle in a farmstead at Les
Granges.

Before this, however, Saint-Cyran had run headlong into trouble
with Richelieu. He demanded that the sacraments should be received
only after a state of perfect contrition, and that attrition which was
conventionally acceptable was 'a man-made invention and a slacken-
ing of the whole penitential system'. This was not a mere dispute of
theologians; Louis XIII could receive the sacraments after merely
expressing his sorrow at his alliances with Protestant powers, but a
demand for perfect contrition would have necessitated a complete
shift in foreign policy. This was what Saint-Cyran sought to achieve,
and he stated his case so vigorously that Richelieu had him imprisoned in Vincennes from 1636 to 1642. He died the year after his
release, and the leadership of the two Port-Royals was consolidated
in the Arnauld family. Mère Angélique in Paris was joined by her
mother, by an aunt and daughter, and by her five sisters, one of

whom, a widow, was accompanied by her six daughters. Among the Solitaires at Les Granges was her brother Antoine Arnauld, a belligerent theologian and Saint-Cyran's most obvious successor, whose weakness was to take himself too seriously and to stand too self-consciously before the throne of God and the judgment of history. There was also her cousin Antoine Le Maître, a lover of poetry and rhetoric, and another brother, Arnauld d'Andilly, who had frequented the salons and combined a dual role of rake and *dévot*, 'loving beautiful souls all the more when he found they so often inhabited beautiful bodies' (Mme de Sévigné). He arrived at Les Granges in 1646 having first won over a powerful aristocrat, the marquis de Liancourt.

For all their apparent faults, the Solitaires were men of learning and devotion who sought practical means of expressing both, and when they were joined by men such as Lancelot and Nicole, their Little Schools became a famous centre of education. Their best years were from 1646 to 1656 with about 50 pupils a year, but because of the controversies in which Port-Royal became involved they were closed by 1660. With the closing, however, the teachers were free to reflect upon their methods and to publish them. They were severe in their theology and only the strictest education could prevent a lapse from grace, and they demanded full control over their charges, one teacher living with five or six pupils under his constant surveillance. But their harsh doctrines were mitigated by a genuine love of children and by a technique of instruction remarkable in its emphasis on the needs, the capabilities and the interests of each child.

Lancelot published a series of books on learning foreign languages, asserting that the child should begin with the familiar and progress to the unknown. From the vernacular he would move to good French and on to Latin—and even to Greek, for which the Little Schools were so famous that their Jesuit rivals referred to '*la secte des Hellénistes de Port-Royal*'. The most novel feature was the emphasis given to French. All teaching was in French and translation from Latin and Greek into good French was valued more highly than composition in a classical language. In this the Solitaires, most of them the product of a salon culture, reflected the growing awareness of Frenchmen about the possibilities of their own language. Coustel, who published in 1687 the principles of language-teaching he had practised from 1646 to 1656, wrote: 'Considering the point of perfection which our language has reached it surely deserves that we should cultivate it a little. As a matter of fact it has never been so rich in its expressions, so noble in its phrases, so precise and so pregnant in its epithets, so subtle in its turns and circumlocutions, so majestic in its motions, so brilliant in its metaphors, and finally so natural and so altogether magnificent and lofty in its verse, as it is at present.'

The Solitaires were extremely up to date in other respects, not least in their admiration for Descartes. In the long run Cartesianism was to tell against religion, reducing Christianity to deism by converting a personal saviour into an impersonal abstraction, but the immediate reaction of many Christians was to welcome the new philosopher who had so convincingly escaped from the defunct traditions of scholasticism—still the staple of all university teaching. At the Oratory, Malebranche eagerly defended Descartes, devoting his life to reconciling his more extreme statements with traditional Christian belief, and at Port-Royal des Champs the response was equally enthusiastic. Antoine Arnauld and Nicole collaborated to produce the Port-Royal *Logique* which enshrined the new logic of Cartesianism; Arnauld and Lancelot attempted a Cartesian examination of the laws of language in their *Grammaire générale et raisonnée*; but it was for theological reasons that Descartes was most loudly acclaimed. Arnauld believed that the *Méthode* was the most effective weapon 'to sustain God's cause against the *libertins*', since Cartesian reason could be invoked to support the notion of God's existence, and the duc de Luynes, a fervent Jansenist, translated the *Meditationes* into French in order to give them greater currency.

The *Traité des Passions*, however, was hotly contested because Descartes affirmed the power of the soul to control the passions. Corneille, too, had already popularised a similar theory by dramatising the conflict of will against desire. Against them both, the Jansenists maintained their pessimistic belief in the total inadequacy of mankind to resist temptation without divine grace. Moreover, the titanic struggles endured by Corneille's characters, instead of re-

ducing them to a proper degree of humility, made them appear to
be a race of supermen. 'All the plays by M. de Corneille, who is
without doubt the most *honnête homme* of all the dramatists', wrote
Nicole, 'are nothing less than vivid exhibitions of the passions of
pride, ambition, jealousy, vengeance and above all of that Roman
virtue which is nothing else but an exaggerated form of self-love.'
He complained that there was no place given to Christian virtues,
and that when saints were represented they were given 'speech
more proper to the heroes of ancient Rome than to the saints and
martyrs'. Yet, as Knox points out a little maliciously, they were not
altogether unlike Corneille's heroes: 'These good Christians, the
slaves of God's will, but of no other, were too much the captains of
their souls, like their contemporaries the heroes of Corneille'—and
what could be more Cornelian than Antoine Arnauld's response to
Nicole when, in a lull in the conflict which burst upon them, Nicole
urged him to accept a compromise in order to let them rest a little
in peace: 'What! But we shall have all eternity for resting in!'

As Descartes dissected the mind, the men of Port-Royal probed
the soul and analysed the nature of man. What was a game to many
in the salons became with them an intense preoccupation. It was
Nicole and his colleagues to whom Mme de Sévigné referred when
she wrote of Port-Royal: 'Never has the anatomy of the human
heart been done better than by those gentlemen there'; and Nicole's
clear perception and psychological insight anticipated the more
famous analyses of Pascal and La Rochefoucauld. 'Out of self-love,
one can wish to be delivered of self-love; out of pride one can wish
for humility. *Il se fait un cercle infini et imperceptible de retours sur
retours, de réflexions sur réflexions dans ces actions de l'âme, et il y a toujours en nous un certain fond, et une certain racine qui nous demeure
inconnue et impénétrable toute notre vie.*'

There were other experts in psychology outside the ranks of
Port-Royal, and chief among them were the Jesuits. Their great
achievement, for all the danger of its being misunderstood or mis-
applied, was to attempt to bring *la raison classique* to bear on the
problems of the confessional where a universal moral law had somehow to be applied to a variety of particular cases. There was moreover

the additional problem of making a reasonable and humane adjust-
ment of rules conceived in an age of asceticism to a society which
claimed the legitimacy of pleasure. This at least is how the Jesuits
put it, but there were critics who maintained that they were merely
lowering moral standards. 'We have now a more easy and agreeable
theology', wrote Balzac, 'one that can be better adjusted to suit the
humours of the great, which can accommodate its maxims with their
interests, and is not so rustic nor so harsh as the old theology.'
With the best type of Jesuit their religious fervour was too strong,
their own good sense too sound, to let the art of casuistry become
what Balzac had criticised. As experts in psychology, they recognised
the naturalness of sin; as experts in theology they maintained that
salvation was not beyond the efforts and attainment of all men. To
mitigate the severity of the commandments and to overcome the
neuroses of remorse, the priest was therefore required to employ
psychological insight in deciding what allowances to make in each
case.

This view was sharply contested by Bérulle and Condren who, like
most orthodox Catholics, disliked all humanist notions which
minimised man's fallen condition. The Jansenists were naturally
more vehement still, and pledged themselves to defend the doctrine
of omnipotent grace against the Jesuit version of casuistry and free
will. Port-Royal, in some respects more Jansenist by association
than by conviction, was dragged into the fray by Antoine Arnauld
on the strength of a conversation overheard in a salon, in which one
lady said that her Jesuit confessor permitted her to attend balls after
Mass on the general principle that for every lapse she could confess,
be absolved and again communicate. This seemed to be a wholly
improper extension of the doctrine of attrition, which itself had been
attacked by Saint-Cyran, and in the year of his mentor's death,
Arnauld published his *De la Fréquente Communion* (1643) as a challenge to the Jesuits. His argument was not against frequent communion but against its reputed use by Jesuits as an easy panacea for
frequent transgressions.

It was a vigorous polemic, deliberately written in French to reach
as wide an audience as possible, and it succeeded so well that the

Jesuits were driven to reply. *Pénitence Publique*, a feeble riposte by Petau, did more harm than good, and so they were compelled to seek other means of discrediting both Arnauld and his associates at Port-Royal. This they did by an astute attack on those sections of Jansen's teaching which most closely resembled the doctrines of Calvin, and it was not too difficult to secure, in 1653, a papal condemnation of five propositions derived from the *Augustinus*. Arnauld agreed that the propositions were heretical but denied that they could be found in Jansen's book. The conflict became more violent. A curé who sided with the Jesuits refused absolution to the duc de Liancourt, because of his association with Port-Royal, and the Jesuits arraigned Arnauld before the Sorbonne to answer charges of heresy. On 14 January 1656 Arnauld, for all his lucidity, for all his pugnacity, knew the game was up. Anne d'Autriche, Mazarin and Fouquet had declared support for the Jesuits, and the Sorbonne had demolished his point that the heretical propositions were not in the *Augustinus*. It was only a matter of days before the rest of his case fell to the ground, and he therefore turned to his friend Blaise Pascal, begging him to take his cause away from the packed tribunal of the Sorbonne and to expose it to the commonsense opinion of reasonable men across France.

Pascal was born at Clermont-Ferrand in 1623, the son of Étienne Pascal, a *président* of the Cour des Aides. The family moved to Paris in 1631, where Étienne became the friend of Descartes, Mersenne and other scientists. He educated his children at home to prevent them learning nonsense in the schools, and with so many men of genius in constant attendance at the house the children grew up in an atmosphere of intellectual excitement. Blaise was a child prodigy. At the age of 11 he wrote a treatise on the sounds of vibrating bodies, and at 15 an original study of conic sections. In 1638 a dispute with Richelieu over the *rentes* threatened Étienne's career, but all was smoothed over—apparently by his daughter Jacqueline who won Richelieu's favour by her performance in a private production of *L'Amour Tyrannique*. Whatever the reason, Étienne became a Treasury *intendant* and went to Rouen, where his house was still a centre for scientists—and for dramatists too, since Corneille became a visitor.

Blaise invented a computer, a *machine arithmétique*, but his health was poor. A nervous collapse in 1647 induced temporary paralysis, and thereafter he was never free from ailment. About the same time, his father was confined to the house with a broken leg, and the family was visited frequently by two of Saint-Cyran's converts who exercised great influence, particularly on Blaise, and the connection with Port-Royal was strengthened by their return to Paris soon after. Étienne died in 1651, and Jacqueline, after great opposition from her brother, entered Port-Royal as sœur Sainte-Euphémie.

Pascal was left in a state of nervous fret, bordering upon despair. He had been greatly influenced by Saint-Cyran's disciples, but he had also enjoyed the Stoic humanism current among his father's friends and in the salons. For a while he was fully occupied by his study of atmospheric pressure, publishing his *Traité sur le Vide* to disprove Descartes's contention that there were no vacuums in nature, but increasingly he became dissatisfied with science and also with philosophy. Aware that the abstract god of the philosophers offered no comfort to him he began a serious study of the Bible. Two men from Port-Royal, Singlin and the duc de Luynes, called regularly to advise him in his reading, and invited him to join them, but he jibbed at taking so final a step—and this no doubt explained his hysterical opposition to Jacqueline's vows. The issue was resolved by an emotional experience. In November 1654, after the shock of an accident to his coach on the Pont de Neuilly, Pascal had a vision of God. Until this date he had chosen what he termed '*les sciences de raisonnement*', in which he could freely argue, question and experiment, as opposed to '*les sciences d'autorité*', such as theology, which derived all their truth from the Bible alone. Now, on a parchment which he carried with him for the rest of his life, he wrote his new declaration of faith, beginning, 'God of Abraham, God of Isaac, God of Jacob, not of the philosophers and wise men'. In December 1654 he joined the Solitaires, and a year later he accepted Arnauld's appeal to undertake his cause against the Jesuits.

On 23 January 1656 he published the *Lettre de Louis de Montalte à un Provincial de ses amis*, the first of a series of letters known as *Les Provinciales* which represented a new peak in the development of

French prose. The other masters of prose, such as Balzac, Voiture and even Descartes, had always begun by forming their ideas in Latin, because all the best literature was in Latin, and their sentences betrayed the influence of Latin constructions and Latin authors. Pascal, however, did not set out to write literature. The *Lettres Provinciales* were deliberately polemical, directed not to the Sorbonne but to the general public who, if ignorant of theology, could nonetheless recognise common sense when it saw it. For this reason Pascal adopted the tone and the manner of the salon conversation and avoided such conventional models of eloquence as Quintilian or Cicero. He wrote directly for *les honnêtes gens* of the salons, combining the skill of a rapporteur of conversation and a superb mastery of sarcasm with the freedom, vigour and urgency of his scientific treatises.

They were immediately successful. The simplicity, the precision, the irony and the invective were the qualities of the *conversations d'esprit* transformed into literature. In the first place they had that lively narration of conversation which only Mme de Sévigné could rival. 'At these words the Jesuit Father returned, laden with books. He offered me the first, saying, "Read Père Bannay's *Somme des Péchés* which I have here—and it's the fifth edition too which shows it's a good book." "What a pity", murmured my Jansenist friend, "that it has been condemned both in Rome and by the bishops of France".'

*Les Provinciales* were greatly enjoyed for their irony. Pascal made great play of a doctrine, supposedly maintained by the Jesuits, that sins were not truly sins when committed without thought of offending God. '*Béni soyez-vous, mon Père, qui justifiez ainsi les gens! Les autres apprennent à guérir les âmes par des austérités pénibles: mais vous montrez que celles qu'on aurait cru le plus désespérément malades se portent bien. Ô la bonne voie pour être bien heureux en ce monde et en l'autre! J'avais toujours pensé qu'on péchât d'autant plus, qu'on pensait le moins à Dieu. Mais, à ce que je vois, quand on a pu gagner une fois sur soi de n'y plus penser du tout, toutes choses deviennent pures pour l'avenir.*'*

---

* How blessed you are, Father, for vindicating men so! Others tell us that souls are made better by painful austerities, but you show that those whom we would have

The blend of conversational nonchalance, irony and theological debate was sometimes abandoned, when Pascal switched abruptly from the mood of sweet reasonableness to one of passionate condemnation. If the earlier extracts recall the skill of Mme de Sévigné and Molière, this next is a Cornelian *tirade* in prose. After describing all the precautions taken in a murder trial to secure the appointment of independent judges, he continues; '*Voilà, mes Pères, de quelle sorte on dispose en justice de la vie des hommes: voyons maintenant comment vous en disposez. Dans vos nouvelles lois il n'y a qu'un juge, et ce juge est celui-là même qui est offensé. Il est tout ensemble le juge, la partie et le bourreau. Il se demande à lui-même la mort de son ennemi, il l'ordonne, il l'exécute sur-le-champ.* . . . *Et enfin, pour comble de ces excès, on ne contracte ni péché ni irrégularité en tuant de cette sorte sans autorité et contre les lois, quoiqu'on soit religieux, et même prêtre. Ou en sommes-nous, mes Pères? Sont-ce des religieux et des prêtres qui parlent de cette sorte? Sont-ce des chrétiens? Sont-ce des Turcs? Sont-ce des hommes? Sont-ce des démons? Et sont-ce là des "mystères révélés par l'Agneau à ceux de sa société", ou des abominations suggérées par le Dragon à ceux qui suivent son parti?*'*

After his initial success in urging Arnauld's cause on the issue of omnipotent grace, Pascal realised that that particular horse was dead, and began to expand generally, as we have seen, on the topic of Jesuit errors and scandals, exploiting these unfairly but to great effect. For the Jesuits it now became a point of honour not merely to

believed to be sick beyond hope are in fact in the best of health. Oh what a good way to be happy in this world and in the next! I had always believed that we sinned all the more grievously for thinking less of God, but from what I understand, when we have persuaded ourselves no longer to think this way, everything becomes pure for the future.

* See, my Fathers, how justice is dispensed among men; see now how you dispense it. Under your new laws there is only one judge and he himself is the one who has been offended. He is at once the judge, the plaintiff and the executioner. He demands for himself his enemy's death, orders it and carries it out straightway . . . and finally, to crown all these excesses, no one commits any sin or irregularity in committing murder in this manner, without authority and against the law, provided he is in orders or a priest. What should we make of it all, my Fathers? Are these men clerics and priests who speak in this way? Are they Christians? Are they Turks? Are they men? Are they devils? And are these things 'mysteries revealed by the Lamb to members of His society', or are they abominations proposed by Satan to those who take his part?

silence Pascal, but to close down Port-Royal. In this they were supported by Mazarin and Anne d'Autriche who disliked the spiritual nonconformity of the Jansenists, and who regarded them not merely as a source of heresy but as a centre of sedition. Many Frondeurs, such as Conti and Mme de Longueville, went to Port-Royal to seek direction in a life of penitence, and the more violent the excesses of their earlier life the more extreme the regimen they adopted. This of course compromised Port-Royal in the eyes of the government, and when Louis xiv came into his own he authorised the issue of a formulary condemning the five heretical propositions in the *Augustinus*, and demanded the universal subscription of the clergy. When the Port-Royal community refused its assent, the schools were closed and the nuns confined at Port-Royal des Champs, until in 1669 a compromise was arrived at which gave them a decade or so of limited freedom.

By this time Pascal had died, but not before writing a second masterpiece. Whatever the literary qualities of the *Provinciales*, they were religious only in a superficial sense, and by 1657, when the last one appeared, Pascal had become more concerned with his own spiritual experience than with ecclesiastical polemics. In that year his 10-year-old niece, Marguérite Périer, was afflicted with an unpleasant and painful fistula which affected the eyes and nose. The nuns of Port-Royal possessed a thorn, supposedly from the crown of Christ, and when one of them took it and touched the young girl's eyes the fistula was miraculously healed. The miracle of the thorn, as it was known, was attested by diocesan officials who authorised a *Te Deum* to be sung, and it proved to be the final stimulus to Pascal to write a defence of Christian faith. His health was poor and getting worse, but he struggled at the work until his death in 1662 when the unfinished manuscript of his *Pensées* was edited by his friends.

His object was to combat the cultured scepticism, the sophisticated Stoicism, he had met, and indeed shared, in the salons. Once again, therefore, he wrote for the *honnêtes gens*, with the same innate faith in the power of reason to convince others. In this respect he was still in the Cartesian tradition, as adapted by Port-Royal, by regarding reason as an essential guide to the conduct of life, and man as preeminently superior to the rest of creation by virtue of his power of thought. '*L'homme n'est qu'un roseau, le plus faible de la nature, mais c'est un roseau pensant*—Man is only a reed, the weakest to be found in nature; but he is a *thinking* reed. It is not necessary for the whole of nature to take up arms to crush him: a puff of smoke, a drop of water is enough to kill him. But, even if the universe should crush him, man would still be more noble than that which destroys him, because he knows that he dies and he realises the advantage which the universe possesses over him. The universe knows nothing of this. All our dignity, then, consists in thought. It is upon this that we must depend, not on space and time, which we would not in any case be able to fill. Let us labour, then, to think well: this is the foundation of morality—*Travaillons donc à bien penser: voilà le principe de la morale.*'

But *le roseau pensant* discovers he cannot comprehend the purpose of the universe, and reason staggers before the contemplation of the infinitely minute and the infinitely vast: '*Le silence éternel de ces espaces infinis m'effraie.*' Descartes's decision to appeal to 'the sole light of reason' is therefore found to be inadequate; it is a claim for human self-sufficiency which Pascal has to repudiate, and does so with tremendous effect: '*Connaissez donc, superbe, quel paradoxe vous êtes à vous-même. Humiliez-vous, raison impuissante; taisez-vous, nature imbécile . . . et entendez de votre maître votre condition que vous ignorez. Écoutez Dieu.*' For all his powers, man cannot prove the existence of God by reason, and it is here that Pascal parted company with his colleagues at Port-Royal. In place of the Cartesian assumptions about our 'natural, clear and certain idea of God's existence', which Nicole had embodied in the Port-Royal *Logique*, Pascal proposed a simple gamble on the issue of God's existence and the immortality of the soul. To win is to win everything; to lose is to lose nothing.

Pascal's final conclusion agreed with the doctrine associated with Jansen and with the whole community of Port-Royal that God is essentially God the Redeemer, and that man is nothing but the unworthy object of His redemption. In a dramatic contrast between *La Misère de l'Homme sans Dieu* and *La Félicité de l'Homme avec Dieu*, he brings to bear not only Jansenist theology but great powers of analysis and psychological observation, but that which separates him, even from his colleagues at Port-Royal, is the black mood of pessimism which runs through the *Pensées*. It is as if Pascal wanted to humiliate mankind as much as possible in order to enhance the power of God's grace, and to destroy once and for all the illusion that man can do anything at all towards his own salvation.

Pascal was chided for this extreme pessimism by Mme de Sablé: 'When important people want to make you believe that they have some special quality which they have not, it is dangerous to show that you doubt them, for in depriving them of the hope of being able to deceive the rest of the world you also deprive them of the desire to undertake such fine actions as are appropriate to the quality they affect to possess.' From a Jesuit this would have been misinterpreted, but Mme de Sablé was a devout Jansenist and a close friend of Pascal. Her salon surpassed all but the Hôtel de Rambouillet for its literary and aristocratic associations, but it was unfortunately short-lived and irregular in its sessions as she never liked having too many people around her, and in 1656 she took private rooms within Port-Royal itself. Contemporaries agreed that she was extremely attractive, and Mlle de Scudéry portrayed her as Parthénie in *Le Grand Cyrus*, whose 'conversation was no less charming than her features'. She was also well read. Arnauld consulted her about the introduction to the Port-Royal *Logique*, and her close friend was Conrart, the bibliophile, who kept a detailed record of the salon's activities. It was she who established a fashion for condensing thoughts and experiences of life in maxims, which, as opposed to epigrams, were not supposed to sacrifice truth to wit. Her own were indifferent; '*L'amour est à l'âme de celui qui aime ce que l'âme est au corps qu'il aime*'; but in her salon Pascal polished up many of his *Pensées*, and the greatest exponent of the genre was another close friend, La Rochefoucauld.

François, prince de Marsillac, later duc de la Rochefoucauld, had a disastrous career, largely due to his own folly. On behalf of Anne d'Autriche he engaged in plots against Richelieu, and later, as a passionate lover of Mme de Longueville, he intrigued against his former mistress in the Fronde. Eventually he became disenchanted with the whole business, tried but failed to reconcile Condé and Mazarin, was wounded and retired to his estates. In an attempt to justify his record he wrote a history of the Fronde for circulation among his friends, but it was pirated and published in the Netherlands, with many fictitious additions which harmed his reputation.

For all his proud title and ancestry it was a pension from the bourgeois Fouquet which saved him from penury and allowed him to return to Paris in 1656 to enjoy the one consolation left to him in life, the conversation of the salons. He described this as one of the greatest pleasures, although he added with characteristic honesty, 'what makes so few people agreeable in conversation is that each one pays more attention to what he wants to say than to what is being said'. Mme de Sablé had already begun her semi-retirement within Port-Royal, but he became a constant visitor to her rooms. He also attended the Hôtel de Nevers whose hostess, Mme du Plessis-Guénégaud, was married to a Treasury official and was therefore closely linked with the fortunes of Fouquet. Despite this, her salon was very much a centre for Jansenists, and she helped to disseminate the *Lettres Provinciales*. In her house La Rochefoucauld met Mme de la Fayette, who became the most brilliant novelist of the century and with whom he found true happiness. Their long and platonic friendship was the one thing to save him from complete despair in his old age when he became chairbound by illness, and when his sons, especially his most precious son by Mme de Longueville, were killed in the Dutch war. Of their friendship Mme de la Fayette wrote; '*Il m'a donné de l'esprit mais j'ai réformé son cœur*', not that he was dissolute or corrupt in heart, but that he was near to despair until she had reconciled him to the value of existence.

The composition of maxims, or sentences as they were called in the salons, enjoyed a brief popularity, the *jeu des sentences* rivalling the *jeu des portraits*, but La Rochefoucauld discovered in himself a particular skill in this genre. Encouraged by Mme de Sablé—with whom he discussed them so much that he once wrote that 'The maxims only become maxims after you have approved them'—he conceived the idea of publishing a collection, not to divert but to

26. Versailles—a performance of Lully's *Alceste* within the original *cour d'honneur* of Louis XIII's Château

27. Versailles—the Salon de la Guerre by Charles Le Brun (see page 252)

provide moral instruction. Then, as he saw less of Mme de Sablé, his enthusiasm faded, though in 1663 he took out the manuscript to rewrite it. In 1664, when he learned that a pirated version was being published in Holland, he swiftly issued his own edition in the same year and continued to expand, revise and reprint it until his death in 1680.

A certain shyness of character had long encouraged him to imagine himself the disembodied observer of mankind, and the salons had developed not only a taste for psychological analysis but, after a generation of *conversations d'esprit*, considerable practice in using language with economy, precision and epigrammatic skill. Voltaire described the *Maximes* as 'one of the works which most contributed to form the taste of the nation and give it a spirit of nicety and precision.... The little collection was read with eagerness; and it accustomed people to think and to express their thoughts in a vivid, concise and elegant manner.' As for content, a dominant influence was the memory of his own disjointed career, of what he termed *la comédie du monde*, the swift reversals of fortune, the inconstancy of friends, the uncertainties of war and the ingratitude of the great. This cynical pessimism was corroborated by the severe strictures on humanity made by the Jansenists of Port-Royal, and made him as ruthless as Pascal in stripping away man's self-delusions and hypocrisy. The *Maximes* were debated not only with Mme de Sablé but with another Jansenist, Jacques Esprit, as rigorous as Pascal in his view of man's incapacity without grace, and it was Esprit who encouraged him to publish them so that their corrosive analysis might destroy for ever the *libertin* belief in the 'natural' virtues supposedly enjoyed by ancient Romans and other pagans.

*L'hypocrisé est un hommage que le vice rend à la vertu.*

*Nos vertus ne sont le plus souvent que des vices déguisés.*

*Le plus grand effort de l'amitié n'est pas pour montrer nos défauts à un ami: c'est de lui faire voir les siens.*

*Nous nous consolons aisément des disgrâces de nos amis lorsqu'elles servent à signaler notre tendresse pour eux.*

*On a fait une vertu de la modération, pour borner l'ambition des grands hommes et pour consoler les gens médiocres de leur peu de fortune et de leur peu de mérite.*★

In these highly polished phrases which charm even as they wound La Rochefoucauld destroys mankind's pretensions to virtue. He reveals moreover a strong element of fatalism. Echoing Pascal—'The most important thing in life, the choice of a job, is determined by chance'—he wrote: '*L'homme est conduit lorsqu'il croit se conduire*'; but he went further, influenced almost certainly by Descartes's *Traité des Passions*, in describing man as subject as much to his own inner passions as he is to forces of chance. The case for man the automaton is stated in its most succinct form.

*Toutes les passions ne sont que les divers degrés de la chaleur et de la froideur du sang.*

*La force et la faiblesse de l'esprit sont mal nommées: elles ne sont, en effet, que la bonne ou la mauvaise disposition des organes du corps.*†

'What corruption there must have been in his heart and in his soul to have imagined all this', wrote Mme de la Fayette in anguish; and the cheerless philosophy was condemned as universally as its expression was admired. Port-Royal could of course claim, as Jacques Esprit had intended, that the destruction of 'natural virtue' made all the more necessary a belief in the omnipotent power of grace but, for all his close association with Port-Royal, it is not altogether certain that this was La Rochefoucauld's ultimate intention. Rather, the object of his moral instruction may well have been to show man what a depraved, selfish thing he was in order that he might rise above his abandoned nature—not for fear of punishment

---

★ Hypocrisy is a tribute which vice pays to virtue.

Our virtues are only too often our vices in disguise.

The greatest service of friendship is not to reveal our faults to a friend but to show him his own.

We console ourselves very easily when the sufferings of our friends provide an occasion for us to demonstrate our concern for them.

We have made a virtue of moderation in order to limit the ambitions of the great, and to console the mediocre for their lack of luck and for their lack of merit.

† The whole range of our passions only reflects the warmth or coldness of our blood.

Strength and weakness of character are badly named: they represent nothing more than the good or bad disposition of our body's organs.

nor for love of God but because this is required of anyone presuming to be *honnête homme*. Such a man will not be content with displays of good manners and conversational finesse; he will be absolutely honest with himself and with others. '*Les faux honnêtes gens sont ceux qui déguisent leurs défauts aux autres et à eux-mêmes; les vrais honnêtes gens sont ceux qui les connaissent parfaitement et les confessent.*'* Thus, although the *Maximes* are not unchristian and owe a great debt to Pascal and Mme de Sablé, it seems that ultimately the ideal of the salon triumphed over the ideal of Port-Royal. '*Ainsi*', wrote Lanson, '*les Maximes sont comme le testament moral de la société précieuse. Elles sont aussi son testament littéraire.*'

So literary was the milieu of Port-Royal and so well-read its members that it is difficult to believe that one of them, Nicole, could write: 'Novelists and dramatists publicly poison not the bodies but the souls of the faithful. . . . Poets are the masters and the apostles of self-love. . . . Poetry is the art of lying.' We know in fact that Nicole had written most moderately about Corneille, but the point is that as a matter of principle the Jansenists mistrusted pleasure, in all its forms. It was not enough to mortify the body, to discipline it by depriving it of its pleasures; as thorough-going puritans they condemned pleasure itself and followed the Cistercian tradition of maintaining that the arts are dangerous vanities which, by giving pleasure, can seduce the soul. Agnès Arnauld expressed this clearly when she wrote: 'The more we deprive the senses, the more we enhance the soul, and with every pleasure we derive from visible things so we impoverish the life of grace.' But as it was well nigh impossible for these sophisticated men and women, most of whom had lived in the salons, to repudiate the arts altogether, they declared them acceptable if they aided devotion. This meant that there could be neither frivolity nor falsehood, no paganism, no fantasy, no nudity. It was not surprising, therefore, that Port-Royal stood in stark opposition to the baroque.

We have noted already that the sophisticated eclecticism and abandonment of the rules which characterised painting and architec-

---

* The bogus *honnêtes gens* disguise their weaknesses from others and from themselves; the true *honnêtes gens* know them by heart and admit them.

ture in the mannerist period was accompanied by a new awareness of spiritual needs which found no solace in the optimistic humanism of the High Renaissance. The Church welcomed this new mood of meditation and quiet ecstasy, but was unable to exploit it. In the period of the Counter-Reformation something more aggressive, more dramatic and more convincing was required if the senses and emotions of the people were to be fully engaged. A church could not remain a retreat for private meditation, nor even an auditorium for sermons; it had to appear before the faithful as the House of God in all the splendour and panoply appropriate to the houses of great kings.

The propaganda effects of architecture were first exploited by the Jesuits in della Porta's church of the Gesù (1568), but the style reached its magnificent climax at Rome in the seventeenth century with architects like Bernini and Borromini. In planning a church to be the focal point of the neighbourhood, it was not enough to design an imposing façade, nor even to raise a mighty dome above the roof-tops; the planning had to extend beyond the building to the flights of steps, the balustrades, the fountains and the squares. No longer was one form placed by another to satisfy a logical principle, or to establish a mood of serenity and balance; the overriding principle was the creation of moods of splendour, drama and power. To achieve this the baroque architects swept away the conventional rules, not in the sophisticated, self-conscious style of the mannerists, but with a supremely self-confident recklessness. Instead of articulating the storeys with the appropriate orders, they not only ran colossal pillars up the entire façade but dramatised the effect by grouping them in pairs or by carving them into spirals. Straight lines were replaced by curves, and Borromini's façades were a complex study in concave–convex forms.

Art which is wholly baroque is always part of a whole, a detail which loses its meaning when detached from its context in a greater organic unity; consequently it is difficult to consider a baroque painting in isolation from the building or room it was designed for. In the ceiling of the Jesuit church of the Gesù, for example, the volutes and lozenges of the roof are painted in, to be broken in the centre as though the roof had opened to admit a heavenly host, some of whom are seen as against the sky while others appear to ride on clouds within the canopy of the church itself. Baroque painting can be generally identified, therefore, as decorative painting in the grand manner. It is expansive and naturalist, and, in order to create striking illusions of reality, it uses light with dramatic effect.

Baroque swept swiftly through most of Catholic Europe, and even affected the art-forms of Protestant states, but it made very little impact on Paris. For one thing the chronology of stylistic development in France had become confused; mannerism had been imported before classicism had been fully established, and the classical style of which baroque was so directly a development was only just being achieved by de Brosse, Mansart, Vouet and Poussin. Artists and patrons alike were therefore reluctant to abandon something which to them was new and which so readily satisfied their needs, and we have seen already that those who returned from Italy soon modified their style to suit French taste. Great artists of course have frequently succeeded in educating their own people to appreciate new styles, but there was a particular resistance to baroque because of its association with the more emotional and demonstrative features of the Counter-Reformation. French Catholics had too great a love of order, and too great a respect for the intellect, to approve the spiritual hysteria and the passionate mysticism to be found in Spain and Italy. Their mood was more akin to that initial and austere phase of the Counter-Reformation which had been so short-lived at Rome, and they regarded with an equally cold eye both the devotional excesses of Saint Teresa's followers and the portrayal of her ecstasy by Bernini.

Nor was this mood a passing one. The French tradition of valuing intellect above emotion was deeply rooted. In the twelfth century St Bernard had opposed the unrestrained soaring to the heavens of Benedictine architecture, and Suger's defence was no less characteristic. It served, he explained, to raise not only the heart but also the mind to God. Similarly, André Suarès writes of Notre-Dame de Paris, whose Gothic façade reveals vertical and horizontal divisions as clearly stressed as in any composition of the classical period, 'if classicism represents a sense of order imposed on feeling by reason, a calculation elaborated by the intellect to bestow upon passion the divine privilege of immortality, Notre-Dame is the most classical of churches'.

The baroque, therefore, was rejected because its emotional and theatrical qualities were regarded as an unwelcome distraction from spiritual communion and meditation. More often than not a church was repaired or rebuilt in its original Gothic style, even by the Jesuits whose links with Rome were especially strong, but some Italian ideas were introduced from time to time. Étienne Martellange was a Jesuit priest who had spent 14 years in studying Roman architecture at first hand, and from 1604 he toured France as a kind of inspector of the Society's buildings until his succession by Père Turmel in 1635. Martellange imposed no plan but always collaborated with a local architect, and thus there is no uniformity about his churches at Le Puy, La Flèche and Avignon. The church of the Gesù was of course a dominant influence because its aisleless nave was particularly suitable for the dramatic re-enactment of the Mass, which was a feature of Jesuit worship, since it allowed a clear view of the altar by all the congregation. His greatest church was perhaps the Saint-Paul-Saint-Louis in Paris, which he built with Père Durand. Louis XIII laid the foundation stone in 1627, and Richelieu celebrated its first Mass in 1641. It has a massive aisleless nave whose height recalls the Gothic churches, though the colossal Corinthian pilasters which rise to the entablature and gallery are clearly derived from Rome. Unlike the Gesù, however, the church has transepts, and the illumination from the dome above the crossing throws a special light upon the altar.

The introduction of the dome was perhaps the most obvious and the most popular of baroque motifs, and Lavedan suggests that as Gothic architects had rivalled each other in raising the height of their cathedrals, so in seventeenth-century Paris there was a similar battle of the domes. The first was a simple half-sphere of wood and plaster for the church of Saint-Joseph des Carmes (1613–20), and this was followed by those at the Sorbonne and the Val-de-Grâce. Here, as we have seen, Le Mercier achieved the effect of greater height by terminating the dome of the Sorbonne with a spire in place of a cupola, and by constructing at the Val-de-Grâce a false timber dome above the masonry of the inner shell. The ultimate victory went to Mansart's great-nephew, Jules Hardouin-Mansart, who created a double drum for Les Invalides which makes the two-storeyed façade appear to be no more than a simple podium. This of course was a logical development since there was no point in constructing a dome if a lofty façade obscured some of it from view— a baroque concept, perhaps, which led Richelieu to clear a space for the Place de la Sorbonne so that his new church and its dome could be seen to advantage.

The religious painting of the period was dominated to a great extent by Vouet, as we have seen, and though there were marked characteristics of the baroque in his earlier work he soon conformed to the more restrained and formal tastes of his public. One of his pupils who achieved considerable success in the same genre was Eustache Le Sueur, a quiet, simple man who had none of Vouet's taste for fashionable society. His father was a turner, his son became a grocer and he himself remained unpretentiously artisan. His early work at the Hôtel Lambert was a competent pastiche of Vouet's decorative style, and later, though he never went to Italy, he modelled himself closely on Raphael. His religious paintings, however, were among his best because they were the least decorative of his works. In them he reveals greater maturity, combining an interest in the psychology of his subjects with an essentially classical approach to their construction. He stands midway between the ecstasy of the baroque and the asceticism of Port-Royal, introducing a degree of tenderness which just avoids becoming sentimental. His most re-strained and most talented work in this genre was the provision of 22 scenes in the life of St Bruno for a cloister of the Charterhouse of Paris. These, damaged by exposure to the air, were later transferred to the Louvre, but they do not need their original surrounding to inform us of their purpose. They recall quite simply and with origin-ality a mood of monastic calm and meditation which is rarely found in seventeenth-century painting.

The artist most admired at Port-Royal was Philippe de Cham-

paigne. In 1643 he was attracted to Port-Royal by the sincere devotion and strict life of its members, and stayed in close touch with
them thereafter. His work, which had already begun to shed the
baroque traits derived from Rubens, became increasingly austere
with no trace of ecstasies, visions and *putti*. In his severe compositions,
the cool, strong colours, the clarity and lucidity, the intellectual
appeal, all indicate an independent advance towards a classical style
similar to that which Poussin was perfecting in Rome.

Many of his later works were portraits of the Port-Royal leaders
—which raised an interesting question. Nicole maintained that it was
nothing less than an indication of overweening pride to have one's
portrait made, but it was finally resolved that the propaganda value
of the portraits, engraved and disseminated among the faithful
minority across France, justified the spiritual danger. The portraits,
of course, are singularly free of wordly affectation, emphasising the
character of the face, and it is not surprising that some were done from
mortuary masks. The sobriety and the sharp observation also
appealed to many of the Parisian bourgeois, and not just to those
who were buying Poussins, but to many sober *officiers* who sympa-
thised with the Jansenists against their ultramontane rivals and who
were glad to commission an artist in favour at Port-Royal. If they
were often self-important they were also aware of the sin of pride,
and they demanded neither glorification nor extenuation of their
features. Consequently Champaigne's three great studies of the
Paris *échevins* and his individual portraits of lawyers and merchants
reveal great sensitivity to character, and a gravity of manner which is
accentuated by the black clothes and the sombre backgrounds. In a
few he used a Dutch technique of *trompe-l'œil*, letting the sitter's
hand rest on the frame, but generally the pose was wholly classical
and without suggestion of movement.

He painted a 'Last Supper' for the nuns, and a stark 'Crucifixion'
in the year of his death (1674), but his spiritual masterpiece was
inspired by a second Port-Royal miracle and one of particular importance to himself. When his daughter who had joined the nuns
was struck with paralysis, Mère Agnès, Angélique's sister and successor, successfully declared a novena that she might be cured. In

commemoration of the event, Champaigne re-created the scene in a
manner which represents the Jansenist riposte to Bernini's swooning
saint. The composition could scarcely be more simple. Mère Agnès
kneels at right angles to the chair where the artist's daughter lies,
each in black and grey against a plain background of grey walls.
They wait motionless and calm: only the half-perceived ray of light
which falls between them tells that a miracle is taking place.

*seven*

# Classicism

One of the most important features of French classicism in the seventeenth century was the universal veneration of reason. 'We must always have recourse to reason', wrote the Jansenist, Nicole. 'It is simple and certain and by its light we discover true natural beauty.' Balzac declared it to be 'a holy thing', and Boileau urged everyone to admire it:

> *Aimez donc la raison: que toujours vos écrits*
> *Empruntent d'elle seule et leur lustre et leur prix.**

Descartes, too, had written in praise of reason, asserting the superiority of mind over matter and assigning to reason the power of discovering general truth, but Cartesian rationalism should not be identified too precisely with the reason extolled by Boileau. There was of course a close association of ideas: there seemed to be a direct application of *l'esprit géométrique* to the art of landscape and town-planning, and Fontenelle maintained that 'the order, the neatness, the precision, the exactness prevailing in good books for some time may well be due to that geometrical spirit which is now more widespread than before'. Jean-Baptiste Rousseau, however, complained that 'Descartes's philosophy has cut poetry's throat'. In the event they were both mistaken. It was Malherbe and the Académie Française who robbed poetry to pay prose, and the prose of that great

* Let us therefore love reason; let your writings always borrow from her alone both their lustre and their value.

geometer, Pascal, owed more to the conversations of the salons than to mathematics.

It was not Cartesian logic therefore which underlay and informed the classical mood so much as a general regard for good sense. 'We all believe that good sense, clear thinking and reason are one and the same thing', wrote Bussy-Rabutin to Corneille. When the French expressed their love of reason they were demonstrating in fact their profound respect for the power of the intellect. Even in religious matters, and at a time of considerable spiritual revival, they avoided the emotional excesses of devotional fervour by firmly subordinating sentiment to intellect; and their religious teaching, whether Jesuit or Jansenist, encouraged the taste for self-examination and psychological analysis which lies at the heart of French classical literature. The salons, as we have seen, cultivated the same quality. The *jeu des sentences*, the *jeu des portraits* and the *questions d'amour*, for all the occasional triviality, were intellectual exercises in which the universal ideal was a standard of calm, dispassionate observation— as extolled by Boileau:

> *Qu'est-ce que la sagesse? une égalité d'âme*
> *Que rien ne peut troubler, qu'aucun désir n'enflamme.**

Emotional restraint was an essential corollary to the intellectual quality of French classicism, since it was the classic's determination to see the whole of life reasonably and calmly which prompted him to suppress private emotion lest it distort his vision. The literature of the period tells us little of the lives and personalities of its authors. Malherbe always maintained that the Pléiade had overdone the public expression of its private emotions, and he set a standard of restraint which became generally universal by mid-century. Apart from the savage outburst on his son's murder, no one could know from his other works of the randy old bear, M. Luxe, with a reputation for unkind repartee. It is misleading, too, as we have seen, to examine the plays of Molière in the hope of discovering his personal testament; it was not an age of Confessions, and even the *mémoire* writers concentrated more on the observation of events than the

* What then is wisdom? An equanimity of mind which nothing can trouble and no desires inflame.

revelation of their own responses. Although La Rochefoucauld transposed his own personal experience into generalised statements, so polished were these, so disembodied and so cold, that we can scarcely discern the disillusioned Frondeur, and still less the devoted inseparable friend of a lonely, sick woman.

This is because the classical writer emphasised the universal, not the particular. Man is studied as a universal phenomenon, not for the individual characteristics which separate him from other men, but for the common traits by which mankind is bound together. 'I was delighted to see', wrote Racine in the preface to *Iphigénie*, 'by the effect on our stage of everything which I have imitated from Homer or Euripides, that good sense and reason are the same in every century. Taste in Paris turned out to be in line with that in Athens.' Such literature is therefore social literature; in seventeenth-century France it was also socially conformist. Accepting as wholly natural the social and political institutions of the time, it produced neither revolutionaries nor prophets, but gifted observers of the human condition.

In painting, the taste for historical, religious and mythical scenes demonstrated the same point. Man in his many moods and situations remained the chief object of the artist's interest, and even the landscapes of Poussin are essentially *paysages humanisés*. The classical style in architecture was one in which man was aware of himself as the measure of the building: he was not imposed upon nor reduced to awe but reassured and satisfied by its order and balance. Château Maisons was such a building and Voltaire in describing it expressed the essential character of classicism:

> *Simple en était la noble architecture*
> *Chaque ornement en sa place arrêté*
> *Y semblent mis par la nécessité:*
> *L'art s'y cachait sous l'air de la nature*
> *L'œil satisfait embrassait sa structure*
> *Jamais surpris et toujours enchanté.**

* Its noble architecture was simplicity itself. Each ornament held in its place seemed to be there by necessity. Art hid behind a natural appearance. The eye, regarding the whole structure with satisfaction, was never taken unawares, was always enchanted.

Malherbe's rules on caesura and *enjambement* and the clear articulation of a façade, with string-courses to strengthen the horizontal line or pilasters to emphasise the vertical, both reflect a preoccupation with order and clarity which is another hallmark of classicism. Linked with it was a vital sense of balance and proportion. Fléchier, bishop of Nîmes, in a funeral oration on Julie, duchesse de Montausier, referred to the special qualities of her mother's salon at the Hôtel de Rambouillet: it was, he said, 'a select court, well attended but not crowded, modest but not constrained, learned but not proud, polished but not affected'. This, not merely for what he says about the salon, but for what he chooses to say, exemplifies the spirit of classicism. Unlike the romantic who creates in the full vigour of his emotion, the classic subordinates emotion to his intellect and he seeks to distil the essential nature of his experience. Moreover he must express it simply and without pretension, for as Boileau wrote, 'an author spoils everything by trying to do too much'—which is as valid a comment on the façades of Jacques Androuet du Cerceau as on the verses of a salon poet. To achieve this the classic returns endlessly to polish a phrase or to check a design, knowing that the more intense his emotion the greater the care he must exercise in communicating it. It is to this rigorous self-discipline, therefore, that we owe the craftsmanship, the clarity and the apparent simplicity of classical masterpieces like the *Maximes* and the Château Maisons.

Frenchmen of the classical age believed they were making universal statements about nature, including human nature, but if nature was their model it was subjected to a great deal of intellectual screening before it was portrayed in word or on canvas. Whatever was accidental, ephemeral or local had to be removed, along with whatever seemed ugly or deformed. This was to subordinate nature to art, a view expressed by Félibien in an influential study of aesthetics, *L'idée du peintre parfait*: 'Although nature is the source of beauty, art surpasses nature because we find in nature that individual objects are usually imperfect in some way; nature intends that everything should be perfect but is frustrated by accidents.' This critical view was echoed by many Frenchmen: Colbert bemoaned nature's irregularity when issuing instructions to his *intendants*; and

Malebranche, Descartes's principal apologist, followed his mentor
in describing beauty as the imitation of order, and in pointing out
that, 'the visible world would be more perfect if the seas and lands
made more regular figures; . . . if, in a word, there were fewer
monstrosities and less disorder'.

This matter was not confined to painters or poets. The abbé
d'Aubignac, in his *Pratique du Théâtre*, declared: 'It is a generally
accepted principle that the theatre is not concerned with truth.'
What he sought to emphasise by this was the vital distinction which
we have already examined between *le vrai* and *le vraisemblable*.
D'Aubignac pointed out that whatever ghastly scenes occur in life,
the stage is not the place to show them all, and that the coincidences
of real life appear false in a play. People do drop dead, 'but anyone
who brought a play to a conclusion by making a rival die of apoplexy would be mocked at by everyone'. Art must improve upon
reality, and it was for doing this that Balzac praised Corneille's recreation of ancient Rome: 'You have been able to do this by the
conventions of an art which refines and embellishes the truth, and
which sometimes suggests that you copy directly and at other times
improve upon your model.' Perhaps the most important dictum on
the subject was that in the *Sentiments de l'Académie sur le Cid*, when it
advised an author who dealt with an historical episode 'to reduce it
to the bounds of decency without bothering too much about the
truth, and to alter the whole thing entirely rather than to leave
anything which might clash with the rules of his art, which, by
offering a universal view of things, purifies them of the faults and
individual irregularities which history, by its own strict code, has
to endure'.

Indeed, it was not enough merely to select from nature what was
beautiful or desirable. Rapin in his *Réflexions sur la poétique* reminded
poets that 'nature has hidden charms which you must uncover for
yourself'. Raphael, for example, had revealed how he did this when
he wrote about his Galatea to his friend Castiglione: 'I must tell you
that whenever I have to paint a beautiful woman it is necessary that
I see a number of beauties (with the stipulation that you be present
to choose the most beautiful!). Since, however, there is a dearth of

such accomplished connoisseurs of woman, as well as of beautiful women themselves, I depend upon a certain ideal and idea that I have in my mind.' Everything therefore depends upon what 'ideal' or 'idea' the artist or writer has in his mind. All styles of art, whether realist, romantic or classical, involve selection since none sets out to reproduce nature in its totality; the difference between them is determined by the principles which govern the process of selection. French classicism accepted two such principles—the good example of past masters, especially the ancients, and the rules deduced from their practice or arrived at independently in the light of reason.

This interest in classical masters did not spring from any blind enthusiasm for the past. The *honnêtes hommes* abominated pedantry and associated it particularly with classical scholarship; moreover, while the fervour of the Catholic revival induced a greater suspicion of a pagan culture than was evident in the sixteenth century, the scientific revolution discredited much of its authority. Few agreed with de Viau in his reference to ' *la sotte antiquité*' but their attitude was neither awe-struck nor nostalgic—indeed nostalgia for the past was a particular feature of romanticism. The French studied classical models as Poussin did: not to copy them but to discover how the problems which confronted them had been solved in the past. In their endeavour to distinguish the essence from the accidental in nature they believed that works which had so successfully withstood the test of time must embody what is constant and universal: 'The antiquity of a writer is no certain guarantee of his merit', wrote Boileau, 'but the long-standing and constant admiration in which his works have always been held is a certain and infallible proof that we too ought to admire them.' It was this respect for the practical achievement of the classics of antiquity that prompted Corneille to write: 'I owe them respect as men who blazed the trail and cleared the rough countryside which they have left to us to cultivate.'

The French looked to classical antiquity for inspiration and help. They did not intend to reproduce it. When La Fontaine, for example, advised his son to study Cicero, Horace and Virgil he did not expect him to write like them but to learn from them the qualities of precision and clarity. Similarly, when the French formulated rules from their observation of antiquity and from their own common sense and experience, their intention was simply to make their own task that much easier. Just as France finally gave acceptance to the concept of centralised royal authority, not on account of any Divine Right theories but because it seemed reasonable and altogether preferable to the alternatives of noble anarchy or provincial autonomy, so French writers and artists accepted the authority of the rules and practice of the ancients, in so far as they were of use to them. '*La règle?*', said Chapelain, 'It is common sense become law.' To rely on it was not a sign of impoverished inspiration; on the contrary, the stronger and richer the inspiration, the more necessary it was to regulate it.

Although the rules were an important feature of French classicism it was only the later academicians who believed that their literature and art was classical *because* of the rules it observed—and it was Molière's character who exploded the unnecessary mystique which surrounded them. 'It would seem from listening to you that these rules of art [ie poetry] are the greatest mysteries in the world, but in fact they are only a few commonsense observations on things which might otherwise impair the pleasure we get from these poems.' The cardinal aim affirmed by artists, poets and playwrights was to give pleasure. The rules were designed to assist this, but men of talent were not indissolubly bound to them. 'I like to follow the rules', wrote Corneille, 'but far from making myself their slave I stretch or twist them according to the needs of the subject. As for the rule about unity of action, I break it without any qualms if its severity in my opinion interferes with the creation of dramatic beauty.'

Nicole, in the preface to an anthology of religious verse, went to the heart of the matter. He argued that whatever one's theories about poetic beauty, the important thing was that a poem should be able to stir the reader's emotions—endorsing Pascal's remark, 'You can never prove that you ought to be loved by simply setting down the causes of love'—and he insisted that the appreciation of beauty involved 'something altogether more subtle than the rules, and

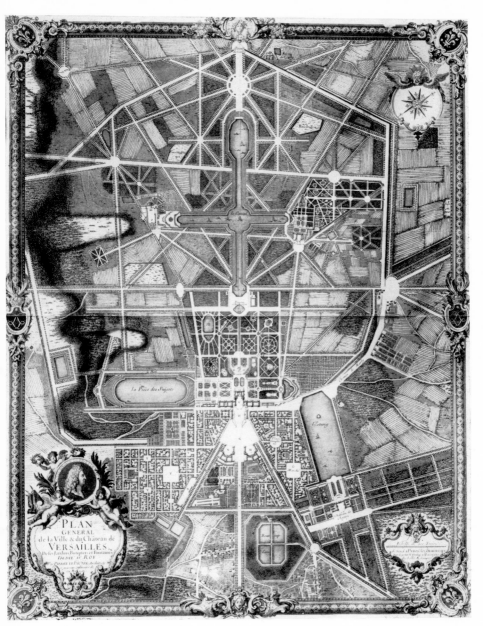

28. Versailles—general plan of Le Nôtre's gardens (see pages 223–6)

29. Versailles—the Orangery, designed by François Mansart (see page 224)

which I call *sentiment* or *goût*'. *Goût*, taste, or the secret of giving
pleasure was of course as ill-defined, even in that age of analysis, as
was *esprit* in the conversations of the salons. La Fontaine tried to
define it as 'something piquant and pleasurable', but this was mere
tautology for, as Pascal admitted, 'no one really knows the nature
of the pleasure given by poetry'. The same problem faced Roger de
Piles in his treatise on aesthetics: 'In painting there ought to be
something out of the ordinary, something piquant, something truly
great, which can take us by surprise, please us and instruct us, and
this I call *le grand goût*: it is this quality which makes ordinary things
beautiful, and beautiful things marvellous and sublime.' Frenchmen,
therefore, in an age which so highly respected definition and regulation, were reduced to a perpetual reference to *je-ne-sais-quoi* in
order to communicate their sense of the indefinable quality of great
art and literature.

In our preoccupation with the intellectual basis of French classicism, its rigorous craftsmanship, its regulation and restraint, we may
well overlook its emotive qualities. These may be less obviously
evident when set against the work of Romantic poets or baroque
painters, but without them classicism would never have triumphed in
mid-century France. The patrons of the period were turbulent and
passionate to excess, and no matter how profoundly they came to
respect the virtues of order and restraint in the arts, they were not
prepared to endure boredom. Poetry, it is true, suffered badly from
the reaction against personal statements of emotion or frivolous
flights of fancy, but there was a compensating delicacy and vigour
in the theatre. Racine emphasised that 'the principal rule is to give
pleasure and stir the emotions'; Corneille's *tirades* had no other
purpose but to arouse passion; and Molière stated the case for lively
involvement with characteristic bluntness: 'Let us go frankly for
things which grip us by the entrails, and never bother to find reasons
to stop us enjoying ourselves.' Intellect may control passion; it does
not kill it. Indeed, by refining, it may intensify it. Château Maisons
arouses an emotional response by its very clarity and order, and the
works of Poussin, the most restrained, at times the coldest, of French
artists, have an intensity of their own. 'The sensuality, which in

Rubens's paintings is totally overwhelming, is none the less powerful in Poussin's for being severely held in check' (André Gide).

It was Poussin more than any other painter who embodied the
qualities we have associated with French classicism, even though he
spent most of his life in Rome. A peasant's son, born in 1594 near
Les Andelys in Normandy, he was brought up without any thought
of an artist's career. It was not until he was 17 that a minor painter,
Quentin Varin, came to work in the village church, and this apparently aroused Poussin's interest to such a degree that within a
year he had left for Rouen, thence to Paris, to serve his apprenticeship in an artist's workshop. His movements after this are not clear.
He made one visit to Florence in 1620 and another to Lyon in 1623—
abortive efforts to reach Rome—and in the intervening years was
employed with Phillippe de Champaigne at the Luxembourg. He
was given commissions too by Marie de' Medici's Italian poet,
Marino, but from what survives there is no indication of genius in
his work, which was merely competent decoration in the mannerist
style of Fontainebleau.

In 1624 Poussin reached Rome at last, but to no good effect.
Marino, on whom he had intended to rely for employment, introduced him to the influential Cardinal Francesco Barberini, but died
within a year, and Poussin found it impossible to settle happily into
the style of baroque composition demanded by the Italians. When
Barberini secured for him a much-envied commission to paint a
martyrdom of St Erasmus for St Peter's he was unable to rise to the
occasion and produce the great masterpiece which might have made
his name. For several years he suffered poverty and illness and, above
all, the frustration of an artist unable to find a style congenial to his
own nature and talents. In 1630, however, his marriage to the daughter
of a French chef seems to have been the turning point in his life. He
no longer undertook the large altarpieces and allegorical wall-paint-
ings for which he had no aptitude, but began instead to paint relatively small pictures for a learned and sophisticated group of patrons
who centred around Barberini's secretary, the Commendatore
Cassiano del Pozzo, and who shared his enthusiasm for the sculpture
and architecture of ancient Rome. It was this type of clientèle that

Poussin was to find the most congenial, and for the next ten years he painted scenes from mythology and the Old Testament—notably the 'Golden Calf' and the 'Crossing of the Red Sea'—in which he began to demonstrate a surer sense of style, moving away from the mannerism of his youth and the baroque of his environment to a style more reminiscent of Raphael, and developing not only a talent for balanced composition but also a taste for psychological observation.

It was not surprising therefore that his pictures began to attract interest in Paris. Richelieu had already bought the 'Bacchanals', but it was Paul Fréart de Chanteloup, owner of the 'Israelites collecting the Manna', who became his most devoted admirer. As secretary to Sublet de Noyers, the *surintendant des bâtiments*, responsible for the decoration of all royal palaces, de Chanteloup was in a strong position to bring Poussin's work to Louis XIII's attention. The result was an official invitation to Poussin to return to Paris, and a triumphal reception on his arrival in 1640. But everything went wrong. Poussin was not only beset with too many commissions but most of them were of the kind he had failed with in Rome—a series of allegories for Richelieu, a number of altarpieces, and the large-scale decoration of the Grande Galerie of the Louvre. His sense of inadequacy was made worse by the jealous opposition of Vouet and Le Mercier, who resented his influence with Louis and Richelieu, and after 18 months he abruptly abandoned everything and left for Rome.

The visit to Paris had one fortunate result since Poussin was able to meet Paul Fréart de Chanteloup, and his brother Roland who was a scholar with a tremendous interest in the arts. Roland made several visits to Italy and published, among other works, a translation of da Vinci's treatise on painting, with a long preface dedicated to Poussin and, significantly, a *Parallèle de l'architecture antique et de la moderne*. Around these two brothers had evolved a small group of merchants, minor civil servants and small bankers, modest bourgeois in the main who could not afford to build *hôtels* but who satisfied themselves with the purchase of paintings. Their taste reflected the ordered pattern of their lives, their respectability and their high regard for intelligence and craftsmanship, and it was for them that

Poussin, after his return to Rome, produced the paintings which are generally considered to be the very embodiment of French classicism —namely the second series of the 'Seven Sacraments' (1644-8), the second of the 'Arcadian Shepherds' (1650), the 'Holy Family on the Steps' (1648) and the 'Ashes of Phocion' (1648).

After 1648, Poussin began to paint almost exclusively for his own satisfaction, exploring the logical development of the features of his style, and becoming increasingly unconcerned about public reaction. Perhaps this was due to living in Rome and to sharing in the elevated view which Italian artists held of their own calling, but more simply it was due to his independent spirit, and in this he showed himself untypical of the artists and writers of France. Such was his studiously intellectual attitude to his work that he was clearly pre-occupied with problems of composition and colour and gave little thought to what the public would make of it. He was therefore fortunate, as he acknowledged, to discover in the cultivated circles of Cassiano del Pozzo and of Fréart de Chanteloup a group of patrons who found his work intelligible and knew how to appreciate it.

It is all the more remarkable that so individual a genius with an extremely personal philosophy of art, and one who moreover lived comfortably outside France, should nonetheless have reflected so admirably the mood of French classicism. 'Sound judgment is very difficult', he wrote, 'if we do not combine a great deal of theory with practical experience in this art', maintaining that the satisfaction of the senses and the communication of emotion were not enough unless reason too were satisfied. 'My natural temperament inclines me to look for and to love things which are well ordered', and as he grew older he tended to regard a work of art primarily as a rational composition. This was not so disastrous as might appear, since he had so powerful an imagination to stimulate his artistic responses that he could take it for granted; what required his attention there-fore was not the initial inspiration but its regulation and application according to the principles of reason. In his earliest work his use of colour was sensuous, in the style of Titian, but as logic and order became increasingly important to him in the presentation of sub-jects, interest in colour for its own sake declined. Everything about the picture had to be logically derived from its subject and, if this were a harsh, cold one, then nothing in the treatment, including the colour, should suggest sweetness and warmth.

One consequence of his preoccupation with the subject-matter of his paintings was his interest in the theory of modes which we have already referred to for its bearing on compositions for the lute: 'The Dorian mode was wise, grave and severe; the Phrygian, wild, vehement and warlike (during the next year I want to paint something in the Phrygian mode—some fearful battle scene perhaps). The Lydian mode was melancholy, the Hypolydian sweet and joyful—suited for celestial, glorious matters. The Ionian was for dances, bacchanals and feasts.' But the creation of mood alone was not sufficiently intellectual for him. He liked above all to reconstruct a situation from the past in order to crystallise the critical moment and to demonstrate its historical significance, very much as Racine and Corneille attempted to do on the stage. The 'Last Supper', for example, emphasised the two essential incidents of Jesus blessing the cup and of Judas leaving the room, but this analytical interest in the subject-matter could be carried too far as when he set out, in his 'Israelites collecting the Manna', 'to represent the misery and hunger to which the Jews had been reduced, and at the same time their joy and delight, the astonishment with which they are struck, the respect and reverence which they feel for their lawgiver'. He was first attracted by scenes from classical mythology and by the dramatic episodes of the Old Testament; after his return from Paris his pictures were inspired by the central themes of the New Testament and by Stoic philosophy; but whether he painted bacchanals or Bible pictures he never ceased to engage the mind of the spectator, insisting that his pictures be read as well as seen.

In all his works Poussin accepted the current distinction between *le vrai* and *le vraisemblable*. In his resolve to achieve perfect clarity of exposition, to state the essential and omit the incidental, nature had to be purged of its imperfections and oddities. This could not be done without some criterion to assist the screening process, and for this Poussin selected the ideals of classical antiquity, and in particular of the statuary available in Rome which he studied at great length and with great admiration. 'When a painter has made a drawing from the living model he should try to make another study of the same figure on a separate sheet and should try to give it the character of an ancient statue.' This advice, given by one of Poussin's disciples in the Académie Royale de Peinture et de Sculpture, reflected only one part of the master's technique. Poussin in fact went further than this and made models from these sketches, rearranging them as on a stage until he was satisfied that their individual proportions and poses embodied the qualities of the classical statuary in which he was so expert. He then began to paint from the model itself, since 'he felt that if he painted from life he would lose his image of this ideal. This unusual method explains many of the features of Poussin's style: its classicism, its marble-like detachment, and also its coldness, which at some moments comes near to lack of life' (Blunt).

All this intensive preparation and preliminary study was proof of his high standard of craftsmanship. 'It is not something you can do as you whistle, as your Parisian painters do', he said in a sarcastic reference to the hustle he had endured during his visit to Paris. To discover the detail of a classical building for a part of a painting, the correctness of a robe or, as in the 'Last Supper', the fact that the disciples would have lain on couches and not sat on chairs, gave him intense satisfaction, and he prided himself, perhaps a little too self-consciously, on the comprehensive range of his craftsmanship: 'I have neglected nothing.' But throughout the polished construction, throughout the intense concern with the intellectual significance of his work, Poussin never failed to communicate emotion nor to please the senses. His 'Ashes of Phocion' embodies so much of French classicism. Its subject-matter demands interpretation by the intellect, and its brilliantly restrained and balanced composition no more admits of alteration than does the façade of Château Maisons. But these are not ends in themselves. The quiet majesty, the tragic calm of this carefully ordered landscape creates its own emotion, nonetheless moving for being motionless, and all the more abiding for striking the heart through the mind. 'The heart', said Pascal, 'has its reasons'; here, in this superb painting by Poussin, the mind has its emotions.

Since genius is the ability to give a universal quality to things particular and transient, it is often the men of lesser talent who mirror more exactly the features of their environment. Poussin embodied the best qualities of French classicism, but to learn more of the attitudes of the classical age we should turn to the life of Nicolas Boileau. He was born in 1636 into a family of lawyers and qualified as a lawyer himself, but his father died when he was young and left him a fortune sufficient to release him from the need to work. Consequently he was able to spend his life as a lively, pleasure-seeking member of the salons, developing a free wit and a ready invective all his own, and writing a great deal of literary criticism in verse—including the *Satires* (1660–6), the *Épîtres* (1669–95), and the *Art Poétique* (1674). His significance has been exaggerated. It was once believed that France acquired her classicism in the so-called 'school of 1660', led by Boileau, Molière, La Fontaine and Racine, but the theory overestimated the friendship of these four, disregarded the fine arts altogether and ignored the obvious establishment of classical tastes well before 1660. Boileau's *Art Poétique* merely restated the doctrines of Malherbe and the Académie, but from him we learn how to understand the classical spirit of mid-century France. He was so imbued with this spirit that, in an age when 'at least half of the plays which were applauded by the contemporaries of Molière and Racine were in a greater or lesser degree totally different from those which posterity has chosen as representative of the classical drama' (Mornet), Boileau not only identified and condemned the tendencies opposed to classicism but with remarkable judgment applauded the very authors whom we today consider to have been the best.

The first two *Satires*, written for private circulation, attacked *préciosité* for its excessive refinement, burlesque for its excessive vulgarity, epics for their dullness and historical romances for their insipidity. Throughout he advocated good taste, *bienséance*, restraint and order, and did so with a malicious wit 'which earned for satire its patent of nobility' (Montgrédien). He had learned as Pascal had done that if they were to have their proper effect, serious subjects must be treated in such a way as to entertain the salons. Hence he

wrote the most quotable literary criticism of all time. Of the
melancholia demonstrated by many poets in love, he wrote:

> *Pour quelque Iris en l'air faire le langoureux,*
> *Et toujours bien mangeant meurent par métaphore,*

and of Chapelain's mammoth epic,

> *La Pucelle est encore une œuvre bien galante;*
> *Et je ne sais pourquoi je baille en la lisant.*\*

His destructive skills were matched, especially in the third satire
and his later works, by a constructive analysis and defence of classicism. Appropriately enough he renewed the dicta of Malherbe on the
importance of construction. Indeed, he gave the impression at times
that craft was more important than inspiration but, like Poussin,
he never lacked for inspiration and could take it for granted. What
mattered was its orderly presentation:

> *J'aime mieux un ruisseau qui, sur la molle arène,*
> *Dans un pré plein de fleurs lentement se promène,*
> *Qu'un torrent débordé qui, d'un cours orageux,*
> *Roule, plein de gravier, sur un terrain fangeux.*
> *Hâtez-vous lentement; et, sans perdre courage,*
> *Vingt fois sur le métier remettez votre ouvrage:*
> *Polissez-le sans cesse et le repolissez;*
> *Ajoutez quelque-fois, et souvent effacez.*†

He encouraged poets to study how the classical poets of Rome had
dealt with their problems and insisted that their subject-matter be
ruled by reason. Individual fantasies were to be suppressed along with
all references to whatever was ephemeral, accidental or local, so that
poetry might be both universal and intelligible. He did not deny that
it was poetry's function to give pleasure, but maintained that this

---

\* For some imaginary Iris they pine away and, while they eat like horses, die by
metaphors. . . . *La Pucelle* is indeed a very notable work, and I do not know why I
yawn while reading it.

† I much prefer a stream in the gentle valley which slowly meanders through a
field full of flowers, to a bursting torrent whose stormy course, full of stones, rolls
across the miry ground. Make haste slowly, and, without losing heart, return your
work a score of times to the anvil. Polish it ceaselessly and polish it again; sometimes
add something, often take something away.

was achieved provided the poet would imitate what was beautiful in nature. In deciding what was beautiful, of course, he must remember the distinction between *le vraisemblable* and *le vrai*, and conform to the dictates of reason and good taste.

It seemed that Boileau had all the qualities of a critic and none of the poet; he was so thoroughly bourgeois, a man of overpowering common sense untroubled by metaphysics, mysticism or mystery. Yet he did not lack the poet's eye for detail, and there are sections in the *Satires* which reveal so keen and accurate an observation of his immediate surroundings that they would serve admirably to accompany the etchings of Parisian life by Abraham Bosse:

> *En quelque endroit que j'aille, il faut fendre la presse*
> *D'un peuple d'importuns qui fourmillent sans cesse.*
> *L'un me heurte d'un ais, dont je suis tout froissé;*
> *Je vois d'un autre coup mon chapeau renversé;*
> *Là, d'un enterrement la funèbre ordonnance*
> *D'un pas lugubre et lent vers l'église s'avance;*
> *Et plus loin, des laquais, l'un l'autre s'agaçants,*
> *Font aboyer les chiens et jurer les passants.*
>
> *Là, sur une charrette une poutre branlante*
> *Vient menaçant de loin la foule qu'elle augmente;*
> *Six chevaux attelés à ce fardeau pesant*
> *Ont peine à l'émouvoir sur le pavé glissant;*
> *D'un carrosse, en tournant, il accroche une roue,*
> *Et du choc le renverse en un grand tas de boue,*
> *Quand un autre à l'instant s'efforçant de passer*
> *Dans le même embarras se vient embarrasser.*

The comedy continued with the arrival of a score of cars, a herd of cattle and, finally, a troop of horseguards sent to clear the road: chaos was worse confounded and Boileau, covered in mud, fled for his life.

> *Et n'osant plus paraître en l'état où je suis*
> *Sans songer où je vais, je me sauve où je puis.*★

★ Wherever I go I have to squeeze through a crowd of tiresome people who swarm unceasingly. One strikes me with a plank so that I am black and blue, and my hat

But such a finely observed, nicely presented study of life in its individual detail was not in Boileau's eyes the proper subject of his verse since it lacked the reflective, analytical and universal qualities of classical poetry. It was akin to the *bambochades*, the work of the genre painters, and could not be called art. His talents were devoted therefore to the analysis of literature, and especially to the service of an ideal based on reason and universal truth. This meant that as a judge of the classical mood he was brilliant, but as an exponent of it merely second-rate since, though his verse did not lack vigour or wit, the freshness of his observation might have been used to greater effect in another genre.

Some of the best illustrations of French classicism come neither from painting nor poetry but from the arts of town-planning and landscape gardening. As with classicism in general, a Cartesian influence can be detected in part for it was Descartes in the *Discours* who condemned haphazard urban growth: 'These ancient cities which, having begun as small villages, have become with the passage of time large towns, are usually so badly planned that . . . when you observe the indiscriminate juxtaposition of the buildings you would say it was chance, rather than any human will guided by reason, which led to such an arrangement', and there is no doubt that the human will guided by reason can be most happily employed in the laying out of new roads and squares. Henri IV, of course, would have echoed this.

Town-planning, however, was practised on so small a scale that it permitted few opportunities to demonstrate the principles of reason and order, and we see them achieved to better effect in the landscaping of parks and gardens. These '*jardins de l'intelligence*', as

---

I see knocked off by another blow. There, the funeral procession advances to the church for a burial with dismal and heavy tread and, further off, some lackeys, each provoking the other, make the dogs bark and the passers-by curse. There on a wagon a swinging beam menaces from afar the crowd which it is about to augment; six horses harnessed to this heavy burden can scarcely move it on the slippery paving stones. In turning it catches against the wheel of a carriage and the collision throws it over on to a great pile of mud, when another carriage trying to pass at that very moment lands up in the same predicament. . . . No longer daring to appear in the state I am in, I flee where I can, paying no heed where I go.

Corpechot calls them, were as much a product of the classical mood as Château Maisons or the dramas of Racine and, as we might expect, they had a respectable pedigree in antiquity. Félibien's studies of Pliny's country house and garden were extremely popular, although initially it was from the Boboli gardens in Florence, the Vatican garden, and the landscaped estate of the Villa Maderna on the slopes of the Monte Maria that French gardeners had first derived their inspiration. The gardens served a practical purpose, for recreation and for the growing of vegetables—since these outnumbered flowers until well into the seventeenth century—but the most important thing was the desire to impose an intellectually conceived order upon nature in the raw, so that the gardens should be not only a joy to the eye but a source of satisfaction to the mind.

One of the first experts in France was Bernard Palissy who published in 1563 his *Recepte Véritable*, 'by which all Frenchmen may learn how to add to their treasures by designing a useful and delightful garden'. He made good use of flowing water in his plans, and laid out series of crosswalks whose angles were neatly emphasised by the siting of garden houses, but his most ambitious creation was the *cabinet de verdure*. For this he trained several rows of young elms to a determined height, at which they were lopped and the tops of the trunks heavily scored with deeply cut rings. The scars which resulted soon resembled capitals, and above them the new shoots and branches were trained across the rows and intertwined in order to create an enclosed garden walk.

A more delicate form of decoration was developed by Claude Mollet who designed the gardens of Saint-Germain, Fontainebleau and the Tuileries for Henri IV. He grew miniature box-hedges in lines to give the appearance of embroidery, creating the most elaborate patterns along the ground which were appropriately known as *parterres de broderies*. His sons succeeded him in the art: Claude became head gardener to James I of England and André to Louis XIII. André had an unexpected taste for hydraulic booby traps and revolving fountains, but his importance lay in his realisation that it was not enough to design individual features of a garden. *Parterres de broderies*, for example, lost most of their effect unless they were laid out where they could be seen from above, and he emphasised the need for an overall design. His *Jardin de Plaisir*, published in 1651, transformed gardening into landscaping for, in planning the approach to a great palace, he suggested not only the double or triple lines of elms, 'which ought to be laid out at right-angles to the front of the house', but that 'at the beginning of the avenue there should be a large semicircle or square so that the general design can be better appreciated'.

Boyceau de la Barauderie, who laid out a massive *parterre de broderie* at the Luxembourg and served both Louis XIII and Louis XIV, was as skilled in the theory as in the practice of his art and published, in 1688, a *Traité du Jardinage selon des raisons de la nature et de l'art*. He repeated the views of André Mollet in insisting that a *parterre de broderie* be seen from above, but emphasised more emphatically the need for an overall design: 'All things, however beautifully they may be chosen, will be defective if they are not ordered and placed in proper symmetry.' To this end he demanded that all gardeners be given formal training in the art of design. He even proposed mathematical rules for the width of avenues, calculating that for a length of, say, 800 yards an avenue should be approximately 16 yards wide, and that the width of avenues should diminish as they converged upon the centre of the park.

Boyceau's views on the training of gardeners were exemplified, quite fortuitously, by the career of André Le Nôtre, the classic exponent of the art of landscape gardening. Le Nôtre's grandfather was a gardener to Catherine de' Medici, his father to Louis XIII, but he himself showed promise of being a painter and was bound apprentice to Vouet. He then worked for an architect, unknown to us, who taught him to prefer the beauty of rational proportion to the mere decoration of a surface, but Le Nôtre could settle neither to painting nor to architecture. In 1637, aged 24, he returned home and came to the conclusion that if he joined his father in the family occupation there would be, as he put it, 'plenty of scope for using the talents of a painter'. As a child he had heard little talked of but gardening, and so it was not difficult to pick up the threads as his father's assistant. Within six years, after working for both Anne d'Autriche and Gaston, he received a *brevet* from the young Louis XIV which affirmed that 'because of the great skill and experience he has in design, His Majesty, on the advice of his mother the queen regent, retains him in the rank and office of designer of plants and parterres in all his gardens'. Meanwhile he had married a bourgeois girl who brought him a dowry of 6,000 livres, and this, in addition to his royal employment, established him as both prosperous and successful.

In 1657 he became *contrôleur général des bâtiments* and had already been commissioned by Fouquet to design the grounds at Vaux. From there he was summoned to Versailles by Louis XIV, directed to Sceaux by Colbert, and brought back to Versailles, virtually for good, in 1663. Colbert was greatly opposed to the expensive plans of Louis and Le Nôtre and with every justification poured scorn on the site itself: 'It is the most miserable and most thankless place in the world; there are no views, no trees, no water and no land, for there is nothing here but quicksand and quagmire.' But Louis was excited beyond measure by Le Nôtre's plans for reducing nature to the will of man. According to one account he kept shouting , 'Le Nôtre, I must give you 20,000 livres', at every stage of Le Nôtre's explanation of his plans, until Le Nôtre interrupted, 'Sire, I cannot tell you any more just now: it would ruin you'. Their close relationship, almost indeed a friendship, persisted, and Louis frequently sent for him if only to enjoy his company, for a tradition of frank conversation had been established between them which no courtier would have dared to imitate. Le Nôtre became a most respected figure. He was ennobled, his pupils became court gardeners in Russia, Austria and Germany, he was begged by Charles II to visit Hampton Court, and when he accompanied the duc de Nevers to Rome in 1679 he was given a splendid reception by the Pope. Le Nôtre enjoyed Rome. His nephew reported that he 'admired the public squares, the abundance of beautiful fountains, the magnificent churches, several palaces, fine pictures and famous statues which entrance all lovers of art'—but added that Le Nôtre considered their gardens inferior to his own.

The distinguishing classical feature of Le Nôtre's work was his prime concern to give an intellectual significance to his landscapes.

Incidental motifs he came to dislike because the more attractive they were the more they distracted from the overall plan, which in his view not only related the garden to the house but both to the surrounding countryside. Moreover the appeal of turbulent cascades and *parterres de broderies* was directed to the senses, whereas his concern was to organise the diverse elements of his gardens in such a way that the logic of their relationship should satisfy the mind. Alexander Pope mocked his achievement:

> *Grove nods at grove, each alley has a brother,*
> *And half the platform just reflects the other,*

but there was far more to Le Nôtre's designs than symmetry alone. Because he conceived of the whole rather than the part he displays a sense of mass and a taste for rational proportion which reminds us of Mansart, while his attitude to nature is essentially that of Poussin. Nature he tamed and reduced to order not because he despised it but to give form to what he believed was best in it. The landscape of the 'Ashes of Phocion' finds a parallel in Le Nôtre's work, and because human reason so obviously controls the processes of selection, concentration and clarification, his gardens are not only *'jardins d'intelligence'* but, in Corpechot's other phrase, *'paysages humanisés'*.

From the changes he wrought in the Tuileries gardens we can see the nature of his achievement. Du Cerceau's plan reveals a patchwork quilt of separate, self-contained parterres of different sizes and shapes, on land which fell several feet towards the Seine. Le Nôtre raised the lateral terraces on the river side and replaced the fussy grotto mazes and little square parterres immediately in front of the palaces by two major parterres, to give a more balanced and impressive entry into the garden. Then, by means of a well-defined central alley, with emphatic lateral axes and two round-points, he succeeding in co-ordinating the separate features into a satisfying whole. Moreover, he gave the garden a second point of interest in that on one side it led to the Tuileries and on the other to a terrace from which three great avenues were planned to radiate. The first of these was the Cours de la Reine flanking the river, which at that point altered course slightly to the south-west. It was 1,500 metres long with a massive round-point, 100 metres in diameter, in the middle, and was flanked by double lines of elms, planted so that the central alley was of 20 metres and the two outer ones of ten. The second avenue, continuing the line of the main axis of the gardens, was the Champs Élysées, but the third, symmetrical with the first, was not constructed.

His most spectacular undertaking was, of course, at Versailles. He began by simplifying the complex pattern of parterres which Boyceau de la Barauderie had designed below the old château and raised them to the level of the ground floor by constructing an artificial plateau, supported by a vast semi-circular earthwork, the Rampe de Latone. This sloped gently away from the plateau, the arms of the half-circle enclosing a pond, the Bassin de Latone, and bearing balustraded terraces to catch the sun and to face across the park. From the ramp the broad avenue of the Allée Royale established the central axis of the overall design. It was cut through trees to a stretch of water, which later became the Bassin d'Apollon, but to terminate the perspective, Le Nôtre then extended it as far as a grassy mound which marked the horizon at that point. The view in retrospect was equally impressive, with the green walls of the Allée Royale leading to the Bassin de Latone and up the curved terraces to the palace behind.

By 1664 the plans were taking shape and the courtiers made many expeditions 'to marvel', said Mme de Sévigné, 'at these leafy palaces which must be called enchanted since nature herself had never had a hand in them'. But Le Nôtre was planning more ambitious projects; the work, he told Bernini, 'was only roughly sketched out', and he was preoccupied with plans to lay more lawns, to create the Jardin du Roi, and to plant a double file of limes and oaks to give greater emphasis to the Allée Royale. This last embellishment only served to make the Allée seem too short, but he was unhappy to remove the grassy mound which terminated it lest the eye rebel against the monotony of the avenue disappearing into the distance. Moreover, behind the hill was a swamp. His solution was deceptively simple: he levelled the hill, drained the swamp and extended the Allée in the form of a Grand Canal, whose surface might carry the eye unwearyingly into infinity. His ambitions, too, seemed to be following the same course. To right and left of the main axis he laid out splendid gardens, forest glades and wooded alcoves, and in 1670 began work on an Orangery, ostensibly to satisfy Louis's passion for the fruit. He placed it to the east of the artificial plateau and Mansart designed the simple buildings to fit in well with the slope of the ground, while Le Nôtre did the parterre. Once it was completed he could not resist the urge to extend the perspective towards the east by once again using a vast sheet of water, the Pièce des Suisses—and, similarly, on the other side of the axis he laid out another garden to match the Orangery, leading to the Bassin de Neptune. These placid waters so fascinated him that he replaced the parterres in front of the palace with two great *parterres d'eau* which mirrored Le Vau's façade.

When Colbert had initially opposed the idea of developing Louis XIII's château at Versailles, he had warned Louis XIV that 'the steep gradient of the parterres and avenues will not allow any further extension and use of the ground unless everything is turned upside down at prodigious expense'. This is precisely what Le Nôtre had done, nor was it a matter of expense alone. His operations required a small army of labourers for terracing, levelling and draining the park. Le Vau recorded 500 at work on the Rampe de Latone, but as the number of projects increased the numbers employed ran to 2,000—and the appallingly high death-rate from fever and pneumonia made it difficult to maintain recruitment. So urgent became the need to keep up to schedule that Louis even won permission from the Church for them to work on Sundays after Mass.

Strangely enough, in view of the swampy terrain, the most serious obstacle in Le Nôtre's way was the shortage of water. A family of Italian hydraulic experts, the Francini, were brought in to advise, but it soon became clear that the water drained from the park was not enough to meet Le Nôtre's requirements. Denys Jolly, master of the Samaritaine, the great pump by the Pont Neuf, was commissioned to build a pumping tower to bring water from a lake at Clagny, and Louis XIV broke off his absorption with a campaign in Alsace in 1673 to write home anxiously demanding that the pumps should work. They did indeed, but the supply was still inadequate, and another team undertook to build the Machine de Marly by

30. Rigaud's portrait of Lully and his fellow musicians (see pages 127–36, 254–8)

31. Versailles—celebration of *Les Plaisirs de l'Île Enchantée* (see page 254)

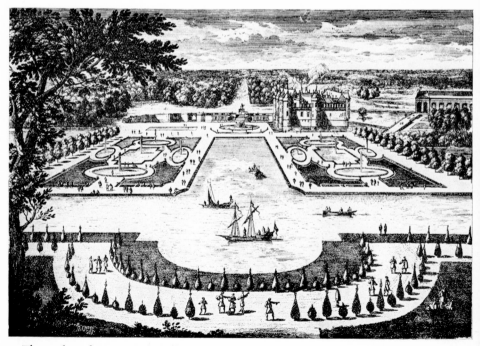

32. The gardens, fountains and canals at Chantilly (see page 272)

which water would be brought across from the Seine, eight miles away. The project took five years to complete, and needed 223 pumps, but still there was not enough water and it became clear that nothing less than a river would satisfy Le Nôtre. Riquet, the greatest civil engineer of the century and creator of the Languedoc canal, proposed to harness the Loire, but Louis finally settled for the more accessible Eure. In 1685, directed by Louvois and members of the Académie des Sciences, Vauban and an army corps began to work in day and night shifts to create a new bed for the Eure, and to build a colossal aqueduct. The project was stopped after three years by the outbreak of a major European war, and never renewed. Meanwhile, ponds and streams for miles around Versailles were drained in order to sustain Le Nôtre's fountains and *parterres d'eau*.

Other commodities which had to be imported were the plants and trees which could not be found in the natural environment of Versailles. Though Le Nôtre disliked fussy ornamentation in his parterres he enjoyed the colour effects obtained by massing flowers and the successes of the Dutch in floriculture by this date had made flower beds a necessary feature in any garden. Michel le Bouteux, Le Nôtre's nephew, achieved considerable success in propagating flowers at Versailles, but it was necessary to import plants in bulk. Colbert, writing on other matters to his agent in Marseilles, added: 'You know that for the ornamentation of the royal gardens we must have a large quantity of flowers. As there are so many varieties in Provence I urge you to buy all the jonquils and tuberoses that you can find, and also any other curious flowers that would contribute to the ornamentation of the gardens.'

More difficult to maintain was the supply of trees; 3,000 orange-trees were imported from Italy for the Orangery, but the demand for less exotic ones was never ending. Le Nôtre wanted his trees grouped in well-drilled geometrical masses, correctly sited and uniform in colour and appearance. The slightest deviation in this respect destroyed the logical unity of the whole and, as Corpechot points out, he was bound by a self-discipline as intense as any artist and could no more dispense his colours freely than could Poussin. To acquire the trees he needed, he plundered Vaux and then ransacked

the forests of France: Compiègne for elms and limes, Flanders and
Normandy for hornbeam and birch, Dauphiné for evergreen oaks,
and Norwegian pine from the Vosges. Saint-Simon recorded that
three-quarters of these died *en route* and had to be replaced, and it is
not surprising that Mme de Sévigné should have complained that on
the roads of France you could not 'escape the forests which they
carry fully grown and bushy topped on the road to Versailles'.

The result of all this effort has been variously assessed. 'Nature',
says Pevsner with deliberate irony, 'subdued by the hand of Man
to serve the greatness of the King, whose bedroom was placed right
in the centre of the whole composition', and it might well seem that
for reason to triumph so spectacularly over nature, across an entire
countryside, was in itself unreasonable. Yet Le Nôtre echoes the
words of Poussin: 'My natural temperament inclines me to look for
and to love things which are well ordered'; and the elements of
logic, intelligence and restraint mingle with a burning creative
passion in his work, as in the work of all the great artists and writers
of the age of classicism.

# eight

# Louis XIV and Colbert

Louis XIV had grown up during the years of French victory in the Thirty Years War and in the war against Spain. Since the year of Rocroi (1643) his generals and his diplomats had won for him both territory and power, and left him with a taste for imperial grandeur. When the Treaty of the Pyrenees recognised French supremacy in Europe and guaranteed that there was nothing more to fear from the Spanish provinces and bases around his frontiers Louis was not content. He determined to acquire these very provinces and bases for himself. His marriage to Marie-Thérèse gave him an opportunity to claim some of them on her behalf when her father was succeeded by the young and sickly Carlos II, and it was under this dubious pretext that Turenne was ordered to invade the Spanish Netherlands in 1667. The army's successes confirmed Louis's ambitions. Turenne captured Lille and occupied the Southern provinces within four weeks; in 1668 Condé overran Franche Comté in three. The major powers of Western Europe, accustomed to many decades of alliance with France against an over-mighty Spain, were aghast at the changed circumstances, and Sweden, Holland and England hastily formed a Triple Alliance to check French progress. Louis was unworried by this but took everyone by surprise by restoring his conquests to Carlos II—a magnanimous gesture only explained by a secret agreement with the Emperor Leopold of Austria to partition Carlos' empire when he died, an event expected daily.

But Carlos survived—indeed until 1700—and it was the Dutch

who were the next to suffer a French invasion, in 1672. This was a move that ran wholly counter to the traditions of French policy but, now that Louis had become all-powerful, personal motives were replacing reasons of state in the direction of foreign affairs. The Dutch in short were to be chastised for their Calvinism, their republicanism, their commercial success and their part in the Triple Alliance. Nonetheless, despite the might of the French armies, the mission failed; the Dutch flooded their Northern provinces, the Emperor Leopold declared war on their behalf and, as other powers joined in, Louis was forced into a defensive war to safeguard all his frontiers. This was an operation carried out with great success, but it became clear by 1679 that although France could not be beaten, it was equally unlikely that Holland could be occupied and held. Peace was made, therefore, at Nijmegen, and Louis refused to be sidetracked on this occasion by the lure of future spoils. Carlos, still sickly, yet lived and Louis demanded possession of Franche Comté and a strip of frontier territory 200 miles long from Dunkirk to the Meuse.

For the next nine years Louis deliberately exploited both his own power and the obvious reluctance of the other states to engage in another war. He succeeded by legal claim, spurious pretext, blackmail and force of arms in occupying towns and provinces piecemeal along his eastern frontier, strengthening his strategic grasp on the Rhineland. It was a policy which gained France valuable pockets of territory, but it drove the other powers into a coalition to defend their interests. When, in 1688, French armies occupied Cologne and crossed the Rhine into the Palatinate the rest of Europe joined to meet France on equal terms, and when peace was made in 1697 Louis was compelled to restore the territories gained since 1679. France, supreme in Europe in 1661, had taught the European states how to redress the balance.

Though it was for his exploits abroad that Louis, in 1679, was hailed as Louis le Grand by a people eager to acclaim a successor to Charlemagne, it was by his domestic policies that he made his greatest impression on his subjects. When Mazarin died, Louis had assumed direct and personal control of his government: 'I resolved never to appoint a first minister', he wrote, 'nor to leave to another the function of royalty while reserving to myself the mere title.' There were to be no more cardinals but, because of the successful endeavours of Richelieu and Mazarin to extend royal authority, the 'function of royalty' was no sinecure; it had become a highly specialised and demanding occupation, as Louis recognised by referring frequently to his *métier du roi*. It involved him in long hours in the council chamber, for the working of the centralised bureaucracy depended upon the decisions of a dozen councils which met, some daily, others weekly, to superintend the affairs of France. In the hierarchy of government Louis insisted that 'the right of deliberation and resolution belongs to the head alone, and all the functions of the other members consist in executing the orders given to them'. Fouquet seemed to challenge this and was reduced to life imprisonment at Pignerol, but if Louis brooked no rivals, nor did he look for sycophants. Mazarin had left him an excellent team of civil servants—Lionne the brilliant diplomat, Michel le Tellier and his son Louvois who reformed the army, and Jean-Baptiste Colbert who controlled every department of internal affairs—and Louis wisely listened to their counsels. He could not rival their specialist knowledge but he developed a genius for exploiting it and, through his councils and committees, co-ordinated their work in a manner which left them permanently responsible to him. As Colbert reminded his son, 'Never as long as you live send out anything in the King's name without his express approval.'

Even Louis's moments of relaxation were directed to maintaining and emphasising the dignity of the crown, and he played billiards, as one lady remarked, with the air of being master of the world. The laws of etiquette which he fostered at the Louvre, and later at Versailles, served an important political purpose since they demonstrated so clearly the inferior rank of all who attended the King. The day began with *petit lever* at which a few privileged courtiers witnessed their master leave his bed; a second group was then admitted while he wiped his hands on an oiled rag, and at each successive stage of his toilet further groups, each one less select than the one before, entered the chamber until 100 or more courtiers clustered together to see their sovereign fully dressed. Ceremonial of such a nature accompanied all the domestic incidents of the day but Louis never neglected to play his role in the perpetual parade. It was a part of his *métier du roi*, and seven days before his death the old and broken King still dined *au grand couvert*—though he could barely sip a little liquid—to demonstrate that the life of the court still revolved around him alone.

Away from the court and the royal councils, royal authority was exercised in the provinces in a manner quite unforeseen in 1598 but, successful though the ministers of the crown had been in this respect, France still lacked administrative uniformity. To achieve this was Colbert's task from 1661 until his death in 1683, and his first target was the fiscal autonomy enjoyed by the surviving *pays d'état*. Instead of abolishing the Estates, Colbert, by bribery, intimidation, infiltration and persistent pressure, won control of their members within less than ten years; the *don gratuit*, which was formerly an independent and voluntary statement of what the province was prepared to contribute to the king, became a matter for royal direction under the guise of local consent. 'They have only to ask what the king requires', wrote Mme de Sévigné of the Brittany Estates. 'No one will say a word, and so it will be done.'

The provinces, *pays d'état* or *pays d'élections*, retained their governors, an office which in Henri IV's day had carried considerable weight and which had been claimed as a right by the most powerful family in the province. Richelieu had rescued the post from the hands of over-mighty subjects, and Colbert completed the work by restricting the term of office to three years. This ensured that the real direction of local affairs was conducted by *intendants* who answered only to the royal council. Nor did they have to suffer interference from the local parlements. The powers of *parlements* had been compromised beyond repair by the collapse of the Fronde: if any case arose in which the crown had an interest it merely transferred the matter to the council and, as Colbert wrote to one of his *intendants*, 'It is no use writing about speeches made in the *parlement*. As you know, the noises made by *parlements* are no longer in season.' As for the boroughs, whose charters of incorporation had granted them considerable independence, the incompetence and dishonesty of most councillors and local officials gave Colbert the chance in 1683 to order each corporation to submit an annual report of its finances. The *intendants* moved in, liquidated the debts accumulated over decades, and assumed control. Ten years later local elections were abolished and municipal offices were sold by the crown as profitable sinecures.

There was, however, another side to Louis's absolutism. The right to govern was transferred by Colbert to men who depended wholly on the king, but the governors, mayors, members of the Estates and *parlementaires* maintained the outward show of power and exercised an inefficient jurisdiction over the vast majority of matters which no *intendant* had the time to deal with. Moreover, absolute control is only possible in an egalitarian society in which each member is equally exposed to the power of the government. French society was a hierarchy, and each class above the peasantry retained countless bulwarks of privilege to defend it against the crown. The nobility, deprived of political power, was still too powerful a class to be reduced to paying taxes, and the *officiers*, the very class on which the government depended for the day-to-day administration of its policies, were entrenched by purchase and inheritance in positions of authority from which they were virtually irremovable. Wise enough since the Fronde not to challenge the government by open opposition, they demonstrated their capacity for passive resistance, exercising an informal surveillance over all royal edicts and ignoring those which in any way offended the interests of their class or their locality.

Not only was it impossible for Colbert, for example, to unify the various codes of law which had survived from the separate kingdoms of the Middle Ages; he could not even enforce uniform methods of procedure. The magistrates resisted him because, having mastered the law once, they were in no mind to master it again, and because they knew to a nicety their perquisites under the old dispensation; individually vulnerable, collectively they could ignore the new edicts with impunity. So it was that a king, against whom all open resistance had ceased, and whose authority was recognised by every institution which had formerly claimed some degree of autonomy, was thus exposed to the silent opposition of those who administered the laws in his name.

Louis XIV's absolutism was to some extent similarly qualified in church affairs. The Gallican Church, for all its protestations of loyalty and its exaltation of the monarchy as a divinely appointed institution, was nonetheless more devoted to maintaining its privileged status than to serving the king. This meant that it would support Louis without reserve in any conflict with the Huguenots, or with the pope for that matter, since it was jealous of interference from Rome, but it was reluctant to assist him in disciplining its own members. There was indeed a ten-year struggle between Louis and the papacy to resolve a conflict of jurisdiction and of revenue, but the outstanding feature of the reign was the persecution of the Huguenots. This was pursued by Louis less for doctrinal than for political reasons. The edict of Nantes had been one of the greatest concessions wrung from the crown by force, and Louis was resolved that what had once been granted out of weakness should be reversed from strength. His theory of the State allowed no room for dissent, and the Huguenots, as a separate community within the Kingdom, were a blatant example of irreconcilable nonconformity. So, too, were the Jansenists in Louis's eyes, for they were exposed to him by the Jesuits as Calvinistic Frondeurs. In this matter, however, the support of other clergy made it impossible to attack Port-Royal outright. His initial attempt to dislodge them in 1661 had failed by 1668, and an uneasy truce prevailed until the end of the reign.

In matters of secular administration, the edicts of a master bureaucrat like Colbert revealed the classical virtues of clarity, order and common sense, along with an excellent gift for comprehending complex problems. Their inefficient enforcement reminds us that the seventeenth-century state, even that of Louis XIV, was a world of disobedience and delay, yet energy and persistence applied to the solution of particular problems could secure remarkable results on occasion, as Colbert proved by his fiscal and economic policies. Nothing could be done, of course, to remedy the basic faults of a system by which the wealthiest were exempt from taxes, since this would have required a frontal assault on the privileged structure of

French society, but Colbert was given a free hand to pursue his own agents who in 1661 were putting into their own pockets more than 53 million livres of the 85 million they collected.

Fouquet's downfall and the commissions of inquiry triggered off by it served Colbert's purpose admirably; in the general panic he was able to introduce new systems of book-keeping which limited the opportunities for peculation. None of his other measures to extend the range of taxes nor to invent new ones was so important or successful as this establishment of good order. Even under the demands of warfare he could only increase the total sum collected from 85 million livres to 116 million, but his administrative reform ensured that the costs of collection did not exceed 22 million. Successful though it was, the system was never foolproof and Le Pelletier who succeeded Colbert reported discrepancies in the accounts. For this Colbert's idealism rather than his efficiency was at fault, and in part it reflects the current distinction in the arts between *le vraisemblable* and *le vrai*; denied the chance to establish good order throughout the administration, it was some small consolation for him to make his books reflect the ideal statement of his intentions.

Colbert's fiscal policy was empirical; his commercial and industrial policies were based on the mercantilist belief that wealth is a limited commodity represented by bullion and, if it was easy for historians of a free-trade era to condemn this view, it is less so now in an age preoccupied with adverse balances of payments. If France could deny bullion to other countries by becoming self-sufficient in the manufacture of her own goods, and if she could produce goods of such good quality that foreigners paid for them with their own bullion, then Colbert believed she would become rich and powerful. Hence he went to great lengths to introduce sugar refining, papermaking, metallurgical industries and the manufacture of luxury goods, but his greatest achievement—and one which is relatively unsung—was the invigoration and extension of the domestic textile industry. Not only did France produce fine cloths at Carcassonne and Arras, and tapestries at Gobelins and Beauvais, but the production of ordinary cloth was greatly improved and increased by a series of first-class edicts, brilliantly compiled and remarkably effective in practice. Trade, like bullion, was also regarded as a limited commodity, and Colbert accepted that the commerce of the day required 20,000 ships: 'The Dutch have of this total 15,000 to 16,000, and the French 500 or 600 at the most.' The moral was obvious, but his trading companies enjoyed only a short life. The bourgeois were suspicious of government-sponsored ventures and their ambition, as we have seen, was to invest their surplus capital in government offices; hence the companies were under-subscribed. During Colbert's lifetime they held their own, and caused anxiety to their rivals in England and Holland, but after his death in 1683 they all collapsed.

For all his importance in the history of seventeenth-century France, Colbert remains a colourless figure. The most talented of Louis's ministers, he was a ruthless and ambitious bureaucrat who drilled himself to stand quietly in the shadow of Louis's greatness, and we can understand why Mme de Sévigné called him Le Nord. Though he exercised lavish patronage on behalf of Louis XIV it seems quite clear that his private enthusiasm for the arts was far less than that of Richelieu or of Mazarin. It is difficult of course to distinguish the private from the public tastes of a politician but it would be fair to say that Colbert built and purchased *hôtels* and country-houses only because it was expected of him. Mazarin left him a *hôtel* opposite to the Palais Mazarin, but in 1665 he bought the Hôtel Bautru, built by Le Vau in the 1630s in his early mannerist style; later he had it extended at a cost of 58,400 livres to make it the Hôtel Colbert, one of the biggest in Paris. He purchased, too, a site behind the Palais Mazarin for 57,000 livres and, from one of Fouquet's unfortunate colleagues, a *hôtel* valued at 150,000 livres when it was confiscated, but bought by Colbert from the crown at 30,800 livres. It is a story in which cautious investment takes precedence over sensibility, and it reveals nothing of Colbert's private tastes.

As befitted his great position he also had his châteaux at Seignelay and Ormoy in Bourgogne, at Châteauneuf-sur-Cher and Lignières in Berry and at Pezcoux and Chanceaux in Maine. Le Vau renovated Seignelay in 1657, while Le Nôtre laid out the gardens, but Colbert, like the careful bureaucrat he was, directed the entire operation from Paris, sending daily instructions on such points as the number of nails required to fix each slate in the roof. Later, in 1670, he resolved that he too must have a country seat near Paris and for 135,000 livres he purchased an estate of 150 acres at Sceaux. This he extended to 850 acres and employed Le Nôtre to landscape it; Le Brun was called in to superintend the decoration and Quinault was commissioned to write a poem in its honour as La Fontaine had done at Vaux—but with accustomed prudence Colbert made sure that the effusion was never published. This threat of comparison with Fouquet haunted him especially in 1677 when a royal visit to sample the new delights of Sceaux awoke memories of the famous visit to Vaux in 1661. Colbert was torn between the need to fulfil his obligations as the king's host and the fear of being charged with ostentation. The occasion in fact went well. It lacked flamboyance but Racine's *Phèdre* was performed in the Orangery to everyone's delight, and the wily Donneau de Visé, who recognised his patron's fears, wrote up the festivities in the *Mercure Galant* with becoming tact: 'One could say that it was magnificent without being pompous and abundant in everything without there being too much of anything.'

One genuine and unrestrained enthusiasm revealed by Colbert was for collecting books, documents and charters. 'As the pleasure of building up my library is almost the only pleasure I derive from the work to which I am attached by the necessity of state and the orders of the King', he wrote to one of his *intendants* in 1672, 'I know by experience that there are sometimes tucked away in the monasteries and important abbeys of the provinces ancient documents of some value which, through the ignorance and lack of knowledge of the monks, are often abandoned in the dust and dirt of the charter rooms.' The *intendant* was accordingly urged to seek them out, exploit this lack of knowledge and buy them up cheaply. Similar instructions frequently occurred in letters to other *intendants*, and to ambassadors on foreign service. His collection was preserved intact after his death and sold for 100,000 *écus* to Louis xv, when it contained 18,219 items, including a Mainz bible on vellum of 1462,

722 charters, 6,117 ancient manuscripts and 524 volumes of Colbert's own letters and memoranda. All these had been scrupulously looked after by his librarian, Baluze, a bibliophile of extraordinary erudition whose own library numbered 11,000 books and who, with astonishing energy, held court with his cronies at the age of 90, demonstrating his unrivalled knowledge of ancient charters and genealogy.

The royal library too enjoyed the benefit of Colbert's attention. His brother Nicolas was appointed *maître de la librairie du roi* and a collection of approximately 10,000 books was increased to 35,589 in 1680, in addition to the collection of 10,000 manuscripts and the purchase of Michel Marolle's vast collection of prints. In 1685 an order was made to all printers and publishers to supply copies for the royal library of all works licensed since 1652. The library was eventually housed in the Palais Mazarin, along with a large section of Mazarin's collection, and in 1688 the two were merged and opened to the public as the Bibliothèque Nationale.

Though his private enthusiasm for art and literature was far less than that of Richelieu or Mazarin, Colbert maintained much more ruthlessly than the cardinals that the State should control the production of art as it controlled everything else. This was partly because he believed that anything directed from the top, be it textiles or literature, would be a better product than anything left to individual caprice. Moreover he abhorred the existence of so many separate clientèles of artists and writers attached to leading families and salons in Paris; just as private jurisdictions had been taken over by the extension of royal jurisdiction, so Colbert wanted the court to become the sole arbiter of public taste and for royal patronage to supersede private patronage as the determining influence in French culture. His motive was frankly political: 'His Majesty, loving the fine arts as much as he does, will cultivate them with even greater care that they may serve to immortalise his great and glorious actions.' To this end Colbert intended to buy up the services of all the best writers, for example, so that even if their panegyrics sometimes lacked conviction, they at least might be restrained from satirical or critical attacks on the régime. The problem was to know whom to employ, and to solve it he commissioned Chapelain, with 30 years' experience of the world of letters, to draw up a list of candidates suitable to become '*les trompettes des vertus du roi*'.

In 1662 Chapelain presented a list of 98 names for annual pensions. There was favouritism, of course, since it included the young Racine—not yet a playwright but a minor poet—for no better reason than his flattering attention to every word of Chapelain's about his verse, but there was generosity, too, in the inclusion of Pellisson, Fouquet's literary adviser who still remained loyal to him. Molière, however, for his part at Vaux, was valued at only 1,000 livres against Corneille's 2,000; La Fontaine was ignored. Chapelain himself received 3,000 livres and, in all, 77,500 livres were made available for both French and foreign writers. In dealing with the foreigners Chapelain advised Colbert that he should not be too obvious in asking them for poems in Louis's honour, 'as if His Majesty's gifts had only been made with the intent of procuring eulogies'; but concerning his compatriots he was more blunt. Some, he told Colbert, seemed to 'think that the favours they receive from the king are nothing more than the recognition of their merit'. Ménage was one of these, and he swiftly forfeited his 2,000 livres a year for refusing to write what was required on the grounds that 'no one trusts praises which have been bought'.

The most generous pensions were paid to men we know little of today but who seemed at the time to exercise particular responsibility for the King's reputation before posterity. One of these was the historian Mézéray, who received 4,000 livres, and was told plainly by Colbert to write less about taxation and be less critical of Louis's ancestors. The response was becomingly obsequious: 'I shall work according to your wishes and according to the rules you have set before me. I will let M. Perrault (Colbert's *commis*) look over my manuscript.' His successors were Racine and Boileau, and it is interesting that they should have been prized by Colbert for work which has no bearing on their literary reputation today. The most highly paid writer was a hack journalist, Donneau de Visé, who wrote for the *Mercure Galant* and was not in Chapelain's original list. He was paid 6,000 livres a year by *brevet spécial* in 1684, and

15,000 in 1697. Not only were the amounts exceptional but he received them at a time when the other pensions had fallen victim to the costs of warfare. They had been given with a flourish in 1663; in the following year the silk purses were replaced with leather, but the total value of the pensions rose to 100,500 livres by 1671. Thereafter the Dutch war and the subsequent wars reduced the amount to less than 40,000, and often there were delays in payment. Corneille wrote an ode on the subject in 1672, addressing his complaint to Louis himself.

> Puissiez-vous, dans cent ans, donner encore des lois
> Et puissent tous vos ans être de quinze mois,
> Comme vos commis font les nôtres.*

In 1673 his name was removed from the list.

The Académie Française was also called upon to serve the King with eulogy and praise. The subjects of the *prix d'éloquence* and the *prix de poésie* were invariably in honour of Louis xiv, and Racine declared of the *Dictionnaire* that 'all the words in the language, all its syllables, seem precious in our sight because we look upon them as so many instruments to serve the glory of our august protector'. Faced with such fulsome devotion, or with the abject humility of a Mézéray, we might well despair of the depths to which artists were reduced by state patronage, but this would be misleading. It was a commonplace of the age for courtiers as well as writers to provide a high-flown line in flattery, and though political patronage is too impersonal and often deadening, yet it offers greater opportunities for making a name in the world and for financial reward than the patronage of private individuals.

The whole problem of motivation was amusingly discussed in Molière's *Le Bourgeois Gentilhomme*, where the Dancing Master demands appreciation more than anything: 'For my own part I must confess that what I long for most is applause; it is appreciation I live for. To my way of thinking there is no fate more distressing for an artist than to have to show himself off before fools, to see his

---

* May you survive to give us laws for 100 years, and may all your years last fifteen months as your *commis* make ours do.

work exposed to the criticism of the vulgar and ignorant.' But the Music Master's retort is also valid: 'I agree, there is nothing more pleasing than the recognition you speak of, but you can't live on applause. Praise alone doesn't keep a man going. One needs something more substantial than that, and, to my mind, there's no praise to beat the sort you can put in your pocket'—and later he adds, 'in any case he is giving us a chance to make a name in the world, and he will make up for the others by paying while they do the praising'. Indeed, Louis's provision of 40,000 livres in poor years, let alone 100,500 livres in the best, was a fair contribution to literature, whatever the motive—and if political reliability counted for more than literary promise, yet it resulted happily enough in the greatest classical dramatist of the reign being kept in comfort as historiographer royal.

Individual pensions represented one form of control, the formation of academies another, and Colbert's sublime faith in their efficacy stemmed from his experience of government committees: 'The desire is that art should have a uniform character, like the state, should produce the effect of formal perfection, like the movement of a corps, that it should be clear and precise, like a decree, and be governed by absolute rules like the life of every subject in the state' (Hauser). Colbert never liked leaving anything to chance. Since France by some miracle had arrived at concepts of good taste and, coincidentally and fortuitously, had also produced men of genius in the arts, it was vital in his view to analyse both good taste and genius so that the intrinsic rules of beauty, and the manner of its attainment, be laid bare for all time. The rule was the same as for textile production: discover the best models, analyse their construction, deduce the necessary rules and apply them uniformly. The academies therefore existed to promulgate doctrine—and classical doctrine at that, since the classical tradition accorded admirably with the requirements of order, discipline and harmony which characterised the ideal of Louis's absolutism. The academies, too, were to become privileged corporatinos, analogous to those of industry, outside of which one was not considered a master, and which would control artists and writers as firmly as the guilds controlled their artisans.

'Like the government of the State, the arts should be uniform, exact and clear; they should be governed by binding regulations; the individual artist, like any other member of society, should not be allowed any freedom, but should serve the State and obey its rules. The duty of the arts was the glorification of Louis xiv, and the Academies were entrusted with the execution of this task' (Carsten).

This compulsive desire to regulate everything led Colbert to revive the Académie Royale de Peinture et de Sculpture, which had fallen on bad times. Le Brun was given virtual control, though he did not become director until 1683, with the task of discovering the best rules of painting and sculpture. This he did by holding a series of *Conférences*, many of which were minuted and published by Colbert, and though the compilation of aesthetic rules by committee would seem doomed to sterility the papers read by Le Brun on human and animal physiognomy and on Descartes's *Traité des Passions de l'Âme* were both interesting and helpful. The error lay in accepting Poussin's assumption that painting is an intellectual affair intended for an educated public, without recognising that this view is tenable only if you possess Poussin's individual genius.

'To produce things worthy of posterity', wrote Félibien in the *Idée du peintre parfait*—an academician's book if ever there was one —'genius must have seen much, read much and studied much', since the Académie was less concerned with stimulating genius to action than with evolving effective methods of refining its operation. Refinement was a process of rational selection, and the Académie owed much to *L'idea del pittore, dello scultore e dell'architetto* by Giovanni Bellori, from whom they learnt the importance at this stage of studying antique models, a practice made famous by Poussin. Students were put to study human anatomy by first studying the Greek forms of ancient statues and friezes, and were not allowed to draw from life until they had become so saturated with the classical ideal that deviation from it was impossible. Even then, lecturers such as Sebastian Bourdon ordered 'that when a painter has made a drawing from the living model, he should make another study of the same figure on a separate sheet, and should try to give it the character of an ancient statue'.

33. A Gobelins tapestry, commemorating a visit by Louis XIV and Colbert, escorted by Le Brun, to Les Manufactures Royales des Meubles at Gobelins (see page 252)

34. Louis XIV in all his splendour, by Rigaud

Drawing was held to be the all-important skill. 'The function of colour', said Le Brun, 'is to satisfy the eye, whereas drawing satisfies the mind'; and the Venetian school was condemned not only for its sensuous use of colour, but also because colour was regarded as a less permanent feature of nature than form. The Dutch, who might have been admired for their draughtsmanship, were condemned for the trivial content of their work; it was insufficiently intellectual to satisfy the Académie, the mirror was held too close to nature without regard to the rules of *bienséance* and *vraisemblance*. Nobility of subject was an important issue, and because the academicians revered Poussin over and above all living artists his choice of subject-matter was the one extolled and imitated. *Peinture d'histoire*, in fact, was a genre ideally suited to the Académie, not least for the possibilities it afforded for psychological and literary interpretation, and by seeking to analyse what Poussin had introduced into his own compositions they formulated the rules for their own practice. This was their weakness. Without his genius and his inspiration they could merely produce a lifeless pastiche.

The lifeless quality of academy painting was accentuated by the proliferation of rules for the handling of details, so that a picture lost its unity in becoming a composite structure of prefabricated parts. Louis Testelin, the secretary of the Académie, undertook an exhaustive study of the means of expressing emotion, and presented his conclusions in meticulous detail. He described the various postures of the body which would best represent such emotions as anger, admiration or affection, and even studied such minutiae as the angle of an eyebrow: 'The most gentle passions are expressed by the lifting of an eyebrow towards the brain: a downward movement of the eyebrow towards the heart represents the wildest and most cruel passions.' Moreover, 'an eyebrow curved in the middle indicates pleasant emotions, but one which rises to a peak in the middle of the forehead reveals sadness and grief'. Doubtless these were conventions subscribed to by many respected artists, but to catalogue them and apply them from the rule book was regulation run mad.

Perhaps the most typical of Testelin's efforts was to attempt to draw up synoptic tables of the rules for 'Great Art'—a *Table de*

*Préceptes* published in 1675—in which the primacy of *peinture d'histoire* over portraiture was established, with landscapes lying third and Dutch genre painting last. Roger de Piles produced a similar work later with an interesting score card on the great artists of the day.

|  | Composition | Drawing | Colour | Expression | Total |
|---|---|---|---|---|---|
| Michelangelo | 8 | 17 | 4 | 8 | 37 |
| Rembrandt | 15 | 6 | 17 | 12 | 50 |
| Titian | 12 | 15 | 18 | 6 | 51 |
| Poussin | 15 | 17 | 6 | 16 | 54 |
| Le Brun | 16 | 16 | 8 | 16 | 56 |

Although Le Brun is put ahead of Poussin, the emphasis given to colour reveals that de Piles, far from reflecting official doctrine, was in fact leading a counter-revolution (see page 270) to re-establish the importance of colour, and his score card indicated Rubens as the champion with a score of 18, 13, 17 and 17.

Much more valuable to artists than the compilation of synoptic tables was the expansion of the royal collections of painting and sculpture, a task for which Colbert was well fitted. The Italian paintings of Francis I and the other royal collections had been augmented by acquisitions from the collections of Mazarin and Fouquet, and represented a most valuable nucleus from which to expand. Colbert bought up private collections wholesale, including that of the Cologne banker Jaibach who, until his bankruptcy, had become the wealthiest collector in Paris. In ten years Colbert acquired 647 of the pictures now on display in the Louvre, and it was he too who made the Louvre the centre of the royal collection by assembling there the pictures from the other royal palaces. By the end of the century French artists, therefore, had the opportunity of studying over 2,400 paintings in one collection—at a date when the English had to wait another century and more before the National Gallery opened with 38 pictures.

A further aid to artists was provided by setting up a subsidiary academy in Rome in 1666. It was a simple establishment led by six painters, four sculptors and two architects under the direction of

Charles Errard, a competent painter who had designed the scenery for *Orfeo* and had decorated a number of Parisian *hôtels*. Here French artists could go to study the Italian masters at first hand, but Colbert wanted more than that. 'We must do what we can', he told Errard, 'to bring back to France whatever is beautiful in Italy'—hence, whatever could not be bought had to be copied. 'Set your painters to work to make copies of everything notable in Rome, and when you have copied everything, if that is possible, start all over again.' Moreover, there was an emphatic warning for students who became bored not to add anything of their own to the statues and paintings they were copying.

One further advantage of the Roman academy was that it removed Errard from Le Brun's way. In the very beginning Le Brun, as we saw, had advocated the formation of the Académie Royale de Peinture et de Sculpture in the hope that it might provide him with an opportunity for power; under Colbert he became its dictator and brooked no rivals. The *brevetés* with whom the Maîtrise maintained an uneasy truce were ordered to join the Académie and thereby accept Le Brun's authority, or forfeit their status and thereby risk prosecution by the Maîtrise. One painter who successfully refused to acknowledge Le Brun's primacy, and who was not to be got out of the way like Errard, was Pierre Mignard, a portrait painter and therefore rated inferior to the *peintres d'histoire*. He had trained under Vouet and at Rome, where Poussin praised his work but thought his heads were lifeless; for a portrait painter this must have been damning indeed, but his reputation grew nonetheless, and in 1656 he was recalled to Paris by Louis XIV. His return was leisurely, spending some time with Molière in the Rhône valley and painting him as César in '*La Mort de Pompée*', but it was hastily concluded at Mazarin's express command in order to dash off a portrait of Louis for the marriage negotiations of the Treaty of the Pyrenees.

Mignard remained thereafter on excellent terms with Louis, but flatly refused to join the Académie and knuckle under to Le Brun. He wrote to Colbert, in what purported to be a spirited defence of the freedom of the individual artist: 'Monsieur, the King is the master and if he orders me to leave the kingdom I am quite ready to depart.

But remember that with these five fingers there is not a country in Europe where I would not be more highly esteemed, and better rewarded, than I am here.' Colbert was too good a mercantilist to export talent, and Mignard was too popular with the King to be disciplined. He made a successful living as court painter and in addition undertook for Anne d'Autriche to decorate the vault of the Val-de-Grâce. It was this which prompted Molière's poem *La Gloire du Val-de-Grâce*, which was in essence a versification from the Latin of *De Arte Grafica* by Mignard's friend Dufresnoy, and which extolled the virtues of classicism as demonstrated by Mignard. Molière also made it an occasion to champion Mignard's stand for independence:

> *Les grands hommes, Colbert, sont mauvais courtisans*
> *Peu faits à s'acquitter des devoirs complaisants.**

But it was not a question in fact of artistic integrity, nor even of a conflict of style, since Mignard had revealed in the Val-de-Grâce a gift for organisation and dramatic composition very similar to Le Brun's; the central issue was the enmity of two artists who would never bow to each other. Mignard was as ambitious, as conformist and as complaisant as his rival. Louis XIV, when sitting for yet another portrait, asked him, 'Do you find me older, Mignard?' With the skill of an accomplished courtier he replied, 'Sire, it is true that I see more victories on your Majesty's brow.' When Colbert died Le Brun lost ground, and as he watched the best commissions being given to his rival he deemed it best to retire from court. He died in 1690 and Mignard immediately abandoned his steadfast hostility to the Académie. On one and the same day he was elected associate, member, rector, director and chancellor.

Painting, sculpture and literature were not the only arts to be regulated by academies. Chapelain and Perrault were appointed to establish an Académie des Inscriptions et Belles-Lettres, misleadingly named since its purpose was to provide visual aids to an understanding of Louis XIV's true greatness; as Colbert crudely stated, 'it

---

* Great men, Colbert, are poor courtiers, ill-suited to carry out works of flattery.

is by the size of their monuments that kings are measured'. Academies were formed too to organise music and drama, and Colbert
contemplated founding an Académie Royale de Spectacles to provide 'tournaments, jousts, affrays, combats, marches, hunts and
fireworks'. One art which had hitherto gone wholly uncontrolled
was architecture. Not even the guilds had claimed jurisdiction over
it, but Colbert created the appropriate Académie in 1671, 'to raise
architecture to a higher degree of perfection than it is at today'.
Nicolas-François Blondel was charged with 'teaching the true rules
of architecture to young men who propose to undertake the profession', and was well qualified for the task. He was primarily an
engineer and a mathematician but he had a great respect for theory.
His *Cours d'Architecture, enseignée à l'Académie Royale* embodied
techniques of instruction akin to Le Brun's and revealed his acceptance of the ideals of classicism. 'Beauty is born from dimension and
proportion', he said, and if he was a little over-rigid in his devotion to the proportions sanctioned by Vitruvius, his austerely
classical Porte Saint-Denis was a very fair attempt at translating
theory into practice.

One other academy of note established by Colbert was the
Académie des Sciences. The history of its formation closely resembled that of the Académie Française, and Colbert's motives were
the same as Richelieu's. The informal group which had met, first
with Mersenne, and then at the *hôtel* of a *maître de requêtes* named
Montmar, was officially incorporated by Colbert in 1661. The
members, who were each paid 1,500 livres a year, met in his library
to debate mathematics on Wednesdays and natural science on Saturdays. Their function, as defined by Colbert, was 'to work for the
perfection of the sciences and arts, and to seek generally for all that
can be of use or convenience to the human race and particularly to
France'. They laid great emphasis on technology and industrial
processes, and their findings were given wide circulation by Colbert
in order to stimulate production, especially in the fields of mining
and metallurgy. After his death in 1683 it fell on bad days but was
reconstituted with 70 members in 1699 and was lodged in the
Louvre.

A corollary to Colbert's determination to direct the administration, the economy and the arts alike from the capital was his resolve to make the capital itself worthy of its exalted position. Since Henri IV had established a framework of plans and building regulations, Paris had improved beyond recognition. Scores of *hôtels* lent a new dignity to the streets and squares and several fine churches ennobled the skyline. The down-town character of the area near the Louvre had been remedied by Richelieu who built his own palace there, and was developed further in 1664 when Colbert commissioned Le Nôtre to apply his talents to the haphazard layout of the Tuileries gardens. The result, and the creation of the Cours de la Reine, made this the most popular area in Paris for an afternoon stroll. So crowded did it become that Colbert thought of excluding the public from the gardens, but was persuaded by Perrault, his *commis*, to deny entrance only to liveried servants and lackeys. As these were the people most given to public affrays, according to all contemporary accounts of life in Paris (see page 217) the decision was a good one, and made the gardens and river walks all the more attractive to the general public. Unfortunately the alleys were not gravelled, and in very hot weather a smothering dust assailed those who had come to take the air. Heavy rain created so much mud that on such occasions the gardens had to be closed.

Mud, of course, was one of the greatest handicaps of life in Paris, for, despite the attempts of Henri IV to control it, the *boue*, that monstrous amalgam of mud and sewage, still made the streets unsightly, unhealthy and dangerous. Parisians accepted it as a natural hazard of town life, and were themselves responsible for perpetuating the evil: 'In the neighbourhood of the Louvre and in many parts of the palace, you see piles of dirt on the steps, in the alleyways, behind doors, upstairs and almost everywhere, and you are assailed by a thousand abominable smells. All this arises from the fact that those who live there, those who frequent the place and those who are passing through use it daily as a place where they can relieve themselves.' This, to be fair, was a biased account since it was written by the authors of a commercial project to provide commodes for the royal palaces, but the following extract from a letter of 1670 indicates clearly the casual attitude revealed, even by ladies of rank, to the problem of sewage disposal: 'Mme de Longueville has berated Mme de Saulx and Mme de la Trimouille because, having been forced to relieve themselves during a performance at the theatre, they then threw everything over into the parterre in order to rid their box of the unpleasant smell, and caused such a rumpus that they were forced to leave the theatre.'

Despite the social habits of Parisians, Colbert found an effective solution by the appointment of La Reynie as *lieutenant-général de police*, whose successes in paving, lighting and policing the capital were equalled by his achievement in removing the *boue*. The regulations about the disposal of nightsoil and similar matters were strictly enforced, and gangs of workmen were employed to shift the accumulated dirt of centuries. La Reynie's efficiency and energy were all that were needed and Paris was almost transformed; unfortunately, after his death at the end of the century, his successors showed none of his qualities and the streets returned to their filthy condition.

What worried Colbert far more than the mud was the fact that in such a fine capital city the Louvre was inadequate to house so splendid a monarch as Louis XIV. Louis himself seemed to realise this too, but his solution was not Colbert's. He hated the palace for the discomfiture he had endured there as a child during the Fronde, and while the minister planned to extend it and to make it the most imposing edifice in Paris, the King sought to escape it altogether, and had already set Le Nôtre to work on the gardens at Versailles (see page 221). When *Les Plaisirs de l'Île Enchantée* were held there in 1664, to the great delight of the court, Colbert sensed that he was losing the game. It was not enough to persuade the King that Versailles was unsuited to his greatness, though this he tried to do—with unconscious irony: 'Your Majesty knows that apart from brilliant achievements in warfare nothing indicates the greatness and character of princes more than their buildings, and that posterity measures their greatness by the size of the superb houses they have raised in their lifetime. Ah! What a tragedy it would be if the greatest and most unknown of kings, indeed one with that special virtue which makes a truly great prince, should be measured by the size of Versailles.' Instead, he proposed as a more positive solution to offer Louis such attractive plans for the completion of the Louvre that he might abandon his passion for what Colbert regarded as an oversized hunting-lodge and spend his money on 'that superb palace which is much more worthy of your Majesty's greatness'.

Only two French architects had the ability for such a task, but Mansart refused to undertake it unless he were given a free hand throughout, and Le Vau, for some reason, was held suspect by Colbert; good mercantilist though he was, however, it was to Italy that he turned for a solution to his problem. The problem, in essence, was to prepare a plan for enclosing the Square Court, begun by Lescot and Le Mercier and continued in part by Le Vau, and to give it an impressive façade and entry on the east side. Four Italians submitted their plans; one by Rainaldi revealed how backward he imagined the French to be since he deliberately introduced domes of strange design and no pedigree along with other elements of the most extreme form of mannerism, but it was Bernini who carried the day, with a design of great visual excitement and baroque splendour. He proposed to build an oval pavilion—with great half-pillars uniting the façade and a massive entablature and balustrade above—from which two elliptical wings curved forward to the corner pavilions. The curves and angles were emphasised throughout by the line of the entablature and balustrade on top, and the flights of steps along the bottom, so massive in appearance that they appeared to serve as a podium for the building.

From Colbert's view it required plans of this sort and an architect of Bernini's stature to distract Louis from his predilection for Versailles, but to solve one problem he immediately created others. Bernini, the man who had completed St Peter's, was not the man to sympathise with Colbert's fears about costs, especially as the extension to the Louvre would involve the purchase of a great deal of property, not merely for the building site itself but in order to clear a space so that the full effect could be properly appreciated. Moreover, the plans had to be altered since Colbert decided that the eastern block, in addition to presenting an imposing façade for Parisians to see, would also have to house the royal suite. Bernini was most unhappy. In Rome he had his own assistants to deal with matters of detail, but in Paris he was expected to meet Colbert's staff in daily committees to discuss such details as the placing of lavatories. Chanteloup and his brother Fréart de Chambéry, who had befriended Poussin on his visit to Paris, did their best to reconcile him to his work, and at last in 1665 he drew up the final plans for Marot to engrave.

In contrast with his first design, Bernini's final one was as massive but much more flat and formal. The complex curves were lost; the flight of steps was replaced by an extraordinary rock-like basement supporting a heavily-rusticated ground floor; the second and third floors, heavily regular in appearance, were linked by a colossal order, and along the skyline stood a row of statues on the balustrade. Impressive but unexciting, it had serious faults. The windows were those of a Roman palace, too small for the sunless days of a northern city; the height was such that on the river front it dwarfed the existing buildings; the new court abutted so abruptly on to the existing parts of the Square Court that no relationship was established between them. Finally, as Colbert pointed out to Chanteloup, while the new court provided magnificent staircases and assembly rooms it was of little value for housing the royal suite: 'We cannot deny that the design is fine and splendid, but in destroying as it were the rest of the Louvre and in spending ten millions we leave the King no better housed than he is at present.'

No one publicly admitted to any second thoughts. The foundation stone was laid in October 1665 and Bernini returned to Rome as planned, apparently well pleased with everything: 'I can say', he wrote to Chanteloup, 'that I received a greater reward for my efforts in six months in Paris than in six years in Rome.' In 1666 his assistant, Matthias de Rossi, made models from the plans and was prepared to execute them, but Colbert began to play for time. From November until February 1667 he avoided seeing the models, and Rossi sensed that it was all over. Louis, too, was firmly opposed to the project. If anything were to be done at the Louvre it would have to be done swiftly and cheaply, so that nothing should interfere with his works at Versailles. Moreover, the outbreak of war in Europe meant that he could not afford to build two colossal palaces simultaneously. In the end Bernini's plans were abandoned and the present east front of the Louvre was built by Charles Perrault. Perrault was not an architect but as Colbert's *commis* in the Surintendance des Bâtiments he had lived with the problem for many years, and the massive basement and the free-standing colonnade of double columns along the upper floors of the present building are in many ways similar to the lower sections of a design originally proposed by Le Vau. The building was much simpler, and much less expensive than Bernini's, and it can be maintained that Perrault has offered not only the economical but also the classical solution to the problem. Certainly it seems to represent a dramatic repudiation of the baroque, especially as there was so little else to indicate thereafter that the great Bernini had lived in France for a year. Indeed, he passed as unnoticed as Rubens had been from 1622 to 1625. Much more to the point, however, the outcome of the Louvre affair represented a victory for Louis over Colbert. There was to be only one great palace for the King, and it was not to be the Louvre, but before we affirm too hastily that the baroque had been defeated, we should first examine the original work at Versailles.

The Roman Catholic Church in Italy had adopted the baroque, as we have seen, in order to impresss the layman with the magnificence of the house of God and with the power of His Church. Others too had noticed the capacity of baroque architecture to arouse awe and admiration and had adapted it for the palaces of princes. Le Vau, who had revealed some baroque tendencies at Vaux, was all the more determined to create an impressive structure for the King at Versailles, and while there is nothing of Bernini in his work his design came as near to the baroque as seventeenth-century France would accept. He did not destroy Louis XIII's château but built around it, enclosing everything but the *cour d'honneur* where the visitor arrived from Paris. On the garden side he built a heavily rusticated ground floor of 25 bays, which served more or less as a basement for a massive first floor marked by pilasters of the Ionic order with double pillars flanking the fourth bay from each end. Above this he ran an attic floor with balustrade, and above it statues repeated the rhythm of the bays and pilasters below. With no roof visible to add a contrasting line the building might have seemed extremely dull had he not set back the 11 middle bays of the first and attic floors to create a terrace above the ground floor.

The effect, as we see it in Sylvester's engraving of 1669, is most satisfying. The ground floor establishes the basic pattern of the building, the recessed first and attic floors give it variety and interest, and the two blocks to right and left, their central bays clearly articulated by the double pillars, are extremely well proportioned in relation to each other and to the whole façade. This is as near as French domestic architecture approached towards baroque in the seventeenth century and, restrained though it was, it was soon repudiated.

There is nothing dull about the classical façade as we saw it at Maisons, for example, but unfortunately, when Jules Hardouin-Mansart* came to alter Versailles in what he conceived to be the classical manner, he only succeeded at the price of a certain monotony. He built the Galerie des Glaces across the recessed terrace on the first floor, and thus brought the central façade forward to make a uniform, uninterrupted line. This in itself might have succeeded, had he not overemphasised it by extending it, without variety, along two wings which trebled the length of the garden façade. The sense of movement and of balance between one part of the structure and another which Le Vau had so skilfully established was now destroyed. In its place there is a mood of disciplined order, reflected in the severely motionless mirrors of Le Nôtre's *parterres d'eaux*. The excessive horizontal line and the unimpaired uniformity of its treatment make it a poor and uninspired example of French classicism.

Within the palace the decoration was directed by Le Brun. Whatever image we might hold of him as Colbert's *intendant* of the arts we must recognise that as a decorator he came near to genius. His gift for painting had been made obvious to the King, not only by his work at Vaux but also by his *peinture d'histoire* of the family of Darius standing helpless before Alexander (1661). In this he had

---

* Hardouin-Mansart was a great-nephew by marriage of François Mansart whose name he added to his own in 1668. He became the one really great architect of Louis's final years, but most of his work lies outside the limit of this study.

demonstrated the fondness for allegory—with Louis XIV identified
with Alexander—the careful observation of expression and gesture,
and the gift for dramatic composition which underlay his work at
Versailles. Moreover, for all his intellectual adherence to the
principles of Poussin, in practice he revealed a freer, more dramatic,
and more markedly emotional style, which comes closer to the
work of such Italian painters as Pietro da Cortona. His Grand
Escalier, for example, subsequently destroyed and known to us only
from the sketches, was a most remarkable feat of *trompe-l'œil* in the
Italian manner, for he painted the walls of the staircase to represent
balustrades and massive pillars, with great crowds of courtiers
pressing forward to observe the ascent of the ambassadors and their
suites.

There still survives his treatment of the Galerie des Glaces, and of
the two adjoining salons, the Salon de la Guerre and the Salon de la
Paix. His ambition was to surpass what he had done at Vaux and,
though the treatment is restrained in comparison with the decoration of Italian palaces, the result is impressive. He takes 30 great
occasions of the reign, and decks them out with the classical and allegorical devices expected of such a genre, so that Louis's assumption
of personal government is made in Roman dress and is proclaimed
by Mercury, but to describe, or even to study, the individual panels
is to misrepresent his main achievement. It was not so much the
detail of any one item or any one room that really indicated Le
Brun's genius but rather the total effect of his combination of painting, sculpture and furniture. It was clear that an organising mind had
planned their relationship to each other and to the room at large.

So great was this talent that Colbert appointed him to direct his
most original foundation, the Manufacture Royale des Meubles de
la Couronne at Gobelins, where everything that might be needed
for the royal palaces was designed and made according to Le Brun's
orders. There were tapestry makers—it was housed in a former
tapestry factory—who reproduced the masterpieces of Poussin,
Raphael and Le Brun; there were weavers, dyers and embroiderers;
there were goldsmiths, marble workers, sculptors such as Coysevox,
cabinet makers such as Boulle, and engravers such as Nanteuil. There

were specialists in every conceivable art or craft of decoration, including one in designing flower panels for over-doors, and the variety of the undertakings is illustrated by the tapestry made there to commemorate a visit by Louis XIV. It was also a school, with 60 apprentices who were given a thorough grounding in drawing and design before going on to anything else, and all those who successfully completed their training were *breveté* and made free of the guilds.

# nine

# The Age of Louis XIV

Versailles was famous not only for its decoration and design but also as the setting for the musical entertainments devised and directed by Lully. He played an important part, for example, in *Les Plaisirs de l'Île Enchantée* in 1664, which set a new trend in court entertainment. It was built around a fantasy of an enchanted island at Versailles, with magic rings, brave knights and wicked sorceresses, until on the third day the spell was broken after a series of six ballets, involving knights, giants, dwarfs, monsters and so on, and a spectacular firework display. The incidental music and the direction of the ballets was undertaken by Lully, who also presented in collaboration with Molière a comedy-ballet, *La Princesse d'Élide*. This was a new development, and a popular one, which combined Molière's gift for comedy—and we too easily forget that plays like *Le Bourgeois Gentilhomme* were first produced in this way—with Lully's inventive talent for light music and dances. It also marked an important stage in the education of public taste. Lully so far had not attempted to reconcile the French to the rich dissonances of Italian opera music nor to the long recitatives, but in his *ballets de cours* he had successfully introduced solo interludes, and even choral ensembles. The comedy-ballet in the years 1664–70 brought him much nearer to the frontiers of opera, since it was necessary to give the vocal side, including a lively type of recitative, precedence over the ballet.

The success of this genre prompted him at last to try his hand at opera. He was not the only one, of course. Italian operas were performed on occasion, and the abbé Perrin was writing libretti for Cambert to score in a manner acceptable to public taste. In 1669 Perrin secured a royal licence to control all operatic performances in France for a period of three years. He ended in prison for debt, however, and Cambert independently produced *Pomone* in 1671 and *Les peines et les plaisirs d'amour* in 1672. Perrin, still in prison, was so angry and disheartened that he finally sold his licence to Lully. This, in conjunction with his powers as *surintendant de la musique*, made him virtual dictator of French music, and an edict of 1672 granted him exclusive rights over all theatrical productions of a musical nature. No company could employ more than six violins without his consent, nor more than 12 musicians in all; and actors, dancers and musicians employed by him were to work for no one else. One immediate consequence was to destroy Lully's successful collaboration with Molière since, in ruthless enforcement of his monopoly, he expelled the playwright's troupe from the Palais Royal (see page 172) and denied them the right to perform their plays with musical accompaniment. For his invasion into the field of opera, therefore, he had to find a new librettist.

His first production was the *Fêtes de l'Amour et de Bacchus* in November 1672, which was little more than a stringing together of several pastoral scenes from earlier ballets, but in 1673, with Quinault to write the libretto, he presented *Cadmus et Hermione*. This, his first full opera, he cautiously described as a *tragédie lyrique*, but his fears were proved unnecessary. Louis was enchanted by it, and insisted that the Palais Royal became a permanent home for opera in France. *Alceste* followed in 1674, *Thésée* in 1675 and *Isis* in 1677. For an imagined slight to Mme de Maintenon in the libretto of *Isis* Quinault was banished from court; until his return in 1680 Lully collaborated with Thomas Corneille, and thereafter continued to produce one new opera almost every year.

*Cadmus et Hermione* established Lully as an operatic composer in the French idiom, and he was careful not to jeopardise his reputation by further experiment. Whatever the theme his treatment never altered. In place of the Italian overture of three movements he invented a shorter, more arresting form designed to hold the attention of an audience as yet unused to these things. After a short but solemn introduction, he gave them a lively, catchy movement, developed more or less as a fugue, and ended with a coda. Then followed the invariable patriotic prologue in which, as in *Armide* for example, la Gloire and la Sagesse hymned the praise of Louis XIV. Once these obsequious rites had been performed, the story could begin. Generally it was a five-act tragedy, observing most of the rules of the Hôtel de Bourgogne, and usually devoted to the theme of mortals striving against the magic powers of sorcerers or arousing the jealousy of the gods. In every case Lully allowed the stage managers the most splendid opportunities to demonstrate their skill in simulating earthquakes and tempests and other manifestations of supernatural powers.

*Armide*, the last of his *tragédies lyriques*, will serve to illustrate the others. Armide herself is a Syrian sorceress who lures brave knights to her enchanted palace and keeps them prisoner. The play begins with the voluntary arrival of Hidraot, prince of Damas, with his suite, to a lively march tune. This is followed by a series of ballets performed by Hidraot's suite and by Armide's, since it was necessary for Lully to reassure his audience that they were not entirely divorced from the well-loved milieu of the *ballet de cour* in which he had first made his reputation. Thus reassured, the audience could then accept a degree of recitative as Hidraot and Armide plot together to destroy a powerful knight named Renault, and the act ends on a dramatic note with the arrival of news that Renault has succeeded in releasing all Armide's prisoners. Act Two begins with Armide casting a spell on Renault, who obligingly falls asleep by the water's edge so that Lully can introduce a ballet of water nymphs who dance and sing around him. Then drama returns as Armide enters to sing an aria of triumph over his prostrate body.

And so the opera continues—and it is genuinely an opera even though the link with the *ballet de cour* is so obvious. In the first place the action of the drama is given musical expression in the recitatives, and this perhaps was Lully's greatest technical achievement. He carried it off by studying the speech rhythms of La Champmeslée,

the greatest tragic actress of the day, and by finding musical equiva-
lents to imitate the emphatic inflections and sonorous vowels which
so delighted the Hôtel de Bourgogne. In consequence his recitatives
demand great flexibility and liveliness of tempo, and the bar values
change almost with every phrase, but the effect was much more
acceptable to French ears which found the Italian recitatives both
heavy and monotonous. Lully's operas deserve the name in the
second place for the manner in which he learnt to use the orchestra
to capture and to reinforce the mood of the recitatives and arias.
Originally he was content to provide a simple obbligato accompaniment, but as he gained in confidence the orchestration became much
richer and more descriptive, indicating the delights of an enchanted
garden or the terrors of a battle scene. In the following example we
see, as Renault falls asleep under Armide's spell, how the muted
strings echo his mood and give particular emphasis to a phrase like
'un son harmonieux'.

Lully's success as a musician was matched by an ability to secure a
reward commensurate with his talents. The monopoly conferred

upon him in 1672, along with his post as *surintendant de la musique*, assured him of considerable wealth, but, like any bourgeois, he coveted more than that. In 1681, after deliberately staging at court exactly the sort of buffoonery and ballet which Louis XIV could not resist, he asked for, and received, appointment as a *secrétaire du roi*; this did not involve him in administration, but was an office which carried with it the status of a noble. After that, he was free to live the part with great conviction, building his own 'place in the country' and marrying his daughter into another noble family. Meanwhile the operas continued to appear each year to universal acclaim until, after *Armide* in 1686, he decided to commemorate the King's recovery from a serious illness by composing a *Te Deum*. It was an ambitious undertaking, but most successful. There is great splendour at times, and the choral sections are powerfully orchestrated, but Lully also reveals his light rhythmic touch in the solo interludes which, apart from illustrating his style to perfection, convey a beautifully balanced emotion. Unhappily, at the performance of his *Te Deum* he struck his foot with the baton. The wound, going unattended, turned into an abscess from which he died in 1687.

Lully's privilege of 1672 had put an end to a successful comedy-ballet partnership, but Molière's company adapted his plays for performance without music, and Molière himself remained high in Louis's favour. Ten years earlier, *L'École des Femmes*, a sequel of sorts to *Les Précieuses Ridicules* with additional caricatures of the nobility, had won him a royal pension of 1,000 livres and, equally valuable, protection in the ensuing intrigues and pamphlet war, as those who imagined themselves to be the victims of his satire joined forces with rival actors and playwrights to discredit him. Encouraged by Louis's benevolent attitude, Molière made a spirited riposte in 1663 with *La Critique de l'École des Femmes*, and then, apparently at Louis's own suggestion, attacked the same targets once again in *L'Impromptu de Versailles*. Louis admired the vigour of his plays and their broad humour, and he was only too happy to enjoy the satirical portraits of ambitious bourgeois and foolish nobles, of misers, doctors and *précieuses*, provided no mockery was made of kings. He stood godfather in 1664 to Molière's son by his marriage to Armande Béjart,

Madeleine's sister, and in the following year gave permission for the company to call itself the Troupe du Roi and to draw a pension of 6,000 livres.

Royal protection became all the more important when, in addition to his other targets, Molière selected for *Tartuffe* the odious hypocrite who battened on the genuine religious fervour of the age. It is the story of a character who ingratiates himself into the house of a certain Orgon as his spiritual director. Once established he takes possession of his property and, very nearly, of his wife, but such is Tartuffe's dominion over his poor dupe that Molière can find no other dénouement than the clumsy device of a royal officer arriving to arrest him for his previous crimes. It is not a comedy at all, and Molière clearly intended it to be a powerful indictment of hypocrisy. Instead, the Church, which already had a prejudiced view of actors and the theatre, interpreted it as an indictment of its spiritual directors: 'M. Molière is one of the most dangerous enemies that the century or the world has raised against the church of Jesus Christ', wrote a Jansenist critic, Baillet, and though Louis XIV took a saner view he was pressed by his advisers to prevent a public performance. In 1667 Molière tried to present it under the title of *Panulfe ou l'Imposteur*, but the theatre was closed down, and it was not until 1669 that with Louis's approval he was permitted 50 performances at the Palais Royal.

*Tartuffe* was very much a *succès de scandale*, only surpassed by the light-hearted entertainments like *Les Fâcheux* and *L'École des Maris* which had been hastily composed to divert the court and which enjoyed 106 and 108 performances, respectively, in Paris during Molière's lifetime. The more solidly constructed plays on which his reputation now rests were more moderately successful; *L'Avare*, for example, was performed 47 times and *Le Bourgeois Gentilhomme* 44, but unlike the '*divertissements royaux*', which were wholly ephemeral, they had enduring qualities and show that Molière was, in his way, as classical a dramatist as Corneille. Not everyone will accept this opinion, but it is an over-pompous view of classicism which interprets the golden rule of *plaire* as the giving of pleasure but which draws the line at hilarity. Just as Corneille made tragedy more than the mere narration of successive miserable episodes, so Molière raised comedy above the traditions of farce, burlesque and buffoonery. What gives his plays their essential unity, despite a degree of sub-plot and minor intrigue which Racine would have abhorred, is his demonstration of the nature of his central character. His plays are not progressions of comic incidents but the development of a single theme around a central character.

In addition, Molière shared the classic taste for anatomising society in general and human personalities in particular. He recognised that life to be successful demands the reconciliation of conflicting forces, and as a true man of his time he accepted a reasonable or logical compromise as the norm—though we must again beware of attributing to Molière personally the views of those characters in his plays who appear reasonable to us. When there is an imbalance of forces, the result is comic or tragic: comic when the consequences are merely absurd, tragic if they are disastrous, and in *Tartuffe* and *L'Avare* Molière came near to exposing the grimmer possibilities of human frailty.

What makes his characters so interesting is that they combine both universal and particular features. When Molière was accused of maliciously portraying people whom he knew he deliberately repudiated the charge and in *L'Impromptu de Versailles*, where he defended himself against his critics, he affirmed that his intention 'is to depict the customs of society without involving individuals'. The individuality that his characters undoubtedly possessed sprang from the creative genius of their inventor. His misers and his social climbers are not merely universal archetypes of avarice or ambition: Harpagon becomes a living, individual miser with a personality all his own. This Molière achieved by combining a gift for comic invention, an observant eye, and a solid professionalism derived from years of experience on the stage. In the first instance, indeed, he established these characters by acting them himself, and it was thus that he met his death, acting against doctor's orders in, of all plays, *Le Malade Imaginaire*.

His death was a crisis for his company. With Lully, like an enclosing landlord, in possession of the Palais Royal they had to take a lease on the Hotel Guénégaud, a tennis court in the rue Mazarine. There they were joined by members of the Marais theatre which went out of business and, for a time, by Thomas Corneille. He was without doubt the most successful author of the century, turning his hand with equal facility to anything from a Spanish comedy of intrigue to romantic historical-tragedy. He wrote several plays for Molière's widow, who had taken charge of the company, until he was lured away to write libretti for Lully. By that time the company was on a sound footing and was joined in 1679 by La Champmeslée —a move which left the Hôtel de Bourgogne without its greatest tragic actress. Louis XIV intervened and ordered all the French actors in Paris to combine in one company and thus, in 1680, established the Comédie Française.

Molière, popular though he was, belonged to a profession which was subjected to much abuse and it was not for his plays, not even for *Tartuffe*, but for his acting that the church authorities denied his corpse the right of burial in holy ground. In contrast, a playwright like Racine, who held the office of historiographer royal, was able to enjoy a much greater degree of social respect which had little to do with his prowess as a dramatist. Indeed, as the duc de Saint-Simon once said: 'There is nothing of the poet about him: he is altogether an *honnête homme*.'

Orphaned at the age of four, Racine was brought up because of family connections as a charity scholar at Port-Royal. Antoine Le Maître, one of the most distinguished of the *solitaires*, had once taken refuge with his parents at La Ferté-Milon and he acted as a father to the boy. He encouraged him in his study of languages, including Greek, developed his interest in literature and advised him to prepare for the bar. In 1658 Racine went to the Collège d'Harcourt to study law, but a few months of this was as much as he could stomach. Through the help of a cousin, who was *intendant* to the duc de Luynes, he secured employment in the duc's service and came to Paris. There he wrote an ode on the marriage of Louis XIV and Marie-Thérèse which won him favourable comment at court, but no matter how assiduously he courted Chapelain and the theatre managers his other poems and plays were universally rejected. As a result he left Paris in 1661 and went to join his uncle at Uzès in Languedoc, intending to become a priest. Despite his uncle's post as vicar general of the diocese, Racine discovered that the fount of patronage flowed slowly and, preferring to be ignored in Paris rather than in the provinces, he abandoned his clerical ambitions and returned to the capital. This time he was lucky. He arrived in time to celebrate the King's recovery from an illness with a loyal ode which earned for him a pension of 600 livres, and in 1664 Molière gave him the chance to stage Le Thébaïde at the Palais Royal.

In the following year Molière's company presented his new play, Alexandre, but so successful was it that Racine could not bear to have it performed only at the Palais Royal. After six days he sold it to the Hôtel de Bourgogne because of its greater prestige as the home of classical tragedy, and not only deprived Molière of his anticipated profit but decamped with Mlle du Parc, the best actress in the company. He then turned on Port-Royal in a scandalous polemic, ostensibly because of Nicole's comments on dramatists and poisoners, but in reality because the archbishop of Paris wanted to discredit Port-Royal and Racine wanted preferment. These acts of ingratitude made him unpopular for a time in Paris, but the court ladies around Mme de Montespan favoured him, and with their encouragement he began to write tragedies like Andromaque (1667)—which achieved as great a success as Le Cid—and Britannicus (1669). In this year Mlle du Parc died, to be succeeded as Racine's mistress by no less a catch than La Champmeslée, the most talented tragic actress of the century, who in consequence abandoned the Marais theatre to act in Racine's play at the Hôtel de Bourgogne. For the next seven years he enjoyed the success he had long struggled for. Bérénice (1670), Bajazet (1672), Mithridate (1673) and Iphigénie (1675) were all acclaimed, and their author was elected to the Académie Française. More valuable still, Louis XIV made him a trésorier de France, an office much in demand since it conferred nobility on its occupant. By now he was living on 5,000 livres a year, had 6,000 deposited with the bankers, and enjoyed a splendid set of rooms in the Hôtel des Ursins.

In 1677 he presented Phèdre, perhaps his greatest play, but the duc de Nevers and the duchesse de Bouillon caballed against it. They championed Corneille's cause as the finest tragic playwright of the century and, to discredit Racine, bought up the best seats at the Hôtel de Bourgogne for the first two nights of *Phèdre* and left them empty. Meanwhile they staged an inferior play on the same subject at the Marais. Racine gave up the theatre. He was hypersensitive to criticism and, even in his most successful days, one adverse comment had been enough to induce a state of melancholy. He always wrote the prefaces to his plays on the day following their production so that he could justify himself, with passionate intensity, against his critics. Perhaps, too, he was affected by his appointment, with Boileau, as historiographer royal, believing it to be unbecoming in a courtier and a historian to have any association with the theatre.

Above all, his conscience nagged him for his treachery to Port-Royal, and he had written an introduction to *Phèdre* designed to advertise the moral efficacy of tragic drama: 'The passions are portrayed merely in order to show the aberrations to which they give rise; and vice is painted throughout in colours which bring out its hideousness and hatefulness. That is really the objective which everyone working for the public should have in mind, and it is what the tragedians of early times aimed at above all else.' Lest the point be missed, he added in conclusion his desire 'of reconciling to tragedy a host of people famous for their piety and their doctrine who have recently condemned it and who would no doubt pass a more favourable judgment on it if writers were as keen to edify their spectators as to amuse them, thereby complying with the real purpose of tragedy'.

He brought about a piecemeal reconciliation with Port-Royal and, as evidence of his reformed character, married a girl of good bourgeois family and—despite his own arguments in its defence—withdrew entirely from the theatre. Instead of plays he wrote the sort of history designed to flatter Louis XIV and made a great success of his career as courtier, being invited to Marly in 1687, which was an honour reserved for those of the highest standing. Mme de Maintenon, who had founded at Saint-Cyr a college for the daughters of army officers, prevailed upon him to write for them 'some poetic drama of a moral and historical nature from which love is totally excluded'. It was a commission that Racine dared not refuse, and in 1689 *Esther* was presented according to specification. It was acted by the girls so well that a special performance was given before an audience of courtiers, and *Esther* became the success of the year. 'All the court is charmed with *Esther*', wrote Mme de Sévigné. 'The Princesse de Conti ventured to praise the opera the other day but she was silenced by being accused of liking love scenes, which are now quite out of favour at Court.' A problem arose in that the young girls of Saint-Cyr had their heads turned by the excitement, and the young nobles of Versailles began to trespass in the grounds in the hope of meeting them. Mme de Maintenon was horrified, and when Louis XIV ordered Racine to write another play for the girls to act, *Athalie* was performed in private before the King alone.

In his preface to *Bérénice*, Racine had urged his audiences to consult their hearts instead of worrying their heads about the rules of drama: 'I urge them to have enough good opinion of themselves not to believe that if they can be moved and given pleasure by a play it can ever be altogether against the rules. The principal rule is to give pleasure and to arouse emotion; all the others are only made to this end.' It was a fair analysis, but the rules in fact created no problems for Racine: they suited him so ideally that they seemed to have been created specially for his type of tragic drama. His aim was to present a simple issue—Will Iphigénie be sacrificed? Will Andromaque marry Pyrrhus?—as simply as possible, and he was angry with those who said that this indicated a lack of dramatic invention. 'They never dream that on the contrary all my invention goes to making something out of nothing, and that laying on a host of incidents has always been the refuge of poets who recognise that their own genius lacks the fluency and vigour to hold an audience's attention for five hours by one simple theme which is upheld by the violence of the passions, by the beauty of the sentiments and by the elegance of their expression.'

Contrived simplicity of this kind is of the essence of classicism and, far from being an intellectual affair, this concentration of emotion arouses the most powerful and passionate responses from audiences. For those of us accustomed to the tragedies of Shakespeare and Corneille—different though these are from each other—this is difficult to understand, since the rigorous exclusion of spectacle, of action and, indeed, in one sense, of rhetoric would seem at first sight to result in dullness. Since the action is limited to the mind, even scenery is abandoned and we are left with nothing but talk. Yet all this is wholly misleading, since it is the talk alone which arouses the excitement. The plays invariably begin at a moment when passions are beginning to mount, and the unities of time and place intensify the mood; no change of scene nor interval of time allows release from the mounting tension. Moreover, the austere economy of characterisation and of vocabulary ensures that nothing distracts from the relentless unfolding of the central theme until its expert and remorseless *reconnaissance*, the unbearable moment of truth when it is resolved.

Racine defined tragedy as 'a simple story with very little to it, which can be shown to happen in a single day and which, as it moves towards its end, is sustained only by the interests, the sentiments and the passions of the characters'. 'There is no need for blood and corpses', since these only distract attention from the torment of the mind and the soul. He did not hesitate to edit his source material. Corneille had chosen extraordinary themes which were acceptable only because they were historically true; Racine twisted both fable and history to serve his purposes, for example, and when criticised, assured his critics that instead of bothering about the changes he had made, they should 'consider the excellent use that these changes serve and admire the ingenious manner in which the story has been related to its subject-matter'. Some things were unalterable, of course, and violent men like Pyrrhus had to be presented in all their ruthlessness, whatever the affront to *bienséance*; but as Racine remarked, 'All these heroes were not made to be Céladons' and 'Pyrrhus has not read our novels'.

In Racine's plays it is clear that passion destroys, whereas in earlier writers it frequently ennobles. This has been explained in terms of a feudal period, dominated by a nobility which applauds the vigorous release of passion, being followed by a period of royal control when everything is regulated; but we do not need to look to Louis XIV's absolutism to find the source of Racine's philosophy, since it stemmed more directly and more personally from the influence of Port-Royal. Though he deliberately rejected Port-Royal until after writing *Phèdre*, and though he lived the life of a voluptuary, he could not release his mind from the thrall of Jansenist theology. Love was never romanticised at Port-Royal and Racine demonstrated that its passion was not the blooming of a generous nature but a madness sent to destroy it—how else indeed could he explain the blackmail by which Pyrrhus, in love with Andromaque, threatens to kill her son unless she marries him? Predestination and the pitiless nature of divine judgment alike inform his plays. Corneille makes tragedy from the clash of wills; Racine finds it in the subjection of mankind to the gods. It is the divine desire for vengeance which makes possible the plot of *Iphigénie*, and ensures that Agamemnon, whatever way he turns, cannot escape from sacrificing his daughter to appease this wrath. When Phèdre declares her guilty passion for her stepson Hippolyte, this is not a tale of sordid lust. Rather, since it is Venus who commands the queen to betray her husband and herself in this way, it is more the story of Phèdre's doomed attempts to resist the unnatural decree of the goddess. More savage and relentless still is the implication that the gods compel mankind to sin, made explicit by Oedipe's widow who cries out about the massacre which the gods decreed:

> *This is the justice of the mighty gods.*
> *They lead us to the edge of the abyss.*
> *They make us sin but do not pardon us.*

Racine could not escape the profound pessimism of Jansenist theology, no matter how he tried to rebel against it, and as a dramatist he drew upon it to give a new dimension to the tragic nature of the human predicament. As a result, his tragedies reveal, as did Pascal, the misery of mankind bereft of a redeemer; but unlike Pascal he introduces no redemption. The gods of Greece and Rome are implacable; they exact their penalties and brook no intercession and even when, at the last, Racine was reconciled to the Church, he goes no further than to present the jealous, vengeance-seeking God of the Old Testament.

The spirit and the form of Racine's tragedies were directly similar to those of the novels of Mme de la Fayette. 'The choice of a definite theme, the ability to expose a situation and to conduct it to a logical climax, and above all the art of portraying the gradual disintegration of the will under the corrosive influence of a grand passion—these were new elements in the novel which now, in imitation of tragedy, attempts something greater than mere fidelity in the reproduction of external detail. . . . The psychological novel is born' (Green). This was remarkable, for, unlike Racine who inherited an established tradition of tragic drama, her only exemplars were the tumultuous and long-winded romances of d'Urfé and Mlle de Scudéry. At first she had nothing to criticise in them, since she was herself a member of that salon society for whom they had written. She was virtually brought up at the Hôtel de Rambouillet, and so unkindly did she take to marriage in 1655, when she discovered that her life was to be spent on her husband's estates in Bourbonnais and the Auvergne, that within three years she had returned to Paris on her own.

Her own salon was attended by the friends of Mme de Sablé, and in particular by La Rochefoucauld. Their friendship we have described, and it is not surprising that her novels reflected to a large extent both the brevity of his style and the pessimism of his philosophy. Her first novel was *La Princesse de Montpensier* (1662) which began at a point where the *romans héroïques* left off—at the point of marriage, which she clearly regarded as an unsatisfactory condition. The heroine is endowed with a deceitful husband, a faithful friend and a faithless lover; in consequence of the dénouement she loses both the friend and the lover and forfeits her husband's respect. Nothing remains but to die of grief. Equally miserable in synopsis is the plot of her most famous novel, *La Princesse de Clèves*, whose heroine marries the prince out of affection rather than love. Despite herself she is attracted to the duc de Nemours, a notorious philanderer, and he to her, though neither wishes to recognise the fact.

At length she tells her husband of her passion, hoping that he may take her away from the court and from temptation; he, poor fool, assumes that she is already guilty, falls ill and dies. The lovers are now free to marry but the princess flies to a nunnery, and Nemours, who has given up for her sake the chance of marriage to the queen of England, is left alone and inconsolable.

There is very little in these tales of suffering and unrequited love— save for the dismal pessimism of their conclusion—to distinguish them from the novels of Mlle de Scudéry and d'Urfé, but it is the treatment, not the subject-matter, which gives them their classical form. There are, for example, no chance meetings, no coincidences, and no *deus-ex-machina* conclusions: instead we have the orderly and logical development of issues inherent in the opening pages. No by-plots distract attention from the single theme of each novel, and the style throughout is succinct, measured and ceremonious. Moreover, as with Racine, the physical setting of the scene becomes unimportant since the action is transferred to the mind. It is not the actions of the central characters which matter but their thoughts and emotions, and it is the psychological insight which she reveals in portraying these which distinguishes the novels of Mme de la Fayette.

She shows for example how, when Mme de Clèves reveals to her husband her love for Nemours, their relationship, hitherto founded on respect alone, becomes paradoxically more intimate as they discover for the first time a more genuine understanding of each other. There is also great perception in the description of a scene in which Nemours has leapt across the room to dance with Mme de Clèves without having been introduced. After the dance they are summoned by Marie Stuart, *la reine dauphine*, who offers to introduce them. Nemours says that he knows who his partner is but that she does not know him. Marie Stuart replies—and the passage is worth quoting to indicate the economy of the style: '*Je crois, dit Mme la Dauphine, qu'elle le sait aussi bien que vous savez le sien. —Je vous assure, madame, reprit Mme de Clèves, qui paraissait un peu embarrassée, que je ne devine pas si bien que vous pensez. —Vous devinez fort bien, répondi Mme la Dauphine; et il y a même quelque chose d'obligeant pour M. de*

*Nemours à ne pas vouloir avouer que vous le connaissez sans jamais l'avoir vu.'*\* Mme de la Fayette's consuming interest in the nature of love and its disconcerting consequences reflected the interest of the salon society in which she lived, and if we find obvious parallels in her work with the *'ravages de la passion'* of Racine, there are strong links too with the pessimistic insight of La Rochefoucauld. The drama which is enacted in her heroine's heart can in fact be summarised in two of the *Maximes*: *'La même fermeté qui sert à résister à l'amour sert aussi à le rendre violent et durable'*; *'Qu'une femme est à plaindre quand elle a tout ensemble de l'amour et de la vertu.'*†

The novels of Mme de la Fayette provided, as she put it, 'a perfect replica of court society and of the way in which we live', and though she derived her plots from the courts of the sixteenth century it was the highly formalised conventions of Versailles which she portrayed. These conventions had done much to make life more decorous and refined, and reflected the standards first established by Mme de Rambouillet; they had, moreover, been encouraged by Louis XIV for political ends, in order to cultivate among his courtiers a taste for order, routine and precedence. Like so much of Louis' work, however, it was overdone. Social life became so formalised that by the time Versailles had been completed the younger nobles were deserting it at every opportunity for the freer, gayer life of the capital. Versailles itself became something of a melancholy white elephant. The splendid palace in which the idol of his people might court his mistresses and accept the plaudits of the world was built too late; the dull respectability of Mme de Maintenon fell like a pall on court society; the messengers who galloped up the spacious avenues from 1688 to 1714 brought news only of defeat at the hands of the European powers who destroyed the French hegemony,

---

\* 'I think she knows your name', said Mme la Dauphine, 'as well as you know hers.' 'I assure you, madame,' went on Mme de Clèves, who seemed somewhat embarrassed, 'that I am not so good at guessing as you think.' 'You can guess very well', answered Mme la Dauphine, 'and it is very flattering to M. de Nemours to be reluctant to admit that you know him without having seen him before.'

† The same firmness of character which resists love, serves also to make love passionate and lasting. How much is a woman to be pitied when she is both virtuous and in love.

and Louis himself grew old in sadness as his sons and grandsons died before him in the palace he had built for them to inherit.

By 1689, when the north wing of Versailles had been completed to balance the south wing, reducing the façade to a state of uninspired conformity and order, the *grand siècle* was already over. That great flowering of French genius in warfare, government, religion and the arts was ended, to be succeeded by defeat, bankruptcy, administrative incompetence and a deadening uniformity which silenced with brutality the individual witness of both Huguenots and Catholics. The men who had made glorious the early years of Louis XIV were dead: Condé and Turenne; Le Tellier and Colbert; Le Vau and Mansart; Poussin; Molière, Corneille and Lully. Le Brun was on his deathbed, and Racine alone survived to add a postscript to the literature of the classical age. For all of them, and for their age, an epitaph is found in Bossuet's funeral oration on Condé, in which he recalls the glories of the past but senses that there is nothing in the future with which to comfort his audience: 'For that flock which I must nourish with the word of life, I can offer nothing but the remnants of a dying flame and a failing voice.'

'A classical period, when it is prolonged, can only degenerate into pseudo-classicism, because when there is no more chaos to transform into order and beauty there is nothing left but to imitate other people's masterpieces according to a set of artificial and superficial rules' (Peyre). This was already true of the Académie Royale de Peinture et de Sculpture, and happily it did not go unchallenged. Roger de Piles, a critic not an artist, rebelled against Le Brun's interpretation of the gospel of Poussin and, as Pascal had once appealed from the Sorbonne to the verdict of the salons, so de Piles carried the conflict from the Académie to that same court. As early as 1673 in a *Dialogue sur les coloris* he attacked Poussin for his failure to understand or to employ colour, and in his argument extolled the virtues of Rubens. Later, in his life of Rubens and in his *Conversations de la Couleur*, he went further by arguing that nature is represented more faithfully by colour than by line. This was not just a simple debate about the rival virtues of Poussin and Rubens, but the symptom of a general loss of confidence in the classical ideal.

After Le Brun had died there was no one to maintain authority as he had done, and conflicting tendencies became clearly visible in the painting of the time. 'The Baroque invades religious and historical subjects; mythological themes are treated with a freedom from classical rules which eventually turns into a rococo lightness; portraiture fluctuates between bombastic variations on the methods of Rubens and van Dyck on the one hand, and naturalistic experiments in the vein of Rembrandt on the other' (Blunt).

In literature, too, new forces were at work: 'Although the garden of literature presented, as it had never done before or since, a prospect of smooth lawns and symmetrical avenues, the winds were bringing back the seeds of wild flowers and strong growths of the forest' (Clark). One of the last great works of the classical period, and the first to reveal genuine traits of social and political nonconformity, was *Les Caractères* by Jean de La Bruyère. La Bruyère was born of Parisian bourgeois parents in 1645, qualified in law at Orléans, and was saved from practice by a legacy from a rich uncle. Instead he bought a lucrative sinecure, becoming *trésorier général de France au bureau des finances de la généralité de Caen* in 1673, and promptly moved to Paris where he entered the society of the salons. Reserved and independent, he acquired a reputation for learning and in 1684 was invited by Bossuet to become tutor to the great Condé's grandson. La Bruyère was no tuft-hunter and had no need of employment but he accepted the job, partly because the princely state of the Bourbons was undeniably attractive, and partly because the family home at Chantilly had a reputation for being a centre of the arts.

Chantilly was not too far from Paris and, since the days of Charlotte de Montmorency, Condé's mother, had been very much an extension of the Hôtel de Rambouillet where guests took part in open-air plays and ballets, and played games of versification. Condé himself had twice retired there—in disgrace after the Fronde and in glory after his victories in the Dutch war—and he filled the place with interesting people. His own interests were very wide: 'His knowledge embraces all things', wrote La Fontaine, 'the court and the camp; the pleasures of conversation and of books; of gardens and of building.' He transformed the old castle of the sixteenth-century

Constable of France into a comfortable residence, and remodelled the gardens and park. Unlike Versailles, Chantilly had a super-abundance of forest and water, and the problem was to give it a sense of composition and order by cutting back the forest and traversing it with great rides, and by channelling the rapid streams into a canal and a *parterre d'eaux*. Excess water was carried away by aqueduct to supply the moat, a set of fountains and an enormous cascade. These waterworks were greatly admired by all, not least by Bossuet, bishop of Meaux, the most outstanding preacher—and the most rigorously orthodox priest—of the day. He came frequently to Chantilly to play chess and to discuss the art of fountains and cascades. Condé lent him his *fontainier*, and Bossuet was able to reply, 'I am now so perfect in the science of hydraulics that your highness will never again have to rebuke my stupidity'; so much were the fountains a feature of the place that in his funeral oration on Condé, Bossuet could not omit a reference to 'those superb alleys where the sound of fountains is never silenced'.

To this idyllic refuge La Bruyère came in 1684, only to find a marked contrast between the ordered gardens and the disordered household. Condé was arrogant and tempestuous; his son was worse, and of him La Bruyère wrote: 'unnatural child, cruel father, terrible husband, detestable master'. The grandson whom he taught was as intolerable as the father, yet all the family were endowed with a genuine love of the arts and with excellent taste. La Bruyère, embittered by the off-hand treatment he received, was yet fascinated by them all, and could never tear himself away. In his anomalous role, neither an equal nor a servant, he cultivated a gift for detached observation, and the penetrating observation of humanity which informed *Les Caractères* was distilled from his experience of life at Chantilly.

As a commentator on human frailty he was following in the tradition of La Rochefoucauld, Boileau and Molière—as he himself recognised: '*Tout est dit*', he began, 'Everything has been said already, and one comes too late after 7,000 years in which men have lived and reflected on their existence. On the subject of human behaviour the best and the better have been harvested, and one can

only glean behind the ancients and the most talented of our contemporaries.' Of his own 'gleaning' he acknowledged his debt to
the society he had observed so intently: 'I hereby return to the public
what it has lent me: I have borrowed from it the material for this
book.' The sense of personal involvement is more pronounced in
*Les Caractères* than in other books of the same genre because, though
there is little that can be directly described as autobiographical, there
is no coherent form to give an air of classical detachment. Instead,
his observations are expressed, according to his mood or because of
his subject-matter, in a variety of ways—in maxims, portraits,
dialogues or anecdotes—which are often dramatic, always lively, and
sometimes brilliantly perceptive.

'If a tax-farmer fails, the courtiers say of him, he is a bourgeois,
a man of no importance, a ruffian: but if he succeeds they want to
marry his daughter.' A similar point is made less epigrammatically.
'Arfure used to go alone and on foot to the great portico of Saint....
and listen from afar to a sermon by a Carmelite or a doctor of
theology whom she could see only obliquely and whom she could
hear but imperfectly. Her virtue went unperceived and her devotion
was as little noticed as herself. Her husband then became a tax-
farmer and made a monstrous fortune in six years. She now arrives
at church in a chariot: someone carries her heavy train: the speaker
pauses while she finds a place: she sees him full face and misses not a
single word nor the slightest gesture.' His dislike for tax-farmers, and
his contempt for those who truckled to them is savage enough to
indicate a personal spite, or at least the resentment of a man who has
failed to make his own fortune. But La Bruyère for all his bitterness
about many things was curiously uninterested in his personal wealth.
His legacy, his office at Caen and his position at Chantilly were
sufficient for his need, and much of the profit from *Les Caractères* was
given to a bookseller to provide a dowry for his daughter. There was
indeed as much sympathy as irony in his comment on those who had
acquired great wealth: 'Let us not envy them: they have a burdensome title to it which would never suit us. To gain it they have
staked their rest, their health, their honour and their conscience: they
have paid too much for it, and nothing is worth such a price.'

Despising the tax-farmer was a truism of seventeenth-century social comment, but La Bruyère went on to attack targets which no other writer of the classical period was prepared to touch, and the mood of *Les Caractères* comes very close at times to the rationalist criticism of institutions which we associate with the eighteenth century. Torture, for example, he described as 'a marvellous invention and quite infallible for convicting innocent men of feeble disposition and acquitting guilty men who are born robust'; La Rochefoucauld might have envied the phrasing, he would not have uttered the sentiments. More fundamental is the criticism of the social structure when La Bruyère attacks the general view that noble birth in itself confers innate qualities: 'Men of spirit despise the high-born nobles who have only their high birth to show.' Warfare is condemned for its unnecessary waste of life and property, and if William III of England and Holland is rebuked for loving war too much, the implication is planted that Louis XIV himself is not above reproach. La Bruyère is not afraid to lecture monarchs on their duty: 'To say that a prince is the arbiter of men's lives is only to say that men, because of their crimes, are naturally subject to the law and to justice, of which the King is the trustee: to add that he is absolute master of all his subjects' goods, is the language of flattery.' No one else but La Bruyère had yet presumed to instruct Louis XIV in his *métier du roi*; no one else had had the insight and the courage to indict him for his failure by asking, 'Is the flock made to serve the shepherd, or the shepherd to serve his sheep?'

As the classical mood began to wane, and as the men who had created that mood were succeeded by those of less ability, there was a corresponding tendency to cling more tightly for security to the precepts of the past. It had never been a feature of classicism to idolise antiquity, but the new generation which lacked confidence in itself tried to dispel its uncertainties by defending the past from criticisms with an emotion verging on hysteria. De Piles had aroused a passionate controversy over colour, and had ended by repudiating the authority of classical antiquity to which his enemies so constantly appealed. Another critic, not of the past but of its adulation by the present, was Charles Perrault. In 1687 he presented to the Académie

Française an ode on *Le Siècle de Louis Le Grand*, innocuous enough in its title but designed to challenge the Académie's authority by repudiating classical antiquity and by throwing open the debate to the salons. It was to the *honnêtes gens* he appealed by emphasising the tedious character of many Roman authors and by comparing them with the brilliant writers of his own day. The feud between the so-called *Anciens* and *Modernes* was a bitter one which lasted for seven years, involving personalities as well as principles. Much of Perrault's case was unexceptionable; the ancients, he said, 'were great men, it is true, but men like ourselves', but it was the tone of his argument which alarmed men like La Fontaine and Boileau, who insisted that the ancients were the only reliable models to follow, and that to study them did not result in imitation but in inspiration. La Fontaine claimed with justice, '*Mon imitation n'est pas un esclavage*', but the number of writers and artists for whom this was becoming untrue increased with every year.

More significant and more dangerous than the social criticism of La Bruyère or the polemics of de Piles and Perrault was the revolutionary assault on the authority of antiquity which was fostered by the scientific discoveries of the century. 'Those whom we call the ancients', wrote Pascal in the *Traité sur le Vide*, 'were in fact quite new to everything and represented so to speak mankind in its infancy, and as we have added to their wisdom the experience gained in succeeding centuries, it is we who represent that antiquity which we revere in others.' From this the next step was an appeal to progress, and it came before the century was out. 'A man of culture is, as it were, compounded from the distillation of all the cultures of preceding ages. Such a man will have no old age; for men do not degenerate and there will be a steady accumulation of sanity and wisdom as one age succeeds the other.' The author, Fontenelle, was Corneille's nephew and a man of great importance in making known to the intelligent layman the work of Newton and others. For the first time in European history the Golden Age was transported to the future, but a belief in progress was not the only consequence of the attack upon antiquity. A scepticism which had no roots in Roman philosophy was bred by writers like Pierre Bayle, who published in the 1690s his *Nouvelles de la République des Lettres* and a *Dictionnaire historique et critique*. The net effect of these was not only to popularise the scientific discoveries of the age but to undermine existing beliefs in philosophy and religion. Bayle's work became a source of inspiration and so quickly was the mood beginning to change that Hazard in a brilliant phrase has written, 'one day Frenchmen were thinking like Bossuet, the next like Voltaire'.

# ten

# Paris and the Provinces

'The Wars of Religion were the last public expression of provincial life' (Lavisse), and when Henri IV had established his authority throughout France and had made Paris the permanent centre for his government the autonomy of the provinces was ended. Thereafter the process of centralisation was completed by Richelieu, Mazarin and Colbert. There was much to admire in their work. The feudal magnates and the municipal oligarchies who were compelled to bow to royal authority were not the champions of any other liberties but their own, and both the public assizes like the Grands Jours d'Auvergne (1665) and the private reports of *intendants* revealed the oppressive nature of their jurisdiction. In this respect Frenchmen were better-governed because of the extension of royal power; but the process continued without stop until it had gone beyond the elimination of local disobedience and local corruption to a stage at which the most minor matters of provincial life were referred for settlement to Versailles. The provinces therefore suffered twice over: not only was local initiative sapped, but the few able men, seeing no future in local affairs, left for Paris to make their fortune.

The cultural parallel of this was the recruitment of the best artists and writers to serve the court and to glorify the monarch. In Richelieu's day the process was not far advanced, and Richelieu's own respect for the arts ensured that policy was moderated by good taste. In Colbert's day policy alone sufficed, and the arts were subordinated to his direction as ruthlessly as were the Estates of Languedoc. Nothing could be left to private and informal control, and the final solution was the multiplication of academies with monopolistic powers not only at court but throughout the provinces. The Académie Française prosecuted Furetière for publishing a rival *Dictionnaire*, and its authority extended over provincial academies founded at Arles (1670), Soissons (1674), Nîmes (1682), Angers (1685) and Lyon (1700). The Académie Royale de Peinture et de Sculpture ruled that no provincial school of art might be established unless its instructors were supplied or approved by itself, and Lully's privilege, exercised through the Académie de la Musique, allowed him to control all musical concerts throughout France.

One consequence of administrative centralisation was to confirm the inhabitants of *la cour et la ville* in their private belief that they were a select and superior community. For a noble to quit the court of Louis XIII had been the act of defiance; to be sent from Versailles was a shameful disgrace. 'Away from you, Sire,' said one unhappy courtier after his exile in the provinces, 'one is not only unhappy but ridiculous.' The nobles of the court looked scornfully upon the *nobles de province* who lived upon their estates because they could not afford to leave them, and who had no other outlets for their interests beyond litigation and hunting. 'Useless to his country, to his wife and himself, often without a roof, clothing or any merit at all, the *noble de province* tells himself a dozen times a day that at any rate he is a gentleman.' This caricature by La Bruyère of the most pitiful of them came very near to the popular view of the country gentry at large. Similarly, the cultural life of the provinces was derided. It was in the provinces, said Boileau, that '*Le mauvais goût* takes refuge like a banished courtier', and Furetière's *Dictionnaire* confirmed Boileau's opinion: 'A provincial is someone who does not have the air or the manners of the court, who lacks polish, who does not know how to conduct himself and who has never moved in society.' Scarron wrote of provincials, 'they are the most tiresome people in the world'; La Bruyère said tersely, 'provincials are fools'; and Mme de Sévigné used the word provincial as a synonym for stupid. 'Do you know whom M. de Lauzan is to marry next Monday at the

Louvre?'. . . Mme de Coulanges said to him, 'This is very difficult to guess. Is it Mme de la Vallière? — Not at all, madame. — Is it then Mlle de Retz? — Not at all! You are very provincial. — Truly I must be stupid as you say.'

The provinces harboured the failures, for there were many, like Molière and the Illustre Théâtre in 1645, who could not survive the competition of others and had to take refuge outside the capital. One such failure was described by Mme de Sévigné in a letter about her travelling companions on a journey from Paris: 'Next to him was a musician of low order who, to avoid starving in Paris, was setting out for his native village in the hope of obtaining money there.' It is a sad footnote to the success stories of others, but she adds: 'his voice was more of a nuisance than the noise of the coach wheels, and he never stopped singing!' One of her own correspondents was also considered to be a failure—Roger de Rabutin, comte de Bussy—who had left Bourgogne with high hopes of succeeding both as a courtier and as a writer, but who was ruined by his very first publication. It was the *Histoire Amoureuse des Gaules*, a salacious and scandalous work which delighted many in secret but was publicly condemned. Committed by Louis to the Bastille for a term, he was then sent home to Bourgogne, where he bemoaned his exile and compared himself with Ovid. In one of his letters he mentioned a few local men with whom he could converse, but added, 'the rest are not worth naming'. It is almost the epitaph on all provincial culture in the seventeenth century.

Parisian contempt for the provinces was of course exaggerated, since it ignored the vigour and variety of a great deal of provincial culture. There were not only two kinds of nobility, the Versailles courtier and La Bruyère's *noble de province*, but many substantial landowners who lived on their estates and made the occasional visit to court, where they observed the latest fashion in architecture and painting and acquired the latest books and the current *bons mots* of the salons. At home they repaired and extended their châteaux, experimented with fountains, built *hôtels* in the provincial capitals, endowed their churches with altarpieces and funeral monuments, and employed men of letters to educate their children and to lend a little tone to their household. It was Chantilly or Vaux on a small scale—but with the important difference that neither Chantilly nor Vaux was in any sense provincial since all the people there belonged to the society of *la cour et la ville*.

A provincial centre which owed nothing but inspiration to the capital was the château of Cadillac on the banks of the Garonne. Jean-Louis de Nogaret, duc d'Épernon, was governor of Guyenne and frequently came to Paris, where Clement Métézeau built him a *hôtel* in the same street as the Hôtel de Rambouillet. Primed with what he saw in Paris, he established at Cadillac what Crozet terms 'a remarkable example of artistic decentralisation', since everything was done by local labour at his instruction, from the building and decorating of the château to the manufacture of tapestries on the estate and the laying-out of the gardens.

The most exciting example by far of provincial patronage by a noble was that of Charles de Gonzague, duc de Nevers, whose vast territories included the duchy of Nevers on the Loire and the independent petty principality of Arches, across the Meuse from Mézières. Such was his wealth that he could afford to build on a scale which rivalled Richelieu. He owned the Hôtel de Nevers in Paris—of which Tallement wrote that 'Henri IV thought it rather too magnificent to have it facing the Louvre'—the Palais des Tournelles at Mézières, châteaux at Rethel and Cassine, and a ducal palace at Nevers, where he enhanced the view by knocking down all the houses between it and the Loire. His most ambitious undertaking was the construction of a new town at Arches, which he called Charleville in his own honour. In 1608 Clement Métézeau arrived from Paris to direct operations, and the new town was laid out symmetrically around a Place Ducale. This idea was obviously derived from the royal squares of Paris, and the treatment followed very much the same pattern. On one side stood the new ducal palace, ornate with Tuscan pilasters; on the other side were houses of uniform design with a ground-floor arcade, slate roofs, dormer windows under pediments, and the style of brick and stone work made popular by Henri IV. There was no difficulty in finding people to live there. Nevers himself was governor of Champaigne, and the principal officers of the provincial government were required to reside around the Place Ducale; moreover, since Arches was an independent franchise, its inhabitants were immune from law suits in French courts—except for serious criminal offences—and the new city therefore enjoyed considerable popularity.

Provincial culture did not depend solely on the wealthy noble with connections in Paris. The bourgeois were eager to imitate what they had learnt of *la cour et la ville*, and derived considerable pleasure from the formation of literary societies and salons, from the building of town houses and from the employment of artists to decorate their rooms and to paint their portraits. Civic pride, too, was an important factor in provincial patronage, though it was rarely as successful nor as ambitious as at Rennes where a public square was created, to be overlooked by the splendid Palais de Justice built by Salomon de Brosse. Elsewhere there were public celebrations and concerts to be arranged, portraits of the city fathers to be painted, and a considerable amount of rebuilding and decoration of town halls and other civic buildings. In addition to all this the maintenance and extension of ecclesiastical property throughout the century, sustained by a stream of pious donations from all classes, was sufficient to employ a small army of artists and masons.

While there can be no doubt as to the extent, and indeed of the vigour, of cultural activity in its widest sense throughout the provinces, we must emphasise that it was almost entirely derivative. During the Grands Jours d'Auvergne in 1665, the abbé Fléchier spent some time at Clermont Ferrand, and, as a minor poet of the Paris salons, was overwhelmed by the local salons who were delighted beyond measure to meet such an examplar of polite society. 'We have so few handsome and refined people in this uncivilised land', they explained, 'that when someone visits us from the court or from high society we cannot observe him enough.' In architecture, too, the point is underlined by Blunt: 'The standards of Paris and Versailles were accepted all over France, and we find little independent initiative in the provinces during this period. When great cities wanted to carry out any important work they usually tried to get a design from the capital and, if they failed, they compelled their own craftsmen to follow the Parisian models as closely as possible.'

If provincial culture was derivative, it was also second-rate. 'From their petty little ways, their affected manner of talking and their extraordinary discourse, we soon realised that this was Montpellier's assembly of *précieuses*', recorded two Parisian travellers, Chapelle and Bachaumont; 'but although they made renewed efforts because of our presence, they only appeared in their true colours as provincial *précieuses* and were feeble in their imitation of ours.' This was unkind but true, and only to be expected when Paris had become the irresistible magnet for all artistic and literary talent. 'In Paris the most outstanding artists were brought together to undertake commissions from the king, the court, the city, the nobility, the churchmen and the bourgeoisie' (Crozet). Here, in other words, was a population of 400,000—in contrast with the 90,000 of Lyon, the second city of France—which included the wealthy, the leisured, the educated and the socially ambitious who had money, fame and appreciation to offer to the best exponents of each art.

Comparative statistics collated recently by Pettinger after studying the case histories of 200 authors in both the sixteenth and the seventeenth centuries demonstrate the accelerated drift of talent to Paris. In the sixteenth century, when provincial life was considerably freer and when provincial culture was less dependent on the capital, 140 of the 200 authors sampled died in the provinces, against 96 in the seventeenth century; and where 47 moved to Paris from the provinces in the sixteenth century, 72 moved in the seventeenth. Moreover it was always the best who moved. Historians such as Baldensperger and Jacquet have tried to discover examples of writers of ability in Lyon and Dijon respectively who did not succumb to the attractive power of Paris, but their efforts were in vain. Crozet, too, has compiled an exhaustive list of artists who never left their province, but we must say of them, as Jacquet admitted of the Dijon poets, 'the glory which they sought did not have much cause to come seeking them'.

The corollary to the loss of cultural independence by the provinces was the dissemination throughout France of the standards and tastes

of *la cour et la ville*. In part this was done by men like the duc d'Épernon who inhabited both worlds, but a more obvious and far-reaching
means of communication was the printed word. For this to have any
effect, however, a degree of literacy was essential, and the extent of
this depended upon the quality of the schools. In seventeenth-
century France the system of education was so inadequate both in
organisation and in content that a description of it is almost irrelevant to a study of French culture and society, except in order to
explain why so few Frenchmen could read.

Primary education was undertaken by the Church through its
*petites écoles*. Fees were low, varying from five *sous* a month for a
child who could read a little to three *sous* for one learning its letters,
and very often the education was given free. What mattered was the
lack of accommodation. Lyon, with a population of 90,000, was
relatively well off: it had 16 free schools to accommodate 1,600
pupils in the care of 100 men and women teachers; but few towns,
and no villages, could equal this. The regional variation in the provision of rival schools was very marked. The north-eastern provinces
which were invariably overrun by armies in every war undertaken
by France were nonetheless the most generously endowed with
schools, and it was in Brittany, Berry, Bourbonnais, Auvergne and
Limousin that schools were few and far between. Where they existed the pupils were at the mercy of teachers whose education had
not gone beyond the primary stage, and who knew no other means
of instruction than a liberal use of the cane. Such a teacher enjoyed
little prestige among his fellow villagers. Often he had to teach in a
stable, or an empty tavern, or in his own rooms; his salary was
frequently paid in kind, and in some areas he had to live with each
of his pupils' families in turn. Not surprisingly, he spent much of his
time in other employment, assisting the priest as sexton or as bell-
ringer, working on the land, playing the fiddle or even, as at Angles
in the Hautes-Alpes, shaving the villagers' beards.

If primary education for the majority was wholly inadequate,
secondary education for the privileged few was remarkably good.
Once a child had been grounded at home in the rudiments of Latin
by a private tutor, he would be sent in some cases to an academy of

the Oratorians or, more usually, to a college of the Jesuits. There, for an average fee of 150 livres a year, he would be given the finest secondary education in Europe, and one which had been shared by Molière, Bossuet, Descartes, Corneille and the great Condé himself. Each college was founded by its own benefactor who provided the buildings, but the Jesuits supplied the teaching staff. All children followed the *Ratio Studiorum*, the official curriculum of every Jesuit school in Europe, which began with six years of intensive study of Latin and Greek. At the age of 16, those who were up to it would undertake what was virtually a university course in the philosophy and science of Aristotle, and if any pupil then sought ordination he would complete his education with a four-year course in theology.

It was an education guaranteed to produce complete facility in Latin and to encourage a taste for rhetoric, the art of effective expression in both speech and writing, but it was not for their curriculum that the Jesuits were famous but for their teaching method. They were reluctant to use beating, and tried to find other ways of encouraging boys to work, by appealing to their pride in the school, by encouraging them to compete with each other in regular examinations and by offering prizes for the best rather than blows for the weakest. Sensibly, too, hours of study were kept to a minimum in order to prevent learning from becoming too burdensome and to diminish the risk of fatigue. The most novel device was to enliven instruction by acting, and the college plays were sometimes the only source of dramatic entertainment to be found in many districts. Moreover, by restricting the size of the classes to ten pupils, the influence of the teacher in stimulating interest in the work was all the greater. There was, of course, no wish to encourage freedom of thought, and the avowed aim of all the teaching was to induce 'humility, obedience, purity, meekness, modesty, simplicity, chastity, charity and an ardent love of Jesus and his Holy Mother'.

For the education of girls there was virtually no provision. At the primary stage they were barred in most dioceses from attending the *petites écoles* alongside the boys, and it was unusual to find a school founded solely for them. The only recourse for the daughters of bourgeois and noble families was to attend the convent schools, but these were unsatisfactory. The Ursulines, for example, whose order predominated in France, were mainly concerned to prepare girls for the cloister. When not in class the girls followed a regimen of silence and prayer, 'and they should often be reminded', ran the Ursuline rule, 'that contempt of the world and its vanities is one of the essentials of the Christian life'. Their education was, therefore, restricted to enough arithmetic to do simple accounts, enough reading to follow a simple work of devotion and enough writing to make a copy of it. This was the best that the convents could offer, but there were many which offered a good deal less. Some were impoverished and sought to improve their finances by taking in pupils though they had no idea how to instruct them, and were contemptuously described by Mme de Maintenon as crèches since the girls were looked after but given no teaching.

Arnolphe in *L'École des Femmes* decided to send Agnès to a convent school precisely because 'they will make her as big an idiot as they know how to', and Mme de Sévigné warned her daughter against sending her children to the Ursulines and urged her to educate them at home. This was excellent if the tutors were good: Mme de la Fayette was taught by Ménage, the grammarian of the salons, and Mme de Sévigné herself by Ménage and Chapelain, but most girls in these circumstances were entrusted to governesses who were generally incompetent to teach them anything. Condé, after his rigorous education by the Jesuits, married Claire-Clémence de Maillé-Brézé who, as a result of being left to her governess, was still playing with her dolls and was unable to read or write when he left her for his first campaign. Mme de Maintenon, who had formerly served as a governess to the royal children, complained to her colleagues at large: 'What sort of education do you think such a governess would give you? As a rule they are peasants or at best *petites bourgeoises* who know nothing beyond making you stand up straight, and lace your corsets properly, or showing you how to curtsey well. ... The greatest fault, according to them, is to upset the ink on the cloth; that is a crime worthy of the cane, because the governess has the trouble of washing and ironing it; but it doesn't matter if you tell lies as much as you like, because that does not necessitate any ironing or mending. . . . But let us go up the scale to our princesses. How do you think they are brought up? They are given as governess a lady of rank, who has often been educated in the way I have described!'

For several years Mme de Maintenon took a close interest in a school at Montmorency, north of Paris, which was run by a Mme de Brinon to train the daughters of the 'deserving poor' for domestic service. It was, however, too far from Versailles for Mme de Maintenon to visit it without inconvenience and so she had it moved first to Rueil in 1681 and then to Noisy, where it adjoined the park of Versailles. She visited it daily and entrusted several daughters of court nobility to Mme de Brinon on the understanding that their education should be practical and unlike that of the Ursulines, for she was as critical of convent schools as she was of governesses. Within a few years the reputation of the school began to grow, and at length the King was persuaded to endow it with places for 250 daughters of necessitous noble families, and to rebuild for them the château at Saint-Cyr—though Mme de Maintenon commented with some insight: 'I know the King's architects; they will give a palace of exquisite external symmetry, lacking in every single convenience of a school.' To ensure that no comparison was made with convent schools, the 36 mistresses wore the dress of respectable widows instead of the nun's habit, and the avowed intent of the five-year curriculum was to produce girls who were 'frank, unaffected, generous, straightforward, open and impartial', and who could hold their own at court or in the salons. One novelty was the use of amateur theatricals to entertain and to instruct, and because Mme de Brinon's plays, though edifying, lacked literary and dramatic qualities, Mme de Maintenon commissioned Racine to write *Esther* and *Athalie* for the girls of Saint-Cyr.

Saint-Cyr, the academies of the Oratorians, the *petites écoles* of Port-Royal and the colleges of the Jesuits, provided an excellent education for a privileged few, but we must see them within the context of an impoverished and inadequate system of education which offered nothing at all to most Frenchmen. The vast majority remained illiterate, and Louis Maggiolo discovered in 1870, from a study of 217,000 marriage contracts dated between 1686 and 1690, that only 29 per cent of the men and 14 per cent of the women were able to sign their own names. The market for books and journals was therefore a limited one, largely confined to the publication of cheap satire, chivalric romances and lewd adventures. The stories of Tabarin, the comic of the Pont Neuf, were pirated by a bookseller in 1622 and ran through 20 editions, and all the comedians of the Hôtel de Bourgogne in its early days published their ribaldry for the entertainment of a larger audience. The market for these ephemera was the Pont Neuf where they were sold from boxes on the parapets, and dispersed throughout the provinces by pedlars who carried their wares in a voluminous sack slung from their necks.

The Pont Neuf was also a centre for the sale of political pamphlets which maintained an unwavering stream of abuse against the government, reaching a hysterical peak at the time of the Fronde, when the market was almost glutted with *Mazarinades* as they were called. After that, the guild of booksellers, always jealous of its freelance rivals on the bridge, made a pious pretence of supporting law and order and had them closed down. With Colbert and La Reynie in command, moreover, the *nouvellistes*—the journalists of the clandestine press—were rounded up, imprisoned, flogged and exiled. Their activities were nonetheless hard to suppress. Evidence of their work is largely confined to the copies confiscated by the police and used in evidence at their trial, but from these it is clear that they were remarkably well organised. Their market was not only Paris but the provinces, and they had provincial correspondents by the score: 'It is a strange thing about the provinces,' said Racine, 'everyone is a *nouvelliste* from the cradle.' The police won the day in Paris, and suppressed the publication of obscene stories, too, so that, as Mongrédien remarks, the average Parisian reader after 1670 had little left to entertain him. There were, however, the almanacs, epitomes of useful information which sold well throughout the century and across the country, and were widely studied for their calendar notes, points of etiquette, first-aid hints, and astrological forecasts.

There was little in the way of official newspapers. In the provinces the only towns to publish their own gazette with government approval were Toulouse (1661), Besançon (1664) and Grenoble (1697). The rest were dependent on the Paris journals and these were few in number. In 1631 Théophraste Renaudot, with Richelieu's encouragement, founded the *Gazette de France* as a weekly record of official news of home and foreign affairs, most of it supplied by the government. There was little of social or cultural interest, though a measure of comment was later supplied by an editorial, but it became popular across France and increased in size from four to 12 closely printed sheets in quarto. In the provinces it was reprinted under contract, and it was necessary to keep an eye on local printers who sometimes reissued it under a different name, as at Rouen in 1632 when a pirated edition appeared calling itself the *Courier Universel*. Renaudot was a match for any competition. During the the Fronde he had to leave Paris on Mazarin's orders in order to publish the *Gazette* from the Orangery at Saint-Germain, but he was so anxious not to lose his custom within the city that he left two sons behind to publish a *Courier Français* which reflected the views of the Frondeurs. It was a tremendous success, and from a contemporary account, 'the pedlars left deposits the night before publication in order to ensure their copies, and all day long on a Friday you could not hear anything else being shouted but *Courier Français*'.

Renaudot had government support; without, it was impossible to escape censure by the police. In 1672, for example, Colleret secured permission to publish a *Journal des avis et des affaires de Paris*. He wanted, he said, 'to instruct future generations in the happy state of their government; the tranquillity of the people; the customs, the greatness and the magnificence of the kingdom, and especially of Paris which is its capital; and the clemency and justice of the King who provides our repose and good fortune'. What more could any government wish from the press? But after two editions which conveyed very little information beyond the details of births, marriages and deaths, the *Journal* was banned. Surprisingly a journal devoted to gossip about life in *la cour et la ville* succeeded in evading the censors, possibly because it was published in verse. This was the *Muse Historique*, written by Jean Loret, which appeared initially in manuscript from 1650 to 1652, and thereafter was printed with four sheets in folio. Loret was a facile rhymester who produced over 400,000 lines of doggerel before his death in 1665. His account of the first night of *Les Précieuses Ridicules* gives some idea of his style—and the final couplet is perhaps one of the finest examples of bad verse:

> *Cette troupe de comédiens*
> *Que Monsieur avoue être siens,*
> *Représentant sur leur théâtre*
> *Une action assez folâtre,*
> *Autrement un sujet plaisant,*
> *A rire sans cesse induisant*
> *Par des choses facétieuses*
> *Intitulé les Précieuses,*
> *Ont été si fort visités*
> *Par gens de toutes qualités*
> *Qu'on n'en vit jamais tant ensemble*
> *Que ces jours passés, ce me semble,*
> *Dans l'hôtel du Petit-Bourbon*
> *Pour un sujet mauvais ou bon.* ★

The *Mercure Galant*, which first appeared in 1672 at 15 *sous* a copy in parchment, 20 in calf, was much more of a newspaper than the *Gazette* and the *Journal*. It carried news of politics and war along with accounts of current fashions, notices of plays, gossip, puzzles, songs and rhymes. It was run by Donneau de Visé, who was joined in 1682 by Thomas Corneille. Their contract for the sharing of profits is interesting for its differentiation of two kinds of profit— 'those from the sale of copies, and those from presents we receive of money, furnishings, jewels and pensions'. It hints at blackmail, but it was quite the reverse; the presents were made not for suppression of scandal but for favourable publicity, and de Visé's pension from the King increased from 6,000 livres to 15,000.

There was one specifically literary weekly, the *Journal des Savants*,

★ This troupe of actors, acknowledged by Monsieur, is staging at its theatre a frolicsome play, entitled *Les Précieuses*, on an amusing subject which induces constant laughter by its witticisms, and which has been visited by so many people of every degree that it seems to me that we have never seen such a crowd for any play, good or bad, as at present in the Hôtel du Petit-Bourbon.

whose editor, Denis de Sallo, intended 'to publicise whatever is new in the republic of letters; it will contain an exact catalogue of the main books to be printed in Europe and, not content with giving the titles only as do most bibliographies at present, it will say what they deal with and for what they will be useful'. The first edition, of January 1665, contained therefore a review by Mme de Sablé of La Rochefoucauld's *Maximes*, but the notion of review articles was not acceptable to everyone. Charles Patin, who was angry about the review of his *Histoire des Médailles*, charged Sallo with sacrilege, on the grounds that he was appropriating the function of the Inquisition. This immediately aroused the interest of the Church and of the Parlement. Patin wrote to a friend; 'After the third edition of the *Journal*, M. le premier président told me man to man in his office: "These chaps are meddling with criticism. They will cause a lot of trouble and we shall soon have to silence them".' In February the *Journal* was closed down. Sallo would not submit to Colbert or the Church on this matter, and it was a friend, the abbé Gallois, who finally gave the necessary assurances to Colbert and was allowed to renew publication in 1666.

Newspapers, almanacs and such scandalous books as *Les Singeries des femmes de ce temps* were generally hawked in the streets, but the sale of serious books was confined to the university quarter and to the precincts of the Palais de Justice. In Paris there were 71 booksellers in the rue Saint-Jacques alone, and 100 in the Palais de Justice. In the provincial towns with universities or *parlements*, and in particular at Aix, Besançon, Bordeaux, Dijon, Grenoble, Metz, Nancy, Pau, Rennes, Rouen and Toulouse, the public was well supplied with bookshops, but in large ports like Le Havre, Toulon and Marseilles— the latter with a population of 80,000—where there was neither a university nor a *parlement*, there were very few booksellers. In such areas the pedlars were at work, though they would rarely carry very much of a serious nature, nor would the haberdashers who specialised in the sales of hymnals and chapbooks.

In the days of manuscript the scriveners, illuminators and binders of the Confrérie de Saint-Jean had had to secure the assent of the doctors of the Sorbonne before releasing their publications for sale.

This system broke down in the sixteenth century because, with the widespread development of printing, the university authorities could not keep pace with the flow of books. For a while therefore the Confrérie was allowed to undertake responsibility for its members' publications and to denounce all works of heresy, sedition or libel before the royal judges, but this created an opportunity for royal control which the King was only too eager to exploit, on the grounds that 'Experience has shown the Kings of France how prejudicial to the state is the liberty of the press'. A measure of control was established in 1618 when the Confrérie was disbanded, to be replaced by a guild of booksellers, printers and binders whose executive officers, the syndic and his four wardens, had to be elected at the Châtelet in the presence of the lieutenant-general of police. The chief agency of control was the Chancellor's department, where an official with the significant title of director of the book trade administered not only the *bureau contentieux de la librairie* which resolved disputes between guild members, but also the *bureau gracieux* where every book was scrutinised before receiving its *privilège* or licence for publication. The *privilège* guaranteed an author's copyright but at the price of universal censorship, and by 1660 the *bureau gracieux* employed four censors, with powers to confiscate, fine, imprison and commit to the galleys. Like everything else in seventeenth-century administration, the severity of the law was sometimes mitigated by the inefficiency of its operation, and it is reassuring to discover at least one example of a departmental lapse when one censor's report ran: 'I have read, by Order of the Chancellor, a work called *The Koran* by Mahomet, and I find nothing in it contrary to religion and morals.'

If the reorganisation of the book trade in 1618 opened the door to royal control of the printers and booksellers, it also ensured that no rivals could challenge the monopoly of production and distribution enjoyed by the members of the new guild. The secondhand bookstalls were tolerated, but a wary eye was kept on the pedlars, who were forbidden to take apprentices or to sell any book of more than eight pages. Their numbers were regulated, each one having to seek registration, and the eight most senior pedlars were permitted to hawk their wares in the precincts of the Palais de Justice.

Within the trade itself there was a short but bitter struggle for supremacy in which the publishers defeated the printers and brought about a remarkable reduction in the number of major printing presses —an activity warmly seconded and assisted by Colbert in the interests of censorship. Of 75 presses in Paris only 36 survived, and each of these was owned by a master printer who had turned publisher; Lyon, a city with a proud tradition of fine printing, was left with 18 presses, and of the other major centres of bookmaking, Rouen had 18 and Bordeaux 12. In the same way, the provincial publishers lost control of their own markets to the wealthier firms of Paris— of Camusat whose list included most things, of Cramoissy and of Despreys who both dealt in theology, the one a Jesuit supporter, the other a Jansenist, and of Barbin, the publisher of Molière, Racine, La Fontaine, Boileau, Malherbe and La Rochefoucauld, and of the *Recueil Barbin*, a five-volume anthology of verse. Lyon, because of its proud reputation, still enjoyed four book fairs every year—there were only annual fairs at Rouen, Nîmes, Saint-Germain and Saint-Laurent—but the local firms no longer dominated them. La Grande Compagnie des Libraires, established in 1519, was able to withstand Parisian competition in its particular field of civil and canon law, and a new family, the Annissons, achieved a unique triumph by making substantial headway against the Lyon branches of the Paris houses; but La Grande Compagnie was the only survivor of the great firms of the sixteenth century, and the Annissons succumbed at length, not to their rivals but to the attractions of Paris. They moved there, and in 1691 were appointed to the Imprimerie Royale.

This allowed the Annissons to join a select group of publishers who were independent of the guild of booksellers and printers. Some were printers 'by appointment' to the Académies, and the coveted prize of being printer to the Académie Française was held for many years by Camusat. It was a status equivalent to that of artists who had been *breveté*, and included the king's own private printers who enjoyed the lucrative right of publishing his edicts. The Imprimerie Royale was rather special and owed its foundation in 1640 to Richelieu's love of fine print and good binding. As the Dutch were then the acknowledged masters in this field, he asked the Dutch ambassador to send him four compositors whom he set up on the ground floor of the Louvre. Their task was to produce books of the highest quality; Poussin, for example, designed the title page and frontispiece of the first one, the *Imitatio Christi*, and the costs of production in the first seven years mounted to 368,700 livres. The press was subsidised, of course, since its products were too expensive to be commercially successful, but Cramoissy who first ran it did not suffer financially: he dowered his daughter with 15,000 livres and left stock valued at over 226,000 livres. A separate and inspired appointment was that of Antoine Vitré as *Imprimeur du roi pour les langues orientales* in 1622. This was not Richelieu's doing but the generous act of Guy-Michel Le Jay of the Paris Parlement who paid for the publication of the French polyglot Bible in ten volumes. In 1647 when both he and Vitré died, the priceless oriental matrices, including Armenian, Chaldee and Samaritan, were handed over to the Imprimerie Royale.

On the production side there was a perennial dispute between the guild and the engravers, who were allowed to print their own plates but who were required to call upon a licensed printer to make the captions. There was a considerable market among the bourgeoisie for prints of the more famous paintings of the day, but the engravers were essentially original artists who composed their own scenes by observing the daily events of urban and provincial life. With something of a journalistic flair they have preserved for us a lively and informative record of street scenes, marriage contracts, christenings and harvest celebrations, although a less domestic and more savage record of the horrors of civil war has also been preserved in the engravings of Jacques Callot of Lorraine. The wide dispersal of these prints and their appeal to the eye made them a useful means of propaganda among the illiterate, and engravers were employed throughout the century by the government to advertise the blessings of internal peace and to commemorate the victorious wars abroad. They also fulfilled a useful function by disseminating the latest fashions, and in particular the new developments in Parisian architecture, throughout the provinces. In addition to the engravings of Jean Marot which made available the designs of Parisian *hôtels*, there was the *Livre*

*d'architecture d'autels et de cheminées*, a fascinating study of architectural details by Abraham Bosse, which inspired rural masons and
their patrons in the most remote areas to graft the new designs on to
their traditional work.

Journals, books and engravings played a vital role in informing
the provinces of Parisian standards of taste; on a much smaller scale,
and with less success, the travelling players brought the works of
Corneille and Molière to the rural outposts of Brittany or Languedoc.
There was great enthusiasm for theatrical entertainment in the provinces, sustained by the amateur productions of the Jesuit colleges
in particular, and a professional company which had failed in the
competitive arena of the capital could make a living by going on
tour. The Illustre Théâtre was an exceptional case, of course, since
it was able to return to the capital, and a more accurate picture of a
typical touring company is given in Scarron's burlesque novel *Le
Roman Comique*. Such companies could acquire the latest scripts
from the Marais or the Hôtel de Bourgogne, but it was quite another matter to imitate the refined standards of presentation which
had become conventional in Paris by 1650. More often than not the
touring company relied for success on the versatility and the obscenity of its comic invention. The abbé Fléchier observed a performance at Clermont Ferrand by such a company. They made a
sorry mess apparently of Corneille, required a great deal of prompting and indulged in repartee and buffoonery *ad libitum*: 'There was
one of their women who could speak very well, and I must give
them due praise for their burlesque because they are better at
clowning than acting.' Significantly he added, 'as they are the only
ones in the province we have to make the best of them'.

Limited though it was in its range of influence, we should not
overlook the dissemination of ideas by correspondence. The letters
of Mme de Sévigné for example were an admirable means of keeping
her daughter's household in Provence in touch with *la cour et la
ville*, but a much wider range of correspondence was that maintained
by Nicolas Claude Fabri de Peiresc, a magistrate of Aix-en-Pro-
vence. In matters of science and philosophy he was constantly in
touch with Étienne Pascal at Clermont Ferrand and subsequently at

Paris, with Gassendi at Digne who maintained in opposition to Descartes the existence of the vacuum, with François Viète, a *maître de requêtes* at Rennes who invented the decimal system, and with Mersenne who superintended the meetings of scientists in Paris. Outside France, 'he knew everything worth knowing about developments in England, the Netherlands, Germany and throughout most of Europe without ever leaving his study' (Dainville). By the same means he was in touch with every development in literary taste, and wrote at great length to Malherbe, Balzac, Chapelain and Corneille. He collected books with insatiable enthusiasm, but unlike most collectors was remarkably generous with his own, and gave no book away without first having it specially bound. Naudé, of course, was a close friend by correspondence, and remarked of his generosity: 'Was there ever a man more skilled in history and philosophy, more endowed with wit, wealth and quality, more ready to assist the student?'

Aix was a remarkably lively centre of provincial culture, owing much to a tradition of humanist scholarship among the magistrates of the city, a tradition going back to Guillaume du Vair and maintained by men of the quality of Peiresc. It also owed much to its position on the route taken by French and Flemish painters, sculptors and architects on their way to and from Italy, since these were glad to break their journey and to undertake a local commission, and would willingly engage themselves to purchase works of art in the Italian cities. Peiresc, who corresponded with Rubens, had built up his own collection, including a portrait done by Van Dyck on the artist's return from Italy in 1621. Barrilly, another magistrate and a friend of Peiresc, was able to acquire 120 paintings, including many attributed to Van Dyck, Titian, Holbein and Leonardo da Vinci, and an equally valuable collection was made by Jean de la Cépède, *président aux comptes*, who housed it in a splendid *hôtel* built in the Paris style. Aix indeed enjoyed an enviable reputation for learned society, for collections of art and for dignified *hôtels* in quiet streets.

More noisy and more important in every sense was Lyon, the second city of France, a prosperous centre of the textile industry, of commerce and of banking, and ideally sited to make independent contact with the cultural centres of Germany and of Italy. In the sixteenth century it had enjoyed tremendous prestige, both politically and culturally, but in the seventeenth its quality and its independence were sapped by Paris. It retained a great sense of civic pride, employing civic artists to embellish civic buildings, and there was no lack of funds available for private patronage, but there was not one work of art or architecture worth setting against anything in Paris. It was well known for its salons—and Baldensperger has made a special study of them in order to affirm their quality—but nothing can erase the damning comment of La Grande Mademoiselle on two *précieuses* of distinction in Lyon, '*elles sont bien faites et spirituelles pour des femmes de province*'. This decorative and inferior status *vis-à-vis* Paris is epitomised by the story of Françoise Pascal. In all accounts of Lyon society she is described as having been a poet, a dramatist, a musician, an artist and a very paragon of the salons, acclaimed and admired without reservation. At length, like everyone else in France with any pretensions to fame, she abandoned Lyon where she had reigned supreme to go to Paris—only to go unnoticed as a *femme de province* of no consequence.

Where Lyon had failed so dismally to compete with Paris, no other city could hope to succeed, and it is pointless to repeat examples of the inferior and derivative quality of provincial culture. Dijon, however, maintained a rare and interesting degree of independence. Bourgogne had formerly been the seat of the power of Burgundy, the middle kingdom of the late medieval period, and it still preserved close links across the eastern frontier with the free county of Burgundy, the Franche Comté, which remained independent of France until 1679, and with the independent duchy of Lorraine. In the sixteenth century it had established a strong tradition of classical scholarship, and the city might have remained self-confident and self-directing in its culture but for the disaster which befell it in the Thirty Years War. From 1632 to 1648, the armies of the major powers spilled over from the Rhineland, and Bourgogne was periodically occupied and sacked. The economic effect of this was to destroy the work of many generations: 'The fields reverted to brushwood; the marshes took possession of the valleys; the barren uplands returned to fallow. The ruined farms and villages were rebuilt as mud hovels, and the villagers fled to the shelter of the castle' (Roupnel). Social and cultural life in Dijon itself was consequently dominated by the fears and disturbance caused by the invasions, and from 1632, in Roupnel's striking phrase, 'la littérature, ce lieu sonore qui enregistre les échos, devient comme silencieux en Bourgogne'. Recovery was slow, and by 1660 the province had in any case been dragooned into line with the rest of France. Nonetheless, the independence of the citizens of Dijon manifested itself in a variety of ways.

It had its salons, its local poet, La Monnoye, and his friend Pierre Legonz who wrote his own Caractères of Burgundian life; but these and the other leaders of intellectual life such as Nicaise, Bouhier, Lantin and Dumay, were serious-minded parlementaires and churchmen, 'who would have cut a poor figure in the Hôtel de Rambouillet. The psychological analysis of love, the delicate refinements of feeling, the affectation and the wit were not their concern at all' (Jacquot). They had no interest in the quarrel of Le Cid nor in the Carte du Tendre; of all the figures of the Paris salons it was Ménage the grammarian who was admired, and Racine was referred to only as the author of the Histoire du Roi.

Paris itself was respected more as a centre of learning than as an arbiter of taste. The sons of parlementaires were sent there to study the law and in this they were remarkably single-minded. Bénigne Bouhier spent two years in Paris, and his only interest outside his studies was to copy or to purchase manuscripts for his father's collection. His father Jean, however, wanted him to acquire some tincture of salon culture: 'there is no place in the world where they talk with such refinement as in Paris; therefore during your stay there acquire a smattering of it.' It was not, however, because Jean held this to be desirable socially; on the contrary, 'It is the best means of winning the most convinced opponents to your own point of view.' Bénigne was in any case suspicious of everything the salons stood for. 'A Dijon student', he wrote, 'does not want to return to his province with his hands in his pockets like an idle fool who is good for nothing.'

The independent quality of Dijon's intellectuals was also apparent in the field of science and philosophy. La Monnoye alone showed any enthusiasm for Descartes, Pascal was totally ignored, and it was the Dutch and the Germans with whom men like Nicaise corresponded. Characteristically perhaps, the twin mentors of Dijon, Leibniz and Bayle, were both public enemies of Louis XIV: Leibniz because, in addition to working on the calculus, he rallied German opinion against the aggression of Louis XIV, and Bayle because his free thinking forced him to take refuge in Holland. The *Dictionnaire Historique et Critique*, coming though it did at the end of the period, was nonetheless the most influential book of the century so far as Dijon was concerned. La Monnoye called it 'a veritable treasury of science and learning', and its author, 'the incomparable journalist who delights all nations'. Bayle returned the compliment: 'Dijon is one of the most civil and most learned cities in the kingdom.'

For all that the cultural interests of Dijon's society were refreshingly different from those of other provincial towns, this diversity was only a matter of degree. Cultural uniformity followed close upon the creation of administrative unity, even in Dijon; Paris attracted to itself the finest artists and writers in the kingdom, and the culture of seventeenth-century France was determined by the standards and the taste of *la cour et la ville*.

# Select Bibliography

# Select Bibliography

ADAM, Antoine, *Histoire de la littérature française au 17me siècle*, 5 vols.
Indispensable work of reference with many enlightening comments.

ASHLEY, Maurice, *Louis XIV and the Greatness of France*, 1948.
A useful introduction to the period including comment on the arts.

AYNARD, Joseph, *La Bourgeoisie française*, 1934.
Analyses sections and sub-sections of the bourgeoisie in detail.

BABELON, Jean-Pierre, *Demeures Parisiennes sous Henri IV et Louis XIII*, 1965.
Indispensable. Excellent reference book, superb illustrations, and enlightening comments.

BALDENSPERGER, F., *Études d'Histoire Littéraire*, 'La Société Précieuse de Lyon au 17me siècle', 1910.
Interesting, but it is of necessity dealing with a rather poor imitation of Parisian society.

BARNARD, H. C., *Madame de Maintenon and Saint-Cyr*.
Author of several studies of education in seventeenth-century France: this book is particularly good on the education of girls.

BÉNICHOU, Paul, *Les Morales du Grand Siècle* 1948.
Very good on Jansenism, Corneille, Pascal and La Rochefoucauld.

BLUNT, Sir Anthony, *Art and Architecture in France, 1500–1700*.
An indispensable and enlightening work of reference. Excellent plates.

———— *François Mansart and the Origins of French Classical Architecture*, 1946.

BORGERHOFF, E. B. O., *The Freedom of French Classicism*, 1950.
An interesting theme: emphasises that adherence to rules much less important than the giving of pleasure.

BOYD, William, *The History of Western Education*, 7th ed., 1964.
Very comprehensive.

BRERETON, Geoffrey, *A Short History of French Literature*.
Especially useful on the early development of the theatre.

BUKOFZER, M. F., *Music in the Baroque Era*, 1947.
Detailed and useful on Italian baroque music, and good on Lully.

CANAT, René, *Une Forme de la Littérature Héroïque: La Littérature Jan-séniste.*

CARSTEN, F. L. (ed.), New Cambridge Modern History, Vol. v, *The Ascendancy of France.*

CAUDWELL, H., *Introduction to French Classicism.*
Deals with literature alone, but is very useful.

CHENEY, Seldon, *The Theatre. 3,000 Years of Drama, Acting and Stagecraft.*

CLARK, G. N., *The Seventeenth Century.*

COLE, C., *Colbert and a Century of French Mercantilism.*

COLES, H. C., *The Growth of Music.*
Useful section on Lully.

CORPECHOT, Lucien, *Parcs et Jardins de France,* 1911.
An excellent and indispensable study.

CROZET, René, *La Vie Artistique en France au 17me siècle* [1598–1661], 1954.
An extremely valuable work of reference, but with little aesthetic comment.

DAINVILLE, *Les Jésuites et l'Éducation de la Société Française.*
Especially useful on the scientists.

DART, Thurston, *The Interpretation of Music.*
Useful on seventeenth-century lute music.

DAVISON, A. T., and APEL, W. (ed.), *Historical Anthology of Music,* Vol. II.

DONNINGTON, Robert, *The Interpretation of Early Music.*
Very technical, but a good section on seventeenth-century techniques of playing and singing.

FLETCHER, W. Y., *Bookbinding in France,* 1894.
Only a short section relates to the seventeenth century but is of interest, especially on Peiresc and Naudé.

GODLEY, Eveline, *The Great Condé.*
Some useful information on Jesuit education, the academies of the Oratorians, and the ménage at Chantilly.

GREEN, F. C., *French Novelists, Manners and Ideas,* 2nd ed., 1964.
Useful on Mme de la Fayette.

GUÉRARD, Albert, *The Life and Death of an Ideal.*
An excellent outline of how French classicism developed, and of its social context.

HAUSER, Arnold, *The Social History of Art*.
Ranges widely over several countries and centuries, but is often enlightening on seventeenth-century French culture.

HAUSER, Henri, *La Prépondérance Espagnole 1559–1660* (Peuples et Civilisations, Vol. x).

HIGHET, G., *The Classical Tradition*, 1949.

HOLSBOER, S. Wilma Deierkauf, *Le Théâtre du Marais*, 2 vols., 1954; *L'Histoire de la Mise-en-Scène dans le Théâtre Français de 1600 à 1657*
Both very detailed and very technical, but most informative.

HOWARTH, W. D., *Life and Letters in France*, 1965.
An excellent survey.

HUGON, Cécile, *Social France in the 17th Century*.
Old-fashioned but helpful.

JACQUET, A., *La Vie Littéraire dans une Ville de Province sous Louis XIV*, 1886.
A study of Dijon.

JACQUOT, Jean (ed.), *Le Lieu Théâtral à la Renaissance*, 1964
Especially the essays by R. Lebègue, 'Unité et pluralité dans le théâtral français'; T. Laurenson, D. Roy and R. Southern, 'Le Mémoire de Mahelot'; A. Beijer, 'Une Maquette de Décor'; and by Jacquot himself, 'Les types de lieu théâtral et leurs transformations'.

KNOX, R. A., *Enthusiasm*.
Not the best man to defend Port-Royal against the Jesuits, but lively.

KRAILSHEIMER, A. J., *Studies in Self-Interest, from Descartes to la Bruyère*.

LAGARDE, A., and MICHAUD, L., *Le XVIIme siècle*, 1962.
Thorough-going commentary on French literature, with good plates and excellent extracts.

LANCASTER, H. C., *A History of French Dramatic Literature in the 17th Century*, 9 vols, 1929–42.

LANG, P. H., *Music in Western Civilisation*.

LANSON, G., *Histoire de la Littérature Française*.
Has clearly been superseded by Adam and Mornet, but well worth reading for the perceptive comments.

LAVEDAN, Pierre, *French Architecture*.
Covers all French history, but the relevant sections, though short, are useful.

LAVISSE, E., *Histoire de France depuis les origines jusqu'à la Révolution Française.*
    Old-fashioned but relevant volumes. Still very useful, and good sections on French culture.

LAWRENSON, T. E., *The French Stage in the 17th Century,* 1957.
    Admirable and comprehensive.

LEWIS, W. H., *The Splendid Century; The Sunset of the Splendid Century.*
    Both useful.

LOUGH, John, *An Introduction to Seventeenth-Century France.*
    Admirable introduction, with a great deal of illustrative material.

—— *Paris Theatre Audiences in the 17th and 18th Centuries,* 1957.
    Highly specialised but fascinating study and most informative.

McGOWAN, M. M., *L'Art du Ballet de Cour en France 1581–1643,* 1963.
    Detailed and very interesting.

MAGNE, E., *La Vie Quotidienne au Temps de Louis XIII,* 1947.

MANDROU, Robert, *Introduction à La France Moderne: Essai de psychologie historique 1500–1660.*
    An original treatment of the period.

—— with Georges Duby, *A History of French Civilisation.*

MONGRÉDIEN, Georges, *Colbert,* 1963.
    Very useful study.

—— *La Vie Littéraire au 17me siècle,* 1947.
    Indispensable and very lively.

—— *La Vie Quotidienne sous Louis XIV,* 1948.

MOORE, W. G., *Molière. A New Criticism.*
    Very lucid and enlightening.

MOREL, J., *La Tragédie,* 1964.
    Very useful.

MORNET, D., 'La signification et l'évolution de l'idée de Préciosité en France au 17me siècle', *Journal of the History of Ideas,* Vol. I, 1940.

—— *Histoire de la littérature française classique,* 1950.

NEF, J., *Industry and Government in France and England,* 1940.

NEWTON, E., *European Painting and Sculpture.*

NOLHAC, P. de, *Versailles.*

PEVSNER, N., *An Outline of European Architecture,* 1943.

—— 'Mannerism and Elizabethan Architecture', *Listener*, 17 February, 1964.

PEYRE, H., *Qu'est-ce-que le Classicisme?* (édition revue et augmentée, 1965).
Brilliant.

POTTINGER, D. T., *The French Book Trade in the Ancien Régime 1500–1791*, 1958.
Indispensable study.

PRUNIÈRES, H., *A New History of Music: the Middle Ages to Mozart*, 1943.

—— *Lully*, 1910.

—— *L'Opéra Italien en France avant Lulli*, 1913.
A first-class and detailed study.

—— *Le Ballet de Cour en France avant Lulli*, 1913.

REYNOLD, Gonzague de, *Synthèse du 17me siècle*, 1962.
Some good ideas, but old-fashioned on the 'school of 1660'.

ROCHEBLAVE, S., *Le Goût en France*, 1914.

ROUPNEL, G., *La Ville et la Campagne au 17me siècle*, new edition, 1953.
Deals only with Burgundy.

SAGNAC, P., and SAINT-LÉGER, A. de, *Louis XIV. 1660–1715* (Peuples et Civilisations).

SAINT-GERMAIN, J., *Les Financiers sous Louis XIV*, 1950.

SMITH, Preserved, *A History of Modern Culture*.
A good deal of useful information here.

STRACHEY, Lytton, *Landmarks in French Literature*.
Worth dipping into for comment.

TAPIÉ, Victor-L., *Baroque et Classicisme*, 1957.
Extremely valuable study, especially of the Mazarin–Colbert period.

TASSÉ, Henriette, *Les Salons Français*.

TILLEY, A., *From Montaigne to Molière*.

—— *The Decline of the Age of Louis XIV*.

TREASURE, G. R. R., *Seventeenth-Century France*.
Not much on French culture but a good synthesis of recent work on French history.

TRIGGS, H. Inigo, *Garden Craft in Europe*, 1913.

TURNELL, M., *The Classical Moment*.

VIER, Jacques, *Histoire de la Littérature Française (XVIme–XVIIIme siècles).*

WEDGWOOD, C. V., *Richelieu and the French Monarchy,* 1949.
One of the few studies of Richelieu as a statesman to mention his interest in the arts.

WILENSKI, R. H., *French Painting,* 1931.
Excellent.

WINEGARTEN, R., *French Lyric Poetry in the Age of Malherbe,* 1954.

ZIGROSSER, Carl, *The Book of Fine Prints,* 1948.

# Index

# Index

Where no sub-headings are given, references to pages of particular importance are set in **bold** type